Readings in International Enterprise

This is a comprehensive, up-to-date compendium of key readings on international business theory and practice. Selected for the Open Business School MBA course on 'International Enterprise', the collection includes some of the most influential articles to have appeared on the subject, drawn from both sides of the Atlantic.

The readings are divided into two parts. The first covers the theory and practice of international business strategies and the human resource management necessary to develop these strategies across the world. The second part of the volume covers different sectors of international enterprise: communications, marketing, production, finance, business ethics.

Readings in International Enterprise will be an essential companion to international business courses both at undergraduate and postgraduate levels.

John Drew is Visiting Professor of European Management at the Open Business School, The Open University. Formerly Head of the United Kingdom Offices of the Commission of the European Communities, he has experience of working in business, government and academia on aspects of European integration.

This reader is part of an integrated teaching system; the selection is therefore related to other material available to students and is designed to evoke critical understanding. Opinions expressed are not necessarily those of the course team or of the University.

If you would like to study the course to which this reader relates or receive further information about Open Business School courses, please write to **The Customer Service Centre**, The Open University, PO Box 222, Walton Hall, Milton Keynes MK7 6YY or telephone 0908 653449/652226.

Readings in International Enterprise

Edited by John Drew

London and New York
in association with

The Open University

First published 1995
by Routledge
11 New Fetter Lane, London EC4P 4EE

Simultaneously published in the USA and Canada
by Routledge
29 West 35th Street, New York, NY 10001

Typeset in Palatino by
Ponting–Green Publishing Services, Chesham, Bucks
Printed and bound in Great Britain by
TJ Press (Padstow) Ltd, Padstow, Cornwall

British Library Cataloguing in Publication Data

A catalogue record for this book is available from the
British Library.

Library of Congress Cataloging in Publication Data
Readings in international enterprise / edited by John Drew.
      p.   cm.
   Includes bibliographical references and index.
   ISBN 0–415–12316–X
   1. International business enterprises.   2. Personnel
   management.
I. Drew, John.
HD2755.5.R384   1994
658'.049–dc20   94–36316
                                                   CIP

ISBN 0–415–12316–x (hbk)
ISBN 0–415–12317–8 (pbk)

Contents

Figures and tables

FIGURES

TABLES

Introduction

John Drew

MANAGING IN UNCERTAIN TIMES

Since the end of the Second World War, there has been an astonishing growth of enterprise across national borders, much of it based on international trade and the development of multinational companies (MNCs). This is not an entirely new phenomenon, as international commerce has existed for centuries. Today's MNCs have forerunners such as the East India Company and the Hudson Bay Company, not to mention the great trading nations throughout history, such as the Phoenicians and the Venetians, and individual merchants bringing goods over lands and over seas. But thanks to technology and its applications in transport and electronic communications, this international activity is set to deepen and widen still further. More states will join regional groupings such as the European Union (EU) (see note on p.12) and the North America Free Trade Association (NAFTA) and the number of such organizations will increase, encouraged by the framework of the General Agreement on Tariffs and Trade (GATT) with it's basic philosophy of free trade and open markets. These developments may prove to be a significant step towards an integrated global economy.

The direction of this historic trend is clear, but the pace of change is difficult to forecast. In industrialized countries, the automobile surprisingly replaced the horse drawn carriage in a matter of decades; few people foresaw the collapse of communism and the Berlin Wall, its dramatic symbol, in the space of a few months; IBM once seemed a paradigm of how international business would develop through a few hundred gigantic companies during the twenty-first century.

We can be sure that international enterprise, however defined, will be exciting; at times confusing; increasingly professional and certainly very complex. Managers working across national borders will need a clear understanding of the contradictions and paradoxes of international wealth creation and economic activity. They will train and retrain in order to operate successfully in an environment where the boundaries between business and government, between the nation-state, regional groupings and international agencies are often difficult to draw. We are moving in just a few decades into an electronic, communications and services based civilization the nature of which will be global. It could in time replace our industrial civilization, which was based on the primacy of the nation-state.

The traditional functional skills we have learned over past decades will be less in demand to the extent that financial, marketing, production, accounting and human resource management activities are underpinned and in part undertaken by ever more powerful software programmes. This will leave space for the development of other qualities and skills necessary for international enterprise: the understanding of the interplay between different cultures, political systems and economic groups; the implications of the growth of technology and how it shrinks distances; language capability; assessment of the role of regional and international organizations, pressure groups, religions and philosophies.

Jobs in international enterprise have traditionally been thought of as the preserve of MNCs, but we are now witnessing the burgeoning of a wide range of other international organizations; public sector companies and non-profit-making organizations, international and regional economic agencies; peace-keeping forces, charitable and relief organizations, professional bodies, small and medium-size companies (SMEs) exploiting international niche markets; companies providing services for long-stay tourists, overseas residents and economic migrants. All these organizations are required to be cost centres, if not profit centres, to create wealth and welfare and to be managed effectively in an international context. Current pressures too are for international operations to be more transparent and to promote justice and morality. All these developments are happening in a world which has broadly accepted the need to reduce barriers to trade and to promote wider and more open markets in the interest of promoting efficiency and growth.

As the pace of change is unpredictable, we need to establish a frame of reference – some marker posts to chart our way. The articles of this Reader can make a contribution. It might also be helpful to establish a personal list of the variables which, often interacting with one another, make up the complex equation of international enterprise. These variables some of which concern the world economy and others the operation of a specific firm in a particular industry sector, can be expressed as a series of continuums, for example:

Local Economy . . . . National Economy
National Economy . . . . Global Economy
National Finance . . . . Global Finance

For any company or organization, nation or region, a line is drawn for each continuum. Thus, in the second example, the line is from 'national economy' at the left of the continuum which moves by gradations to 'global economy' at the right. Current (x) or future positions (y) can be marked, for example:

National Economy . . . . . . x . . . . y . . . . Global Economy

The further x is to the left in this illustration, the more are national considerations paramount. If the present position of an organization or a country on the continuum is x, y might be a prediction of how far it might move by the year 2010. The approach seeks to develop a comprehensive check list of variables affecting a specific international enterprise at a specific time. The criteria for measurement are judgemental and different time scales will change the position of the x or y. For example, labour in the short term is a local or national issue, and sometimes too is finance. In the longer term finance will tend to be more global while labour may be restricted by national or regional legislation.

Some ideas for continuums for assessing the current and future position of an organization or nation are given below. The x and y are merely for illustrative purposes. You would wish to decide yourself how far along each continuum you would mark x to denote the present position or how far y would denote a certain position in the future. This approach is not scientific, but provides a method of looking at a particular industry or nation and comparing its present and possible future position.

Issues affecting the global environment

National . . . . x . . . . y . . . . Global
Frontier capitalism . . . . x . . . . y . . . . Social capitalism
International enterprise . . . x . . . . . y . . . . . International management
Protectionism . . . . y . . . . x . . . . Competition
Material . . . . x. . . . . y . . . . Spiritual

Issues specifically affecting a firm's operations in a specific market

National		*Global*
Finance . . . . x . . . . y . . . . Finance
Marketing . . . . y . . . . x . . . . Marketing
Sourcing . . . . y . . . . x . . . . Sourcing
Production . . . . x . . . . y . . . . Production

If you make a list of your own continuums, the points marked from the present (x) to the future (y) will not necessarily be in the same direction, nor will the distance between them be the same. They will change over time. International activity is uncertain as to the pace of change and in some instances as to the direction of change as well. The following explanations of a few continuums affecting the global environmental show how the approach can be used to describe a fluid situation.

National. . . . . Global

The nation-state has been the fundamental political, economic and social unit of our industrial civilization. The United Nations implicitly recognizes through its 'one country, one vote' rule that nations are the building blocks of any future world order. But their all-powerful role in the twentieth century may not necessarily continue in the twenty-first. In the first instance regional groupings have emerged. The nations of the European Union (EU), for example, have pooled a considerable amount of their sovereignty. They have a common agricultural, commercial and competition policy and are working towards a single currency and a common foreign policy. It is rare already for EU members not to vote as a bloc in the United Nations. EU laws take precedence over those of member states. New regional groupings will proliferate and have to be taken into account by those working across national and regional boundaries.

The global village may still be a mirage glimmering on the distant horizon and yet there are signs of global activity everywhere. Ford designed the Mondio to be the first world automobile which could be sourced, assembled and distributed virtually anywhere. Coca-Cola is to be franchised across the Commonwealth of Independent States (CIS). World brands such as MacDonalds, Scottish Whiskies and French perfumes are universally recognized. Airbus, which is built by a consortium of several European nations, has captured 40 per cent of the world civil aviation business for airliners. The Joint European Taunus (JET) project at Culham in Oxfordshire could lead to half the world's energy being produced by a nuclear fusion process towards the middle of the next century. Mobile telephones will soon communicate via satellite across the world. INTERNET and electronic super-highways are in the process of revolutionizing world communications within a decade.

International standard-setting organizations such as CEN and CENELEC point towards global standards of the future. Currencies are not controlled by individual countries. The President of the USA does not wake up in the morning and decide the dollar/yen exchange rate. Yet the nations of the western economic triangle (USA, EU, Japan) still wage trade wars at the margin to obtain regional economic advantage while at the same time exporting and importing, investing and working in one anothers' countries. There are over 50,000 Japanese living and working in the London area alone. Some capital cities are becoming global cities to judge by their workforce, residents and tourists.

On the other hand we may never have a global economy, nor a United States of Europe. Some nations will break up into tribes or districts. Yet other nations are surrendering power and influence to regional groupings and at the same time there are local pressure to devolve responsibilities to their towns and cities. This centralizing and decentralizing process is sometimes pulling the nation-state in two opposite directions. No clear patterns have yet emerged. A system established today may not be relevant or may not work in five years' time. We are moving along the continuum from the primacy of the nation-state towards a global economy, but where are we on that line and how far and how fast are we travelling?

Frontier capitalism . . . . Social capitalism

Now that communism as an economic system has failed, a new battle emmerges between different types of capitalism. In his book *Capitalisme v Capitalisme*, Michel Albert (Seuil 1991) distinguishes between the Rhineland capitalism of such countries as Germany, Austria, Scandinavia and Japan on the one hand and Anglo-American capitalism on the other. The former is marked by a close connection between business and banking institutions, long-term investment, retained dividends and a collective and consensual approach to stakeholders. The latter is shorter term and profit orientated; dividends are distributed, sometimes when not even covered by profits; return to shareholders is paramount; earnings per share and capital growth are the mainspring of the system. Whether the two types of capitalism will continue to coexist, whether one will prevail or other types develop remains to be seen.

There are pressures to provide ever better social conditions for workers. The Social Chapter of the Maastricht Treaty is widely supported in the Rhineland countries. The more *laissez-faire* approach of the Anglo-American model is being adopted by some emerging economies while others are further along the continuum towards a social economy. Multinational companies in the 1960s and 1970s were closer to what I have called 'frontier capitalism', where markets were developed internationally in a largely unregulated environment. Gradually countries changed their legislative environment to regulate MNC activity through, for example, demanding more local added value and instituting new tax regimes. Social capitalism with its emphasis on workers' rights and strong social security provisions is also under threat through the drive towards international competitiveness.

International enterprise . . . . International management

International enterprise has traditionally been export and import driven and MNCs have played a major role in this process. International organizations proliferate and each year there are more managers involved in international operations, whether in business, government or academia. It is difficult to differentiate between the diverse activities of managers across international frontiers in terms of the skills they require. The multinational country manager, the EU or government official in Brussels dealing with aid programmes, the lecturer arranging an international seminar – all need to understand the environment in which they are operating and to manage in cultures and political and economic climates which may be very different to their own. The hospital administrator running a world conference on AIDS or an environment minister hosting a meeting for regional cooperation on pollution have broadly comparable tasks. Organizing an air lift for a charity to an African country stricken by drought requires many of the same skills as those required by the United Nations officer in charge of peace-keeping in Bosnia. Most of those working across national frontiers, living in different nations and cultures and speaking other languages can be positioned along the continuum from international enterprise to international management.

Protection . . . . Competition

Most goods can be manufactured more cheaply in newly industrializing countries (NICs) than in developed ones. Services industries too are moving activities and therefore jobs in the same direction. Lufthansa and Swiss Air have found it cheaper to do much of their ticketing in countries such as India and the Philippines. How far will developed countries allow this trend to continue?

The conclusion of the Uruguay Round of the General Agreement on Trade and Tariffs (GATT) was a continuing step in the liberalization of world trade, but quotas, tariffs and non-tariff barriers still exist. Those governments wishing to protect home markets argue that to avoid unacceptable levels of unemployment and to prevent social unrest, there must be some element of protection at their national frontiers. Governments at the other end of the continuum see the need to develop skilled workforces to provide high added value services. Lower skilled jobs, they believe, must move to wherever in the world goods and services can be produced more cheaply. The competition policy of the EU favours the opening up of markets and the Union is rigorously enforcing existing European laws. Yet competition is not open in agriculture, many post-office services, energy and airlines, with the result that prices are higher than they would otherwise be. Nations talk with forked tongues as they seek to retain national advantage by covert protection while proclaiming the advantages of open international markets

Unemployment . . . . Full employment

Linked to the issue of protectionism is the problem of employment. At the turn of the nineteenth century, 30 per cent of those employed in the UK were 'in service', working in households as domestics, cooks, gardeners or drivers. With the need for increased production during the two World Wars, women entered the workforce in large numbers. With the growth of equal opportunity legislation and changed social attitudes, female employment has risen in Europe to 40 per cent of the total workforce. Less than 3 per cent of the workforce are now employed in agriculture in the UK. Manufacturing jobs will continue to decline dramatically with increasing emphasis on competitiveness, robotics and computer power. A modern factory contains more machinery and fewer workers. Most employment is now in offices and yet powerful computer systems are also taking tens of thousands of jobs out of banks and other financial services. The emphasis on job creation will vary from one country to another. Demographic patterns become important and training and education is a priority almost everywhere. The Carnegie Enquiry into the Third Age (*Report of the Carnegie Enquiry Into the Third Age*, Carnegie Trust, 1992) suggests new work patterns in developed countries. Work sharing, part-time employment, teleworking, unpaid employment, self-employment, entrepreneurship and outsourcing are growth sectors.

The variables described above are important to understand if we wish to forecast trends in international enterprise. Others might be:

Public ownership . . . . x . . . . y . . . . Private ownership
Individual . . . . x . . . . y . . . . Collective
Totalitarian . . . . y . . . . x . . . . Democratic
Environmentally unconscious . . . . . . x . . . . y . . . . . Conscious
Unethical . . . . x . . . . y . . . . Ethical

You may wish to make your own list. We need to develop flexible frameworks for our thinking on international enterprise because the pace of change is so unpredictable and the pattern so confused. Like the tennis player waiting for a serve, we cannot be sure how fast or slow the ball will come, what sort of spin it will have or exactly where it will land. The need therefore is to train ourselves to keep on our toes, to position ourselves as best we can, continually reviewing and revising our approach.

THE ARTICLES

While the continuum approach seeks to provide a flexible reference framework for a fast-changing subject, the Reader articles are anchored firmly in the current theory and practice of international enterprise. They broaden and deepen in different ways the Units of the International Enterprise course.

Some of them are extremely practical, such as Sharp's 'Business environment assessment'. Others, such as Porter's 'The determinants and dynamics of national advantage' are seminal and suggest a comprehensive theory of explaining the way in which nations and firms interreact in an increasingly global economy. Still others, such as Johanson and Wiedersheim-Paul, suggest models for understanding international enterprise based on extensive studies of how companies become international. Articles by Campanella and Lessard put forward theories on globilization and turbulence and on finance and global competition respectively, based not only on their own theories, but through extensive and wide-ranging references to authorities in their fields. Some articles, such as that by Eames, President and Chief Executive Officer of Coca-Cola, are based on the experience of one person running a major international operation. The Brown and Julius article looks at the changing role of manufacturing, while the Ghoshal and Nohria article is more concerned with organizational forms in multinational corporations as they exist today.

All the articles are referred to in the text of the Units and you may wish to read them as you work through the course at the appropriate time. For the general reader, however, you should bear in mind that each article stands alone and brings together much current thinking and previous research on international enterprise in the specialist function with which it is concerned.

Part I of the Reader deals with strategies and people. The most important consideration in any business is to get your strategy right. If you are in the wrong place at the wrong time with the wrong product, it doesn't matter how efficient your business is: it will not work. If you do not have the right people working for you, even a great strategy will not suffice. Strategies have to be implemented.

Part II covers some of the functions of international enterprise. Of course the malfunction of any part of a business can cause it to fail, but if the strategy is right and the people are good there is a better chance of success through utilizing effectively what are essentially mechanisms for implementing the strategy.

PART I: STRATEGIES AND PEOPLE

In the first article Campanella considers 'The effects of globalization and turbulence on policy-making processes'. She expresses her preference for the institution-building approach based on the possibilities it offers at cognitive and operative levels. She shows how, in spite of the new primacy of economics, policy-making depends on state institutions and national, international and super-national organizations. Her emphasis on the importance of institutions is an important assertion, which counters the frequently held view that in the next century a few hundred multinational companies will dominate the global economy.

The second article is extracted from Porter's *The Competitive Advantage of Nations*. He identifies the fundamental determinants of national competitive advantage in an industry and how they work together as a system. He explains the important phenomenon of 'clustering', in which related groups of successful firms and industries merge in a nation to gain leading positions in the world market. Based on research in over 100 industries worldwide, his findings have implications for both firms and governments. He describes how a company can tap and extend its nation's advantages in international competition. He provides a blueprint for government policy to enhance national competitive advantage.

Porter's explanation of the national 'diamond' is a major contribution to discussion of global competition and the sources of the new wealth of nations.

'Horses for courses: organizational forms for multinational corporations' (Chapter 3) is a description by Ghosal and Nohria of a simple scheme which they offer to classify the environment and structure of MNCs. One of the most enduring ideas of organizational theory is that an organization's structure and management process must 'fit' its environment, in the same way that a particular horse might be more suited to one course than another. The complexity of the firm's structure may not match the complexity of its environment. The article describes four types of MNC environments – global – multinational – transnational – international. This is an important and useful distinction between the different environments in which MNCs operate across the world.

Anthony Eames, President and Chief Executive Officer of Coca-Cola, moves us from the theoretical to the practical (Chapter 4). Competition brings out the best in everyone, he asserts. It demands excellence in everything we do. One thing you learn quickly in international business, he argues, is that in reality each country requires its own textbook. He lists the 'Commandments for Losing' rather than answering the question, 'What makes a winner?'.

In 'The Internationalization of the firm: four Swedish cases' (Chapter 5), Johanson and Wiedersheim-Paul describe and analyse the internationalization of four Swedish firms. They describe the concept of psychic distance, which is defined as factors preventing or disturbing the flows of information between firms and markets. Examples of such factors are language, culture and political systems. They used the research to test their basic assumption that the firms first developed in the domestic market and that the internationalization is the consequence of a series of incremental decisions.

The sixth article, by Sharp – 'Business environment assessment' – is a description of how US multinational corporations structure their assessments of the business environment external to the firm which impact on its international strategy. The Issues Monitoring System (IMS) which was successfully developed and implemented in a large, multinational manufacturing firm is a comprehensive and practical method of ensuring that the changes in the international political, social and economic environment in which MNCs operate are taken into account in developing company strategy. This process, in which the editor of this book was involved with Dan Sharp, is of some importance in strategy development. Business and government are inextricably intertwined in the creation of wealth. The concept of the 'level playing field' is a new and dangerous theory. It claims that all government needs to do is to provide a level playing field and then let the creators of wealth, that is, companies across the world, fight out their competitive battles in the interests of mankind. Level playing fields are, of course, desirable, but games cannot be played on them without rules and referees. These are provided by governments. The relationship of MNCs to governments across the world will be an increasingly important one in developing successful company strategies.

International economic integration is growing and the trend is neither new nor uniform. Henderson, in the seventh article, 'International economic integration: progress, prospects and implications', argues that an economically borderless world does not now exist, nor is it in prospect. The world economy today is further away from full integration than it was before the First World War. Whether and how far the trend towards integration will continue is not predetermined, but depends on governments. While so-called 'trade blocks' are unlikely to be a threat, the drift towards managed trade, especially in the USA and the EU, has yet to be reversed. The most difficult issues of integration relate to cross-border migration, which is now a leading item on the international agenda.

'The cultural relativity of organizational practices and theories' is the title of the eighth contribution, by Hofstede. His article summarizes recently published findings about the differences in people's work-related values in fifty countries. In view of these differences, ethnocentric management theories (those based on the value system of one particular country) have become untenable. This concept is illustrated for the fields of leadership, organization and motivation. What we need, he argues, is more cultural sensitivity in management theories. The convergence of management will never come. What we can bring about is an understanding of how the culture in which we grew up and which is dear to us affects our thinking differently from other people's thinking and what this means for the transfer of management practices and theories. He suggests that this understanding could lead to a better ability to manage intercultural negotiations in multicultural organizations like the United Nations, which are essential for the common survival of us all.

Brewster's article, 'Developing a 'European' model of human resource management' (Chapter 9) concludes this first part. HRM developed initially in the USA and the terminology has spread across the developed English-speaking world and recently into Europe. A range of subject areas in which organizations in Europe are supported/constrained by external factors leads the author to challenge the validity of the American model. A new model of the concept which would encompass Euro-HRM is proposed.

PART II: COMMUNICATIONS, MARKETING, PRODUCTION AND FINANCE

'Tech talk: how managers are stimulating global R&D communication' (Chapter 10) is the title of De Meyer's contribution. It is hard enough to keep the communication flowing in one R&D laboratory, but when you've got thousands of employees in dozens of labs all over the world, the task is Herculean. In this paper, De Meyer reports on the activities of fourteen multinational companies that are trying to improve communications among and within their labs. He describes the six broad areas where companies are seeking solutions and discusses the potential difficulties and rewards of each.

'Rattling SABRE: new ways to compete on information' (Chapter 11) is written by a practitioner who was Senior Vice-President for Information Systems at American Airlines. Hopper asserts that American Airlines built much of its business around massive, centralized proprietary computer systems. The competitive advantage of that era is now over. Thinking guided by 'best practice', as recently as five years ago, is actually counter-productive. On its own, he argues, an information system cannot build enduring business advantage. Soon computers will be as ubiquitous as telephones and as easy to use. He takes as a case study SABRE, which was the world's leading computerized reservations system. Today SABRE is neither a proprietary competitive weapon for American Airlines, nor a general distribution system for the airline industry. It is an electronic travel supermarket. A travel agent can replace SABRE in just thirty days – so how can SABRE create a long-term competitive advantage? As it reshapes the nature of work and redefines organizational structures, technology itself will recede into the strategic background. Information systems will be thought of more like electricity or telephone networks and as a decisive source of organizational advantage.

'*Technik*: managers and management in Germany' by Lawrence is Chapter 12. The word *technik* is a word and concept that does not exist in all languages. This short article is supportive of the interaction approach of international enterprise. The author describes how *technik* exerts a pervasive influence in German firms and on German managerial thinking. It is a force for integration and is perhaps sufficiently pervasive to have some integrating effect between technical and commercial functions.

Lessard's article 'Finance and global competition: exploiting financial scope and coping with volatile exchange rates' (Chapter 13) argues that volatile exchange rates distort traditional measures of current and long-term profitability. This creates illusions that depend on the currency in which strategic alternatives are weighed and operating managers' performance evaluated. In the short run, volatility of exchange rates obscures longer-term trends in the international competitive position of particular industries. It argues for a closer linkage of competitive analysis and quantitative techniques rather than more subjective approaches. A firm's ability to pass on differential financing, costs and taxes is reduced by global competition, but, to compete effectively, MNCs will have to match their competitors' 'cost of capital'. An ideal performance measurement system would hold managers responsible for those aspects of performance over which they have substantial control, but should limit responsibility for performance shifts due to factors largely beyond their control. The increasing integration of financial markets and the continuing exchange rate volatility presents a major threat and challenge to multinational corporations and in particular to the finance function.

The penultimate article is by Dunning. 'Trade, location of economic activity and the multinational enterprise: a search for an eclectic approach', discusses ways in which production financed by foreign direct investment affects our thinking about international allocation of resources. The article argues the case for an integrated approach to international economic involvement and explains the foreign activities of enterprises in terms of their abilities to internalize markets to their advantage. Finally, it examines the effects which MNCs are alleged to have on resource allocation and patterns of trade.

'Is manufacturing still special in the new world order?' In this final article Brown and Julius describe two major shifts in the world economy: geographic and sectoral. The sectoral shift is from manufacturing towards the service sector. The impact of this is exacerbated by a geographical shift, the consequence of the growing comparative advantage of developing countries producing manufactured goods. The authors have identified three key arguments of what they call the Manufacturing Is Special School (MISS). They review arguments for this and conclude that the trend to services is a desirable and natural phenomenon. Manufacturing businesses increasingly will have to locate in low-cost developing countries. This will create pressure for subsidies and protection which should be resisted.

The European Union (EU) has replaced the European Community (EC), which itself replaced The European Economic Community (EEC) as the collective name for the Member States which signed the founding Treaty of Rome in 1957 or subsequent amending treaties. References to the EEC and EC which appear in some of the articles in the reader which were correct at the time the articles were written, have been left in the text unaltered. Similarly, dates are left as given in the original articles.

Part I

International enterprise: strategies and people

Chapter 1

The effects of globalization and turbulence on policy-making processes

Miriam L. Campanella

During recent years analysts of world politics have noted increasing tensions and conflicts between the countries of the OECD area. As the process of globalization is extending to include several new sectors of domestic economies, multilateralism is deteriorating and perhaps, in some sectors, reaching breaking-point. Globalization, widely acknowledged as a powerful engine for the growth of the world economy during the 1970s and 1980s, is now splitting up into trading blocs and much more limited minilateralism. This contribution aims to analyse the extent to which policy-making could be improved so that it can address and deal with the effects of globalization and turbulence on domestic and international environments. Attention is focused on two distinctive sources of turbulence. The first, external-led turbulence, is generated by globalization dynamics and is mainly played out by transnational actors who are particularly visible in monetary issues and financial volatility. The second source, defined as domestic-led turbulence (now highly visible in several difficult trade issues and in the economic recession taking place in many European countries) is being fed by the domestic counter-reactions and maladaptations to new challenges arising from the globalization of markets and production. It can result in a domestication of international politics that could lead to unease and to uncomfortable international agendas being set up (the Uruguay Round is not a unique example of this).

Even though it is true, as Ruggie and Caporaso[1] have recently asserted, that peaceful change has occurred, causing a fundamental geopolitical shift in the post-war era, and that multilateral norms and institutions have contributed greatly to this success, there is frequent evidence that multilateralism is perhaps now nearing a turning-point because of a demand overload which its own success has stimulated. Examples are the difficult Uruguay negotiations and the wider consequences that the erosion of the triadic coalition and the protectionist mood could cause to the newcomers to free market capitalism in Asia, in Eastern Europe and in South America.[2] Today GATT (General Agreement on Tariffs and Trade) has almost five times as many members as it had when it was created. Moreover, the agenda for the Uruguay Round is much more ambitious. While previous talks put most effort into cutting tariffs, today's aim is also to encompass areas of trade that have so far remained outside the GATT structure, such as services, textiles and agriculture. Demand overload on multilateral institutions is creating doubts and is causing several enthusiastic Europeanists to rethink monetary union.

However, there is a certain logic in this state of affairs. In 1942 Theodor Geiger forecast the scenario we have today. He depicted an international, global economy, riddled by tensions between obtaining the benefits of international interdependence and preserving those of national freedom of action in both internal and external affairs.[3] Robert Gilpin describes the scenario of the international economy in similar terms: 'The clash between the integrating forces of the world economy and the centrifugal forces of the sovereign states has become one of the critical issues in contemporary international relations'.[4] As far as globalization is affecting domestic economies, domestic-led turbulence is generating a new source of instability and uncertainty among OECD countries. Policy-makers are still confronted by transnational actors and only now do they have to face the problems created by the domestication of their foreign policy agenda.

EFFECTS OF GLOBALIZATION: OPERATIONAL DEFINITIONS[5]

Even if several theorists of globalization have amply warned about the asymmetries and discontinuities which the globalization process is likely to produce in economic and political governance,[6] the idea still persists that globalization is mainly homogeneous and symmetrical.[7] Globalization for these purposes is assumed to be a process defined in an operational way, so as to avoid ideological shortcomings and panaceas. The definition offered by the OECD selects three main factors:

1 The entrance of new powerful actors such as the transnational corporations (TNCs) onto the political scene.
2 The rapid diffusion of soft technologies in communication and information.
3 The approval of deregulation policies in several OECD countries.[8]

These three factors have been particularly active in OECD area since the 1970s. To take the first point, aggregate data on foreign direct investment (FDI), show a spectacular economic invasion of the TNCs (transnational corporations) in domestic economies. After reaching a peak in 1981, FDI inflows feel during the last four years of the 1980s. European and Japanese firms, attracted by the brighter prospects of the US economy and wanting to gain access to US technology, switched their investment strategy and this brought about a major shift in FDI flows toward the USA and away from the developing countries. As a consequence, the United States became the largest recipient of FDI, receiving almost 40 per cent of the inflows in the first half of the 1980s. At the same time, aided by the dynamism of its TNCs, Japan emerged as a major home country, and its outflows doubled in 1986 alone. Western Europe, on the other hand, became the world's largest source of FDI.

Table 1.1 Distribution of foreign direct investments outflows, by major home countries, 1975–1985

Country groups by region	1975	1980	1981	1982	1983	1984	1985	Annual averages 1975–1980	1981–1985
Developed market economies	98.9	98.1	99.4	96.6	97.3	98.6	98.0	98.8	98.0
Western Europe	36.6	47.2	53.6	59.0	60.5	59.2	50.4	44.4	55.6
France	4.7	5.4	8.3	8.6	4.7	4.9	3.7	4.5	5.5
Germany, Federal Republic of	7.2	7.3	7.6	8.6	8.8	10.0	8.2	7.7	8.6
Italy	1.1	1.2	2.6	3.1	5.8	4.6	3.0	1.0	3.8
Netherlands	8.3	10.4	8.7	10.1	10.1	11.6	5.3	9.4	8.8
Switzerland	—	—	—	—	1.4	2.6	6.0	—	—
United Kingdom	10.9	19.8	22.6	22.0	22.5	18.8	18.7	17.4	20.8
Japan	6.5	4.2	9.1	13.8	9.9	13.7	10.7	5.5	11.0
United States	51.4	38.0	22.9	19.0	9.9	13.2	25.4	42.4	19.0
Developing countries	1.1	1.9	0.6	3.4	2.7	1.4	2.0	1.2	1.8
World*	100	100	100	100	100	100	100	100	100
Billions of dollars	27.6	57.6	54.1	32.7	36.5	43.1	59.9	40.3	45.3

Source: United Nations Centre on Transnational Corporations, based on International Monetary Fund, balance of payments tape; and other official national and international sources.
* Excluding the centrally planned economies of Europe.

The impact of soft technologies as the second major factor of globalization has been combined with the relevant growth of high-value services (banking, financial activities, advertising, etc.). The diffusion of soft technologies has led the shift of transnational activities to services as a major factor of instability of national and supranational monetary systems.[9] The third major factor favouring economic and financial globalization coincided with the acceptance of economic policies based on a growing aversion to government intervention and regulation in economic affairs and on theoretical doubts about the effectiveness of such intervention in terms of the rational expectations of government policies. Deregulation and privatization in the USA, in Great Britain, and other OECD countries, while freeing domestic economies from state regulatory legislation[10] and favouring competitiveness and efficiency of the respective domestic economies, have also exposed them to greater external vulnerability. The net

result is that transnationalization has been greatly increased the interdependence and the interpenetration of free economies, but it has not led
to a corresponding decline in the invisible and visible barriers in many
countries. The Japanese challengers have helped several other players to
profit from the liberalization of trade and tariffs, but they have also
instructed them to protect their own domestic economies through invisible
barriers and unfair rules, as their critics claim. In Asia and Latin America,
while several governments are reinforcing the role of state agencies by
creating what have been labelled as truly 'trading states',[11] cash flows have
increased dramatically in many Asian countries. While Western and
former command economies in Eastern Europe are suffering from severe
capital shortage, some analysts find that small Chinese countries (Hong
Kong, Taiwan and Singapore) are rapidly displacing the Japanese as the
leading investors in most of South-East Asia.[12] Economies in the 1990s
seem to be entering into a phase of global turbulence with advanced OECD
economies facing the big new players now coming from the Third World.

Given the interdependent linkages that globalization has created between actors of different countries, the vulnerability and sensitivity of
countries to each other will increase.[13] As Soediomoto of the United
Nations university of Tokyo observed:

> In the process of interdependence, we have all become *vulnerable*. Our
> societies are permeable to decisions taken elsewhere in the world. The
> dynamics of interdependence might better be understood if we think of
> the globe not in terms of a map of nations but as a meteorological map,
> where weather systems swirl independently of any national boundaries
> and low and high fronts create new climatic conditions far ahead of
> them.[14]

The metaphor can help as long as we recognize vulnerability and, to a less
extent, sensitivity as expressions of the presence of power in interdependence. They can tell us about how and where an actor's strategic
interest is affected, and the extent to which policy responses are effective
in countering the actions of the other actors. By focusing attention on these
two effects of globalization we are much nearer to understanding the *locus
a quo* turbulence originates. The policies adopted by vulnerable actors are
generally ineffective in reducing the negative consequences of interdependence. Sensitive actors are more successful in adjusting their own
domestic economy to the global environment. One of the most frequently
used examples is the impact of the oil price increases in the early 1970s.
This produced sensitivity only in some OECD countries, those which were
less dependent upon OPEC supplies of oil. In others, however, including
several Third World countries, it produced vulnerability. Actors may react
to vulnerability and sensitivity by adopting at least two different strategic
policies. They resort to cooperation and tighter coordination, if incremental
policies are drawn up to adjust and adapt to the global environment. Or,

alternatively, they can resort to conflictual negotiations and isolationist threats if decremental policies are drawn up to deal with global challenges. When cooperation and coordination as well as conflictual negotiations and isolationist threats fail, turbulence sets in. There are several and un-predictable sources of turbulence. Nevertheless, two loci are likely to generate turbulence which is seen in the transnational environment, made up of TNCs and TN actors, and the domestic environment.

I suggest that the two different types of turbulence should be referred to as global or transnational-led turbulence, and local or domestic-led turbulence. The former is mainly generated by the pressure of a global market and by the volatility and fluctuations of financial transactions. An example of this is the mid-September 1992 currency turmoil when central banks were faced with vigorous currency trading. Traders overwhelmed central banks, which were incapable of defending their respective cur-rencies on the world's foreign exchange markets. The domestic-led turbulence originates from the counter-reaction of the exposed domestic economy to the transnational environment. Counter-reactions could take the form of protectionist claims against 'unfair' traders, or aggregate parochial, social and economic groups deciding to nationalize 'strategic' economic sectors, so causing others, such as private corporations, to disinvest and to emigrate.[15] Trade and monetary issues are often more sensitive to global turbulence as they are the two sectors exposed to international interdependence.[16] Global as well as domestic-led turbu-lence are generally believed to hamper the officials' capabilities of adopting a conventional solution to problems. Nevertheless, both kinds of turbulence could offer governments the chance to adopt effective and affirmative policies. Policy-makers could manage domestic constraints so as to benefit from the international arena; or the reverse could be true – they could use international constraints (often the surveillance services of the most highly reputed international institutions, such as the Inter-national Monetary Fund or European advisory commissions, and others) to influence the domestic area (parliament, unions, parties, etc.) so as to implement severe fiscal and budgetary policies. This is not the case for less developed countries. Today Greece and Italy are trying to use external constraints in order to introduce a new deal in their own domestic societies. In conclusion, vulnerability, sensitivity and turbulence reveal the iterative nature of cooperation and conflict, and the new opportunities and chances which globalization offers policy-makers in their successful management of policy agenda.

THE DILEMMA OF GLOBALIZATION

In order to describe the process of globalization and the effects it produces among the actors involved, I have resorted to the epistemology of the system-centred analysis. The obvious reason is that the studies on transnational relations have managed to give primacy to the role and constraints TNCs or powerful actors (hegemonic powers) have exerted on distinctive national governments. Nevertheless, systemic-centred approaches (including the theory of hegemonic stability) at least take account of the international constraints placed on nation-states. Domestic problems, however, even those generated by the impact of globalization on national economies, are scarcely considered. There is a lack of interest consistent with the rationale of the systemic-centred approach, which could cause serious oversights and failure to examine the problematique of governance of globalization. As well as the lack of interest, however, there is an assumption that complex interdependence or globalization would cause an erosion of the authority of nation-states and national polities. This presumption has led systemic theorists to consider the ascendancy of regional and global polities as a corresponding decline of nation-states.[17] By allowing for a sense of symmetry, which has subsequently turned out to be completely inappropriate also for the powerful hegemon, such as the USA, systemic-centred analysts have ended up by accepting a policy of inertia at home, and feverish activism abroad. Further, the systemic-centred approach has promoted in different fields of global governance the view that a multi-layered political configuration, in which the primacy of the nation-state is being replaced, is likely to include every political institution in global governance. Even if, to some extent, this view has been useful in sketching the new map of political institutions, settings and arenas,[18] if does not provide an account of the dynamics created by the globalization processes and the turbulence which pervades domestic factors today.

In this context, the systemic approach underestimates the new role which is being played by state officials and institutions. In the context of European studies, even though several analysts have often recognized the great impetus which institutional entrepreneurs (Monnet or Delors) have given to the acceleration of European political integration, systemic analysts have adopted the visualization of multi-layered political configuration in which national institutions seem naturally to behave as a medium between local and supranational institutions and decision-making. In effect, there is no reason to believe that supranational institutions will replace national polities, and that the latter will be reduced to the 'subsidiary' implementaton of the EU policies, at least in the short run. In fact, the systemic-centred approach fails when it assumes that a lower and local level will necessarily be subsumed within a more global, higher level, or even when, by recognizing a degree of relative autonomy to each level of the whole configuration, it implies a harmonious design of the new world order.

There is no evidence that the actors comply with such an idealized and geometric logic. Studies on foreign economic policy have shown the extent to which government officials within the state, who typically face a national electorate and are charged with the overall defence and welfare of the nation-state, are particularly sensitive to the constraints and opportunities offered by globalization. Yet at the same time they seek to influence the logic of global dynamics, even by playing a key role in shaping new political configurations. Perhaps one explanation for the persistence of the symmetry assumption of the systemic-centred analysis lies in the fact that for a long time the notion of 'national interest' has fallen into disuse and misconception. The literature of the 1960s, 1970s and 1980s abounds with sophisticated and convincing analyses which do not recognize that notion.[19] Nevertheless it is true that high-level government officials who were led to develop a distinctive and autonomous set of preferences cannot be ignored by political analysts in a phase of greater uncertainty and turbulence in the world economy.[20]

It is also true that those officials have continually come up against difficulties in assessing a consistent policy design, and a comprehensive set of alternatives. Although they operate under conditions of limited rationality, those officials are placed in a position to play a major role in managing global links in order to maintain domestic affluence. Yet they fear the effects of these forces as they can undermine the management goals which are being pursued.[21]

MATCHING THEORY AND PRAXIS: THE COGNITIVE ROOTS OF POLICY-MAKING

Even though theory and praxis are believed to be inconsistent and difficult to bring together, a linkage for the cognitive map and the preference rankings and goals being pursued has been found. In my concluding section, I would like to select at least three major lines of reasoning which aim at visualizing the resulting policy outcomes.[22]

- Policy-makers who assume transnational relations as 'first cut' in their representation, are often tempted to emphasize the international agenda, and to be active in international institutions and regimes. An example is the economic foreign policy of dominant or 'hegemonic' states such as Great Britain in the nineteenth century and of the USA after the Second World War. Hegemonic states have a strong preference for liberal economic regimes and they possess the power to create and maintain such regimes, either by providing collective goods (security, energy and others) or by coercing reluctant states to participate.
- Policy-makers particularly aware of the domestic arena are expected to behave differently. As interest groups and coalitions exercise a major influence in agenda-setting and in ad hoc negotiations, policy-makers

concentrate their attention more on the demand for policy than on its supply. Incidentally, such an approach which is particularly sensitive to trade issues can lead to snap decisions and highly inconsistent foreign policies. The protectionist policies being advocated in various parts of the world today are a case in point.

- By seeing interdependence and globalization as elements in a dynamic environment which challenge the capabilities of the participating actors and institutions, policy-makers might feel a duty to act as manager-like actors whose aim is to prevent organizational decline and policy inertia. This is achieved by resorting to cooperation and coordination, and by activating networking and new institutional settings. Such an approach views state institutions neither as a source of authority, nor as obsolete. Policy-makers always manage to adapt state institutions to their objectives. However, the result is not limited to a deterministic state-building, assumed as an active and purposeful process. Policy-makers, while not disliking international commitments, tend to give preference to transnational settings and policy coordination which could influence the domestic economy and political system so that it would undertake painful changes and risk innovations. As a result domestic problems will be tackled looking outward and highly pro-active policies will be promoted.[23]

The approaches described above are suitable for different countries and reflect the different ranking of each country in international competition. Nevertheless, the erosion of hegemonic powers, in particular of the USA, and increasing interdependence, make the first two approaches less attractive. The third approach offers an acceptable explanation of the institutional revival at a local level (state-building), at supranational level (European Union-like), and at global level (redesigning the UN sub-divisions and other international organizations such as NATO). By limiting the analysis to the first and second institutional policies, care should be taken not to overemphasize the momentum of supranational political institutions nor to underestimate the increasing efforts to readjust or redesign state institutions. This is not only the case for some Eastern European countries, in which it is evidence of the need to rebuild the legality and legitimation of public institutions after the collapse of communist regimes. In Western Europe as well the collapse of the Berlin Wall has opened a new phase of state-building, where the role of political parties and unions is expected to be limited and ruled by new state agencies.

There is a lot of evidence that the state institutions are still expected to play an important role in the new context of globalization. As several studies have shown, in some OECD countries, given the established state tradition, the internal hierarchy of the central institutions is adapting to the new transnational environment. As transgovernmental relations have grown constantly during the last three decades, they are beginning to play an increasingly crucial role in every nation's external profile. The traditional monopoly of the foreign ministry on external contacts is challenged by non-governmental actors and by the centralized and decentralized state agencies themselves. In the EU regional governments and sub-regional units have even assumed an external profile within the area of the European Union boundaries, and are developing their own international environment. A recent comparative and longitudinal study of foreign policy management in Sweden and Finland also provides evidence that, at the central level, interdependence causes the role played by foreign affairs in the broader community to be transformed significantly.[24] Transgovernmental relations are becoming an increasingly crucial element of every nation's external profile. There is evidence that the foreign ministry's traditional monopoly of external contacts is now being challenged by several centralized or even decentralized sub-national units. In the EU, regional governments and even non-governmental associations have taken on an external profile, and some of them are pressing for their co-decisional capabilities to be acknowledged (the case of the German Länder).[25]

CONCLUSION

In this brief contribution an attempt has been made to consider the effects of globalization and turbulence on the policy-making process. First, the ways in which they affect the actors involved have been identified. Second, the responses and the different policy activities have been seen at the international, national and transnational level. The author's preference for the institution-building approach is based on the possibilities it offers at cognitive and operative levels. It is also being adopted as the chosen style of decision and policy-making of several top-level countries. Finally, in spite of the new primacy of economics, the forms of alternative assessment and policy-making have been observed once again, falling back on state institutions and actors. Public bodies, even though they are forced to act at the margins, manipulating different types of constraints and resorting to cooperation and networking, are being highly stimulated by appropriate settings (international organizations such as the World Bank, IMF, and supranational institutions) to undertake sustainable policy actions. The linkage between globalization and turbulence and institutional learning could help in understanding the new attitude of several Third World countries toward maintaining formal and legal sovereignty but advocating the adoption of profitable common market agreements, and so creating changes and opportunities for domestic welfare. The case of the North American Free Trade Agreement and the likely inclusion of other Central and South American countries in similar enterprises is not simply a replica of the European Community. It proves that even younger state-actors, but not only them, are more likely to be committed to institution-building at a supranational level. These actor probably resort to institutional learning, active revision of rules and blueprints, organizational innovation and strategic decision-making, thus helping toward globalization of the world economy. This is a process that supranational institutions have stimulated profoundly.

NOTES AND REFERENCES

1   On multilateralism and minilaterism see: John Ruggie, 'Multilateralism: The Anatomy of an Institution', *International Organization*, Vol. 46, No. 3, 1992; James A. Caporaso, 'International Relations Theory and Multilateralism: The Search for Foundations', *International Organization*, Vol. 46, No. 3, 1992; Miles Kahler 'Multilateralism with Small and Large Numbers', *International Organization*, Vol. 46, No.3, 1992.

2   The end of the year number of *The Economist: Looking Back from 2992*, Vol. 325, Number 7791, 1992, comments on the consequences of a failure of the victorious coalition between the United States, the European Community and Japan.

3   Theodor Geiger, *The Future of the International System: The United States and the World Political Economy* [translation], London, Unwin Hyman, 1988, p. 114.

4   Robert Gilpin, *The Political Economy of International Relations*, Princeton, Princeton University Press, 1987.

5   James N. Rosenau, *The Study of Global Interdependence: Essays on the Trans-nationalization of World Affairs*, London, Pinter, 1980; Miriam Campanella, 'Globalization: Processes and Problems', *World Futures*, Nos 1–2, 1991.

6   An example is Martin Albrow and Elizabeth King (eds), *Globalization, Knowledge and Society*, London, Sage, 1990.

7   OECD, *Background Report by the Secretary General, Concluding the Technology/Economy Programme*, C/MIN 891 14, Paris, 1991.

8   United Nations, *Transnational Corporations in World Development: An Overview*, New York, 1988, p. 77.

9   For a theoretical assessment of the shift produced by service activities in the global economy and in the multilateral debate which has developed during the Uruguay Round negotiations, see William J. Drake and Kalypso Nicolaids, 'Ideas, Interests, and Institutionalization: "Trade in Services" and the Uruguay Round', *International Organization*, Vol. 46, No. 1, Winter 1992 pp. 37–100.

10   Andrew Massey, 'Managing Change: Politicians and Experts in the Age of Privatization', *Government and Opposition*, Vol. 27, No. 4, Autumn 1992.

11   R. Rosencrance, *The Rise of the Trading State: Commerce and Conquest in the Modern World*, New York, Basic Books, 1986. On the strategic trade policy and the role of the state, a new school has grown up in the USA advocating managed trade policies. See Paul Krugman (ed.), *Strategic Trade Policy and the New International Economics*, Cambridge, Mass., MIT Press, 1990 and Laura D'Andrea Tyson, *Who's Bashing Whom*, Institute for International Economics, Washington 1993.

12   Joel Kotkin, 'Economies in the '90's: Big New Players from the Third World', *International Herald Tribune*, 3 January 1993. *Tribes: How Race, Religion and Identities Determine Success in the New Global Economy*, 1993

13   The two terms were first introduced by Keohane and Nye: Robert Keohane and Joseph Nye, *Power and Interdependence: World Politics in Transition*, Boston,

Little Brown & Co., 1977; Robert Keohane, *After Hegemony. Cooperation and Discord in the World Political Economy,* Princeton University Press, 1984.

14 Soediomoto, 'Opening Statements', in Michael J. L. Kirby, *The Science and Praxis of Complexity,* contribution to the Symposium held at Montpellier, 9–11 May 1984, The United Nation University of Tokyo, 1987.

15 This was not only the case for Peronist Argentina but also for some OECD countries.

16 Joanna Gowa, 'Public Goods and Political Institutions: Trade and Monetary Policy Processes in the United States', in G. John Inkenberry, David A. Lake, and Michael Mastanduno (eds), *The State American Foreign Economic Policy,* Ithaca, Cornell University Press, 1988; G. John Ikenberry, 'Conclusion: An Institutional Approach to American Foreign Economic Policy', in Ikenberry, Lake and Mastanduno, op. cit., pp. 219–243.

17 Robert Keohane and Joseph Nye, *Power and Interdependence: World Politics in Transition,* Boston, Little Brown & Co., 1977; Miriam Campanella, *Stato-nazione e ordine sociale. Modelli paradigmi delle societa complesse,* Milan, Angeli, 1984.

18 See, for example, Ernst B. Haas, *When Knowledge is Power. Three Models of Change in International Organization,* Berkeley, University of California Press, 1990; Marvin S. Sorrows, *Beyond Sovereignty. The Challenge of the Global Policy,* University of S. Carolina Press, 1986.

19 James N. Rosenau, 'The National Interest', in *Encyclopedia of Social Sciences,* 1968.

20 Stephen Krasner. 'Approaches to the State: Alternative Conceptions and Historical Dynamics', *Comparative Politics,* No. 16, 1984.

21 Bengt Sundelius, *Managing Trans-nationalism in Northern Europe,* Boulder, Colorado, Westview, 1978.

22 The scheme that follows has been freely reworked on the basis of the tripartite presented in Ikenberry, op cit., note 16.

23 Proactive versus adaptive policies are urged in Miriam Campanella, 'Proactive Policy-making the State-actor', *Government and Opposition,* Vol. 26, No. 4, 1991; 'The Globalization Challenges. Globalization, Governance, and Technology Transfer', Monitor-Fast, *Global Perspective 2010, Task for S&T,* 1993.

24 Lauri Karvonen and Bengt Sundelius, 'Interdependence and Foreign Policy Management in Sweden and Finland', *International Studies Quarterly,* Vol. 34, No. 2, June 1990, p. 213.

25 James G. March and Johan P. Olsen, 'The New Institutionalism: Organizational Factors in Political Life', *American Political Science Review,* No. 78, September 1984.

Chapter 2

The determinants and dynamics of national advantage

Michael E. Porter

DETERMINANTS OF NATIONAL ADVANTAGE

Why does a nation achieve international success in a particular industry? The answer lies in four abroad attributes of a nation that shape the environment in which local firms compete that promote or impede the creation of competitive advantage (see Figure 2.1):

1 *Factor conditions.* The nation's position in factors of production, such as skilled labour or infrastructure, necessary to compete in a given industry.
2 *Demand conditions.* The nature of home demand for the industry's product or service.
3 *Related and supporting industries.* The presence or absence in the nation of supplier industries and related industries that are internationally competitive.
4 *Firm strategy, structure, and rivalry.* The conditions in the nation governing how companies are created, organized, and managed, and the nature of domestic rivalry.

The determinants, individually and as a system, create the context in which a nation's firms are born and compete: the availability of resources and skills necessary for competitive advantage in an industry, the information that shapes what opportunities are perceived and the directions in which resources and skills are deployed; the goals of the owners, managers, and employees that are involved in or carry out competition; and most importantly, the pressures on firms to invest and innovate.

Firms gain competitive advantage where their home base allows and supports the most rapid accumulation of specialized assets and skills, sometimes due solely to greater commitment. Firms gain competitive advantage in industries when their home base affords better ongoing information and insight into product and process needs. Firms gain competitive advantage when the goals of owners, managers, and employees support intense commitment and sustained investment. Ulti-

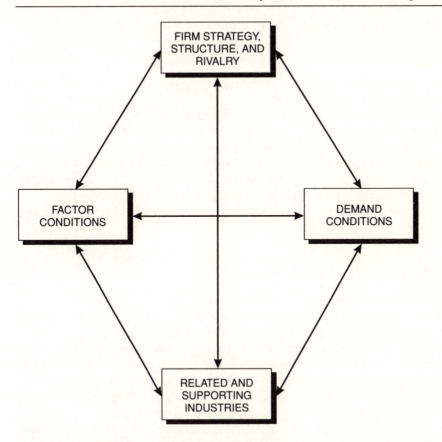

Figure 2.1 The determinants of national advantage

mately, nations succeed in particular industries because their home environment is the most dynamic and the most challenging, and stimulates and prods firms to upgrade and widen their advantages over time.

Nations are most likely to succeed in industries or industry segments where the national 'diamond', a term I will use to refer to the determinants as a system, is the most favorable. This is not to say that all a nation's firms will achieve competitive advantage in an industry. In fact, the more dynamic the national environment, the more likely it is that some firms will fail, because not all have equal skills and resources, nor do they exploit the national environment equally well. Yet those companies that emerge from such an environment will prosper in international competition.

The 'diamond' is a mutually reinforcing system. The effect of one determinant is contingent on the state of others. Favorable demand conditions, for example, will not lead to competitive advantage unless the state of rivalry is sufficient to cause firms to respond to them. Advantages in one determinant can also create or upgrade advantages in others.

RELATIONSHIPS AMONG THE DETERMINANTS

The determinants of national advantage reinforce each other and proliferate over time in fostering competitive advantage in an industry. As this mutual reinforcement proceeds, the cause and effect of individual determinants becomes blurred. The 'diamond' that I use to illustrate the determinants, with its two-way arrows connecting them, is symbolic of these relationships. In reality, every determinant can affect every other determinant, though some interactions are stronger and more important than others.

Patterns of factor creation

The types of factors that are created in a nation are influenced by the other determinants, particularly those types of factors most decisive for national competitive advantage. Investments in generalized factors, such as transportation infrastructure and the secondary school system, are made in virtually every nation, normally as a natural outcome of public policy at various levels of government. What varies is a nation's rate of investment, its desired standard of performance, and how well the institutions involved in creating factors are administered. Though generalized factors are not a sufficient basis for national advantage in advanced industries, they serve as the foundation from which advanced and specialized factors are created. Sustained national investment in generalized factors is therefore essential to national economic progress.

What is important for competitive advantage is unusually effective mechanisms for creating and upgrading factors that are advanced and specialized, such as a world-class research institute in composite materials technology. Investments in advanced and specialized factors are governed in more complicated ways. Unlike generalized factors, investments in them are far from evenly spread across national economies. Nations differ widely in the industries and sectors in which private and social investments in factor creation are made. In Denmark, for example, there are eleven agricultural colleges, the world-renowned Carlsberg Institute engaged in fermentation and biological research, and several professorships of furniture design, all in a nation of only five million inhabitants.

Where do advanced and specialized factors get created and upgraded in a nation? The other determinants of national competitive advantage have an important if not decisive role. Figure 2.2 illustrates several of the most important influences.

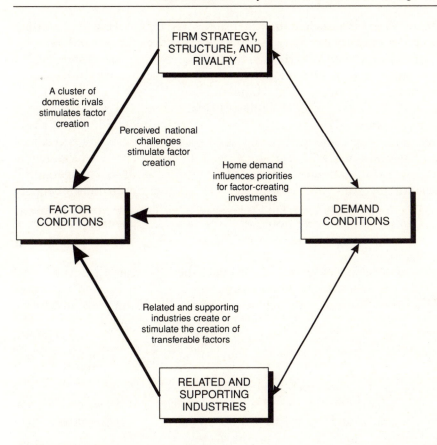

Figure 2.2 Influences on factor creation

Factor creation is perhaps most strongly influenced by domestic rivalry. A number of local competitors in vigorous competition stimulates the rapid development of skilled human resources, related technologies, market-specific knowledge, and specialized infrastructure. Firms invest in factor creation themselves, singly or via trade associations, under pressure not to fall behind. Factor creation will be unusually rapid in industries viewed as prestigious or as national priorities, because the attention of individuals, institutions, and government entities is most attracted. These effects will be most pronounced if the rivals are all located in one city or region. The number of degree programs, data bases, and research efforts in and around New York related to Wall Street is a typical example. There are four specialized university research institutes catering to the auto industry in southern Germany.

A single large firm can have some effect on factor creation, particularly if it is a major economic influence on a town or region. However, a group of rivals usually provides far more stimulation for several reasons. Competition among local rivals spills over into efforts to court and develop relationships with educational institutions, research institutions, and information providers. This competition will boost the rate of factor creation. The presence of a number of rivals not only signals the import-ance and potential of the industry, causing individuals and institutions to take notice, but also reduces the risk of investing in creating specialized facilities and skills. With a group of rivals, there are a number of potential employers for graduates and several supporters and users of specialized facilities, programs, and knowledge. Rivals mitigate each other's bargain-ing power in sourcing specialized factors, promoting an expanded supply. The presence of several domestic rivals may also elevate the political support and consensus for investments in creating specialized factors by government.

The pool of factors and the rate at which they are created are also shaped by the presence of related and supporting industries. Such industries possess or stimulate their own mechanisms for creating and upgrading specialized factors. Some of the factors are usually transferable. The educational programs, skilled personnel, and research capabilities in biology resulting from the Danish food and brewing industries, for example, have been a source of advantage in Denmark's insulin, industrial enzyme, and food additives industries.

The existence of a cluster of several industries that draws on common inputs, skills, and infrastructure also further stimulates government bodies, educational institutions, firms, and individuals to invest in relev-ant factor creation or factor-creating mechanisms. Specialized infrastruc-ture is enlarged, and spillovers are generated that upgrade factor quality and increase supply. Sometimes whole new industries spring up to supply specialized infrastructure to such clusters. Such a mutually reinforcing process is occurring in the United States, where the existence of world-class industries in mainframe computers, minicomputers, microcom-puters, software, and logic circuits has sent public and private institutions scrambling to create software training centers and courses.

Another influence on the particular types of factors that are created is demand conditions. A disproportionate level of demand for a product, or unusually stringent or sophisticated demand, tends to channel social and private investments into related factor creation. Advanced and specialized factors of production grow up to help meet pressing local needs. For example, nations depending heavily on sea transport such as Sweden and Norway have well-developed specialized educational and scientific insti-tutions geared toward oceanography and shipping.

Influences on demand composition and size

Home demand conditions for an industry may reflect many national attributes such as population, climate, social norms, and the mix of other industries in the economy. Yet the other determinants play an important role as well, as illustrated in Figure 2.3.

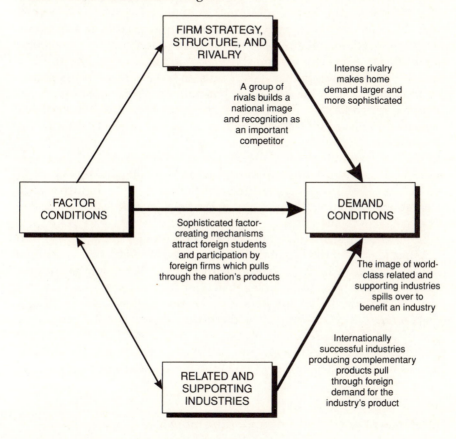

Figure 2.3 Influences on home demand conditions

Perhaps the most important influence is again domestic rivalry. A group of local rivals invests in marketing, driven by an intense commitment and attention to the home market that I have described. Pricing is aggressive to gain or hold local market share. Products are introduced earlier at home, and the available product variety is greater. The very presence of competitive local rivals builds awareness of the industry. Primary demand in the home market is stimulated. Not only is home demand expanded, but saturation occurs sooner and leads to aggressive efforts to internationalize. A good example is the wine industry, where high per capita consumption in wine-producing countries such as Italy and France is due in large part to the presence of local production that is associated with wide local availability of wine and greater product awareness by local consumers.

Active domestic rivalry also upgrades home demand. The presence of a number of aggressive local rivals works to educate local buyers, make them more sophisticated, and make them more demanding because they come to expect a lot of attention. In furniture and shoes, for example, Italian demand has been upgraded by the rapid pace of new product introduction in the home market by the hundreds of Italian companies. Not all Italian firms export, and those that do rarely offer their full line abroad. The net result is that Italian consumers see and learn more and become more discriminating. (In other nations, less competitive local manufacturers offer less choice and quality.) The sophisticated, specialized retailers of furniture and shoes in Italy that I have described earlier reflect intense domestic rivalry in shoe and furniture manufacturing, because local firms were looking for distribution outlets. Retailers compete vigorously and display a wide variety of products for Italian consumers to choose from, educating the consumer in the process. An industry, once internationally competitive, creates conditions domestically which reinforce that competitiveness.

Vigorous domestic rivalry can also enhance foreign demand. A group of domestic rivals builds a national image in the industry. Foreign buyers take notice and include the nation in their review of potential sources. Their perceived risk in sourcing from the nation is reduced by the availability of alternative suppliers. A good example is in cosmetic pencils, where foreign cosmetic companies sought out German suppliers for a new type of pencil because of the group of world-leading German pencil manufacturers in Nuremberg. The presence of successful related and supporting industries can also enhance international demand for an industry's products.

Development of related and supporting industries

The presence, breadth, and international success of related and supporting industries in a nation is influenced by other determinants. Some of the most important relationships are shown in Figure 2.4.

Factor conditions in an industry, especially factor-creating mechanisms, can also influence the development of related and supporting industries. Skills, knowledge, and technology created in an industry spill over to benefit them.

The breadth and specialization of supporting industries is enhanced by the size and growth of home demand for a product. Where home demand is significant, more and specialized suppliers emerge to address unmet needs, replace imports, or perform activities previously carried out in-house more efficiently or effectively. The efficiency of domestic suppliers frequently rises with increasing industry scale.

Once again, the most potent influence on the development of related and supporting industries is aggressive domestic rivals. A group of internationally successful domestic firms, selling worldwide, channels global demand to the domestic supplier industry. For example, the world-leading group of Japanese semiconductor firms has triggered the emergence of world-leading Japanese semiconductor manufacturing equipment suppliers.

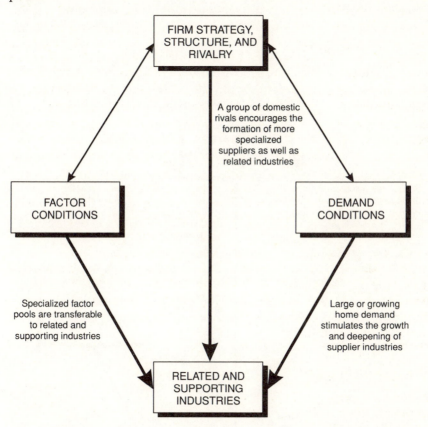

Figure 2.4 Influences on the development of related and supporting industries

A group of domestic rivals is far superior to one dominant firm for encouraging and upgrading home-based supporting industries. The presence of competing home customers reduces the risk of selling to the industry and the bargaining power of any individual buyer, encouraging more entry into supplier industries as well as greater investment and specialization. In addition, the existence of a number of domestic customers, each with some differences in needs, widens the technical avenues explored by suppliers and creates more potential centers of development that speed the rate of innovation.

Cases where internationally competitive supplier industries emerged out of competitive customer industries are numerous. In Germany, for example, a world-leading chemical industry has led to the development of world-class suppliers of pumps, liquid measurement and control equipment, and numerous other products for the chemical sector. In the USA the early success in electronics gave birth to international leadership in such supplier industries as test and measurement equipment.

Influences on domestic rivalry

Domestic industry structure is also influenced by other determinants. Particularly important is the role of other determinants in affecting the number, skills, and strategies of domestic rivals (see Figure 2.5).

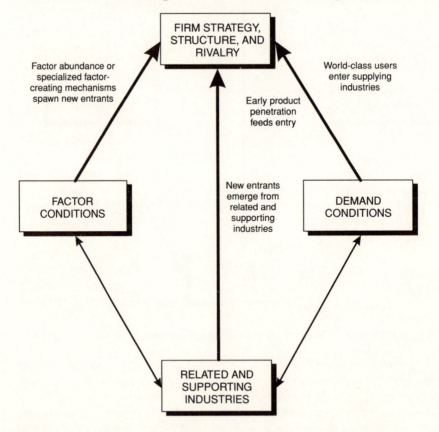

Figure 2.5 Influences on domestic rivalry

Demand conditions enhance domestic rivalry when demanding home buyers seek multiple sources and encourage entry. Highly sophisticated buyers based in a nation may also themselves enter the industry. This is particularly significant when they have relevant skills and view the upstream industry as strategic. A good example is the Japanese robotics industry. Many of the early and leading robotics competitors such as Matsushita and Kawasaki are major robot users. They initially designed robots for internal consumption but then began to sell to others.

New entry into an industry is also encouraged directly or indirectly by strong national positions in related or supporting industries. Entry by established firms in downstream or related industries, which often occurs along with start-ups, produces a domestic industry structure that can be specially conducive to investment and innovation. Suppliers, particularly those which are internationally successful, often enter user industries. In Sweden, for example, Sandvik moved from specialty steel into rock drills, while SKF moved from specialty steel into ball bearings. Supplier strengths in the base industry often provide a competitive advantage in entering downstream industries. Entrants from supplier industries bring with them skills and resources from their core businesses that can reshape competition in the new industry, providing the foundation for competitive advantage. They can frequently share brand names, distribution channels, and technological know-how.

Entrants from a related industry, like entrants from buyer and supplier industries, are particularly desirable types of entrants for purposes of upgrading competitive advantage in a nation. They often possess transferable strengths that lead to higher-order advantages. Many Japanese competitors in personal computers, for example, began as consumer electronics companies. While Japan's overall international position in personal computers is modest, strength is now growing in laptops where compact size and liquid crystal display technology are essential to competitive success.

A third influence on domestic structure is the role of specialized factor-creation mechanisms in spawning new entrants, usually start-ups, into an industry. There are countless examples where a world-class laboratory, academic department, or educational institution was the source of entrepreneurs who entered an industry. The US biotechnology industry, for example, has been built by scientists from top university departments who formed companies.

Domestic rivalry and the national 'diamond'

Among the most striking findings from our research, as I have already discussed, is the prevalence of several domestic rivals in the industries in which the nation had international advantage. Rivalry has a direct role in stimulating improvement and innovation. Its significance is enhanced because rivalry is so important in stimulating firms to reap the benefits of other determinants, such as demanding buyers or sophisticated suppliers. But these benefits of domestic rivalry are only the most direct and more obvious ones. The discussion here makes it clear that domestic rivalry spills over to benefit the nation in many other and important ways that are usefully summarized:

- stimulating new rivals through spin-offs
- creating and attracting factors
- upgrading and expanding home demand
- encouraging and upgrading related and supporting industries
- channeling government policy in more effective directions.

THE DETERMINANTS AS A SYSTEM

Nations achieve success in international competition where they possess advantages in the 'diamond'. Because the requirements for success in industries and industry segments differ widely, and because a limited pool of resources precludes success in all industries, nations can enjoy dominance in one industry and fail miserably in another. Nations can also prosper in one industry segment and lack competitive advantage in another.

Advantages in the entire 'diamond' are not always necessary for competitive advantage in simple or resource-intensive industries and in the standardized, lower-technology segments of more advanced industries. In natural resource-intensive industries and those with low levels of technology, factor costs are frequently decisive.

Competitive advantage in more sophisticated industries and industry segments, however, rarely results from only a single determinant. Usually, advantages in several combine to create self-reinforcing conditions in which a nation's firms succeed internationally. This is because competitive advantage in sophisticated industries depends fundamentally on the rate of improvement and innovation. A nation's firms which lack sophisticated home buyers, capable suppliers, or other favorable determinants face grave difficulties in innovating more rapidly than rivals who do possess them.

Even in more advanced segments and industries, a nation need not always have advantages in all determinants to succeed internationally. In Japanese typewriters, for example, early competitors were well-established companies, such as Brother, that were diversifying out of the related sewing machine industry. They drew on transferable technology, a ready pool of efficient parts suppliers, relatively low wage costs for skilled labor, and established distribution networks. The sewing machine companies were later joined by a number of other entrants, some of whom were Japanese electronics companies seeking a broader position in office automation. The result was fierce rivalry among a large group of diverse domestic rivals.

In small nations, missing domestic rivalry may sometimes be offset by openness to international competition and global strategies in which the nation's firms meet foreign rivals in many countries. Yet the cases in which a nation is successful in an industry where there was never domestic rivalry are comparatively rare. More generally, compensating for a missing determinant is most likely once a nation's firms have achieved international leadership. Here, global strategies may be employed to tap selectively into advantages in other nations, and firms can command the attention and support of foreign buyers and suppliers.

Sustainability

Advantage is sustained because its sources are widened and upgraded. Some determinants provide a more sustainable basis for advantage than others. The current pool of factors, for example, is less important than the presence of specialized and pre-eminent institutions for factor creation. More broadly, conditions that provide dynamic advantages (faster innovation, early mover advantages, pressures for upgrading) are more important than those conferring static advantages (such as factor costs and a large home market). Hence, demand composition is frequently more important than demand size, while the intensity of domestic rivalry is more important than whether firms have an international outlook.

The process of building the system in a nation is often protracted. Once in place, it allows the entire national industry to progress faster than foreign rivals can. The important role of the interaction among the determinants means that the likelihood of achieving and sustaining advantage in an industry depends in part on how effectively the interactions work in a nation. Nations succeed in industries in which they work particularly well. The speed and efficacy with which the entire 'diamond' develops will determine which nation gains advantage.

A multinational with its home base in another nation faces great difficulties in replicating a national 'diamond', even if it establishes a subsidiary in the nation and competes with a coordinated global strategy. Coordination costs and information failures raise the odds against a foreign multinational gaining the full benefit of national advantages from afar. Firms with their home base in the nation will have more fluid and open access to local markets, and be more sensitive to local buyers. They will also communicate with and tap into advantages from local suppliers more easily, draw more readily on local factor creation mechanisms, and be more stimulated and invigorated by local rivals. To beat the odds, a foreign multinational's local subsidiary must in effect become its 'home base'. But this requires that it is given worldwide strategic control of the business as well as core R&D facilities, effectively transforming the subsidiary into a local company.

CLUSTERING OF COMPETITIVE INDUSTRIES

The competitive industries in a nation will not be evenly distributed across the economy. The systemic nature of the 'diamond' promotes the clustering of a nation's competitive industries.

A particularly striking example is in Denmark. Within Denmark there are also clusters of competitive industries related to the home (household products and furnishings) and to health (pharmaceuticals, vitamins, medical equipment, and the like). The health cluster is linked to the agricultural cluster by technology and raw material requirements.

The phenomenon of clustering seems to occur in all nations, including those not part of my sample. In Israel, for example, principal clusters are related to agriculture (crops, fertilizers, irrigation equipment, other specialized equipment and machinery) and defense. The reasons for clustering grown directly out of the determinants of national advantage and are a manifestation of their systemic character. One competitive industry helps to create another in a mutually reinforcing process. Such an industry is often the most sophisticated buyer of the products and services it depends on. Its presence in a nation becomes important to developing competitive advantage in supplier industries. American leadership in consumer packaged goods and consumer durables contributed to American pre-eminence in advertising. The Japanese strength in consumer electronics meant that Japanese success in semiconductors has been skewed toward memory chips and integrated circuits that are used heavily in these types of products.

Competitive supplier industries in a nation also help encourage world-class downstream industries. They provide technology, stimulate transferable factor creation, and become new entrants. One internationally competitive industry also creates new related industries, through providing ready access to transferable skills, through related entry by already established firms, or by stimulating entry indirectly through spin-offs.

Once a cluster forms, the whole group of industries becomes mutually supporting. Benefits flow forward, backward, and horizontally. Aggressive rivalry in one industry tends to spread to others in the cluster, through the exercise of bargaining power, spin-offs, and related diversification by established firms. Entry from other industries within the cluster spurs upgrading by stimulating diversity in R&D approaches and providing a means for introducing new strategies and skills. Information flows freely and innovations diffuse rapidly through the conduits of suppliers or customers who have contact with multiple competitors. Interconnections within the cluster, often unanticipated, lead to the perception of new ways of competing and entirely new opportunities. People and ideas combine in new ways. Silicon Valley provides a good example.

As clusters develop, resources in the economy flow toward them and away from isolated industries that cannot deploy the resources as productively. As more industries are exposed to international competition in the economy, the more pronounced the movement toward clustering will become.

National competitive advantage, then, resides as much at the level of the cluster as it does in individual industries. This carries important implications for government policy and company strategy.

Interchange within clusters

We observed sharp differences across nations, as well as across industries within nations, in how, and how well, clusters work. Nations gain as important national advantage where national attributes are supportive of intracluster interchange. The presence of especially effective interchange in a particular industry or sector, such as in Swedish mining and mining equipment, is a potent predictor of sustained national success.

Mechanisms that facilitate interchange within clusters are conditions that help information to flow more easily, or which unblock information as well as facilitate coordination by creating trust and mitigating perceived differences in economic interest between vertically or horizontally linked arms. Some examples follow.

Facilitators of information flow

- Personal relationships due to schooling, military service.
- Ties through the scientific community or professional associations.
- Community ties due to geographic proximity.
- Trade associations encompassing clusters.
- Norms of behaviour such as a belief in continuity and long-term relationships.

Sources of goal congruence or compatibility within clusters

- Family or quasi-family ties between firms.
- Common ownership within an industrial group.
- Ownership of partial equity stakes.
- Interlocking directors.
- National patriotism.

THE ROLE OF GEOGRAPHIC CONCENTRATION

Competitors in many internationally successful industries, and often entire clusters of industries, are often located in a single town or region within a nation. The vast majority of Italy's woollen textile producers, for example, are located in two towns. While geographic concentration of Italian industries is widely recognized, however, what is less understood is how prevalent the phenomenon is. British auctioneers are all within a few blocks in London. Basel is the home base for all three Swiss pharmaceutical giants.

Geographic concentration of firms in internationally successful industries often occurs because the influence of the individual determinants in the 'diamond' and their mutual reinforcement are heightened by close geographic proximity within a nation. A concentration of rivals, customers, and suppliers will promote efficiencies and specialization. More important, however, is the influence of geographic concentration on improvement and innovation. Rivals located close together will tend to be jealous and emotional competitors. Universities located near a group of competitors will be most likely to notice the industry, perceive it to be important, and respond accordingly. In turn, competitors are more likely to fund and support local university activity. Geographic concentration of an industry acts as a strong magnet to attract talented people and other factors to it.

Proximity increases the concentration of information and thus the likelihood of its being noticed and acted upon. Proximity increases the speed of information flow within the national industry and the rate at which innovations diffuse. At the same time, it tends to limit the spread of information outside because communication takes forms (such as face-to-face contact) which leak out only slowly. The process of clustering, and the interchange among industries in the cluster, also works best when the industries involved are geographically concentrated. Proximity leads to early exposure of imbalances, needs, or constraints within the cluster to be addressed or exploited. Proximity, then, elevates the separate influences in the 'diamond' into a true system.

The competitive advantage of cities and regions

The importance of geographic concentration raises interesting questions about whether the nation is a relevant unit of analysis. The conditions that underlie competitive advantage are indeed often localized within a nation, though at different locations for different industries. Indeed, the reasons why a particular city or region is successful in a particular industry are captured by the same considerations embodied in the 'diamond'; for example, the location of the most sophisticated buyers, possession of unique factor-creating mechanisms, and a well-developed local supplier base. The theory can be readily extended to explain why some cities or regions are more successful than others. The London region is prospering in the UK, for example, because of its advanced demand for many goods and services, its clusters of supporting industries, and the presence of highly skilled labor pools, among other considerations.

But nations are still important. Many of the determinants of advantage are more similar within a nation than across nations. Government policy (such as tax policy and regulation), legal rules, capital market conditions, factor costs, and many other attributes that are common to a country make national boundaries important. Social and political values and norms are linked to nations and slow to change. Yet it is the combination of national and intensely local conditions that fosters competitive advantage. National policies will be inadequate in and of themselves. State and local government can play a prominent role in industry success.

The US case suggests, moreover, that cultural interchange among nations will not overcome the differences among them that underpin competitive advantage. Efforts at European unification are raising questions about whether the influence of nations on competition will diminish. Instead, freer trade will arguably make them more important. While the effective locus of competitive advantage may sometimes encompass regions that cross national borders, such as the region including southern Germany and German-speaking Switzerland, Europe is unlikely to become a 'nation' from a competitive perspective. National differences in demand, factor creation, and other determinants will persist, and rivalry within nations will remain vital.

THE GENESIS AND EVOLUTION OF A COMPETITIVE INDUSTRY

Though sustained national advantage in an industry is a reflection of a well-functioning 'diamond', the whole system is rarely in place at the start. An advantage in a single determinant often provides the initial impetus for an industry's formation in a nation, not infrequently around a single firm. Sometimes chance also plays a role. Once begun, a process is set in motion in which competitors are attracted, other determinants become significant, and advantages accumulate provided the potential is present.

In practice, the formation of a local industry is normally triggered by one of three determinants. An initial advantage in factors of production often provides the seeds for an internationally competitive industry or a predecessor industry in the cluster. The Swedish specialty steel industry grew initially out of deposits of low phosphorus content iron ore in Sweden.

The seeds of competitive industries are also found in related and supporting industries. The Italian ski boot industry grew out of a local industry producing climbing and hiking shoes in the mountainous north-eastern region of Italy.

Demand conditions provide another common foundation for a competitive industry. Substantial or distinctive local demand is an early stimulus to the formation of local firms. Air-conditioning equipment was developed in the hot and humid eastern USA in the early 1900s, at a time when American prosperity made the luxury of air-conditioning more affordable than in other warm regions.

Sustainable competitive advantage can come quickly if a nation either possesses advantages in several determinants right from the start or rapidly develops them. In facsimile, for example, Japan had unique demand conditions and a group of well-established, international companies already competing in essential related and supporting industries.

As advantages are developed in several parts of the 'diamond' and especially as the mutual reinforcement within the 'diamond' begins to take place and cumulate, a national industry can achieve remarkable rates of improvement and innovation for a period of years or even decades.

Chance is often involved in helping to accelerate the process by which an industry upgrades and penetrates international markets. A chance event, such as a demand surge, an input price shift, or a major technological shift, creates a discontinuity that nullifies the advantages of traditional leaders and allows a nation's firms to leap ahead. Japanese TV set manufacturers, for example, capitalized on booming demand and capacity shortages among US manufacturers of color sets to gain a foothold in the vital US market.

It should be clear from this discussion that a nation's basis for competitive advantage in an industry can move around the 'diamond' as the industry evolves, shifting and often cumulating.

A nation that begins such a process early gains the types of early mover advantages I described earlier, such as economies of scale, customer relationships, and a brand name established without the need to sell against rivals. Even more significant, however, may be the opportunity to be the first to create a national 'diamond'. The diamond establishes the conditions for higher-order advantage and is slow and extremely hard to replicate. Once one nation has it, the cost of entry rises substantially.

The development of clusters

The process of industry evolution often breeds new competitive industries and hence builds or extends a cluster. Thus portions of a nation's economy develop a momentum that extends beyond individual industries and is a powerful force for economic development.

Nations differ in the typical path by which clusters emerge, a function of the types of firms in the economy, among other considerations. In Italy, the force behind many competitive industries is sophisticated consumer demand conditions for end products. A vibrant environment for entrepreneurship leads to the rapid proliferation of competitors and intense rivalry. End product industries then spawn competitive support-ing industries.

The formation of clusters extends the surges of progress in individual industries I spoke of earlier. The mutual reinforcement within clusters also leads to surges in innovation (and international competitive position) in whole sectors of a national economy. This is evident today in the consumer related electronics sector in Japan, where waves of innovation are spread-ing from traditional industries such as television sets, calculators, and audio equipment to new industries such as laptop personal computers and facsimile, and back again.

The mobility of technology has led some observers to argue that factor costs are becoming more important in international competition. While the mobility of technology may shorten the imitation lag, firms sourcing technology from other nations are always a generation behind. Moreover, the capacity to deploy technology is what leads to advantage, not mere access. The ability to employ and improve upon imported technology is powerfully influenced by the national 'diamond'. Competitive advantage is increasingly a function not of factors but of the ability to create and apply knowledge and technology to industry competition.

THE LOSS OF NATIONAL ADVANTAGE

National competitive advantage in an industry is lost, however, when conditions in the national 'diamond' no longer support and stimulate investment and innovation to match the industry's evolving structure. The national industry may not perceive needed change, may fail to invest aggressively enough to advance, or may be blocked by having assets and skills that are specialized to outmoded ways of competing and that make responding to change more profitable to newcomers. Some of the most important reasons for eroding advantage are the following:

Factor conditions deteriorate

Factor conditions can deteriorate for a variety of reasons. Most troubling is if a nation falls behind in the rate of creation and upgrading of factors. If the skills of specialized human resources or the base of science and technology related to an industry deteriorate relative to another nation, then competitive advantage will usually fade.

Local needs fall out of synch with global demand

Competitive advantage is threatened if home demand conditions begin to diverge from those in other advanced nations. New buyer needs or new channels emerge elsewhere that are slow to appear in the nation, such as desire for new features, customization, or health concerns. As world demand for cars shifted toward smaller, fuel-efficient, and reliable varieties, US preferences for larger cars delayed the American industry response.

Home buyers lose sophistication

A nation's firms will face grave difficulties in maintaining advantage if foreign buyers become more sophisticated than domestic ones.

Technological change leads to compelling specialized factor disadvantages or the need for new and missing supporting industries

Technological change is often a trigger for shifts in national competitive advantage because it can nullify old competitive advantages and create the need for new ones. A nation's firms, far advanced along one technological track, may find it difficult or unprofitable to jump to another one. Technological change may also create the need for new supporting industries that a nation does not possess, such as software, biotechnology, new materials, or electronic components.

Goals limit the rate of investment

The rate of investment in R&D, marketing, information, and physical assets is influenced by corporate and managerial goals.

Firms lose the flexibility to adjust

Even if a nation's firms know how they must change to sustain competitive advantage, they may lose it if there are barriers to adjustment. Often barriers to adjustment are internal. Entrenched management may grow complacent or find it difficult or unsettling to change.

Failure to innovate may preserve competitive position tied to a particular asset base in the short run but often will ensure that a firm's assets will have little value in the long run. Sustaining competitive advantage demands that firms make their own assets obsolete with new technology or methods before someone else does it for them.

Domestic rivalry ebbs

One of the most common, and often the most fatal, causes of lost national advantage is the ebbing of domestic rivalry, since pressure to improve and adjust is often lost with it. Loss of domestic rivalry is a dry rot that slowly undermines competitive advantage by slowing the pace of innovation and dynamism.

The process of decline

A certain momentum governs the loss of competitive advantage that mirrors the positive momentum I described earlier. Momentum first works to mask decline, because of customer loyalties and the profit enhancing role of under-investment. Decline once begun, however, is hard to arrest because the mutual reinforcement of the 'diamond' works in reverse. For example, a loss of rivalry erodes the quality of the nation's buyers and suppliers, reducing buyer-side pressure, raising input costs, stunting the development of supplier technology, and slowing innovation even further or channeling it in the wrong directions. The industry's problems widen and compound.

Regaining position in an industry where the loss of advantage has gathered momentum is, based on our research, exceedingly rare. The decline may be slowed or stopped by shrinking to the least exposed segments or instituting trade protection, but we found few examples where an industry regained its former strength. Much government policy aimed at 'revitalizing' industries has failed. It is doomed because it does not address the determinants of competitive advantage and is therefore not directed at the true cause of decline.

The insular cluster

Complacency and an inward focus often explain why nations lose competitive advantage. Lack of pressure and challenge means that firms fail to look constantly for and interpret new buyer needs, new technologies, and new processes. They lose the stomach to make old competitive advantages obsolete in the process of creating new ones. They hesitate to employ global strategies to offset local factor disadvantages, or to tap selectively into advantages available in other nations.

The cluster itself, particularly if it is geographically concentrated, may contain the seeds of its own demise. If rivalry ebbs and home buyers become pliant or lose sophistication, there is a tendency for the local cluster to become insular, a closed and inward-looking system. The problem is exacerbated if most firms lack significant international activities and their primary commercial relationships are with each other. Firms, customers, and suppliers all talk only to each other. None brings fresh perspectives. The histories of Sheffield (British cutlery industry) and Lancashire (British cotton industry) are good cases in point. Detroit may well prove to be another.

Declustering

While it is not inevitable, there is a tendency for a cluster of competitive industries to begin to unravel if one or two industries within the cluster that are important to innovation lose competitive advantage. In Sweden, for example, the loss of market position in shipbuilding has led to the erosion or demise of positions in many supplier industries, such as ship brokers, marine engines, and steel. Those supplier industries that are still strong, such as welding products (ESAB), shipboard fire detection equipment (Consilium Systems), and shipboard cranes (Hägglunds), were ones that had already established strong global positions and were organizationally able to make major adjustments.

Clusters are most vulnerable if many firms lack global strategies and do not have significant activities located in other nations. This was the case, for example, in the British shipping cluster around Glasgow, where the failure of the shipbuilding industry led to severe consequences for most of the supporting industries.

Those industries in the cluster that have the most vigorous rivalry and the most global outlook and customer base will have the greatest likelihood of avoiding the domino effect, because their contacts with foreign buyers or suppliers can partially replace or offset a diminished national environment. The industries that enjoy the strongest early mover advantages may also persist. In Britain, industries such as tobacco, whisky, and confectionery have sustained position, for example, because of well-established brand names, global marketing presence, and the absence of any significant shifts in technology or buyer needs that would provide new competitors with the ability to overcome them.

THE DIAMOND IN PERSPECTIVE

At its core the system of determinants of national competitive advantage I have described is a theory of investment and innovation. Gaining advantage in the first place requires a new approach to competing, whether it is perceiving and then exploiting a factor advantage, discovering an underserved segment, creating new product features, or changing the process by which a product is made. Sustaining advantage requires still further improvement and innovation to broaden and upgrade the sources of competitive advantage through advancing the product, the production process, marketing methods, and service.

The determinants in the 'diamond' and the interactions among them create the forces that shape the likelihood, direction, and speed of improvement and innovation by a nation's firms in an industry.

The availability and interpretation of information are central to the process of gaining competitive advantage, and the 'diamond' captures some of the salient aspects.

Competitive advantage emerges from pressure, challenge, and adversity, rarely from an easy life. Selective factor disadvantages, powerful local buyers, stringent local needs, early saturation, capable and international suppliers, and intense local rivalry can all be essential to creating and sustaining advantage. Pressure and adversity are powerful motivators for change and innovation.

I have shown how the determinants of national advantage are a dynamic system. The self-reinforcement of the 'diamond', as an industry evolves, holds the key to upgrading and sustaining competitive advantage. The influence and reinforcement of the determinants leads to the phenomenon of clustering, and to the prevalence and importance of geographic concentration. I have described how the extent of mutual reinforcement is itself a function of particular determinants and of the presence of mechanisms in a nation that facilitate interchange within clusters.

While the examples I have discussed have emphasized the explanation of past competitive advantage, the 'diamond' is also a tool for predicting future industry evolution. A nation has the prospects for competitive advantage if the underlying determinants are favorable or can be developed. Nations lose advantage, for example, if home buyers have lost sophistication, demand is evolving away from global needs, technological change is exposing missing supplier industries, institutions for factor creation do not respond by providing training in relevant skills, and so on. While unpredictable chance events such as acts of invention are also important to industry development, the 'diamond' influences their likelihood of occurring in a nation. More importantly, the diamond allows predictions about whether chance events will result in a competitive industry.

Chapter 3

Horses for courses

Organizational forms for multinational corporations

Sumantra Ghoshal and Nitin Nohria

About two decades ago, business academics told managers that when it came to organization design, one size did not fit all. Different companies, racing different business demands, needed different kinds of organizations. More complex and turbulent environments called for more complex organizational approaches, and the nature and extent of organizational complexity had to match the firm's strategic complexity. In its initial formulation, before the hedge that 'it all depends' made it too complicated to mean anything at all, this contingency theory of organizations provided managers with some simple guidelines to help them decide on the kind of organization they should adopt.[1]

For multinational corporations (MNCs), such guidelines were available in the 'stages model' proposed by Stopford and Wells[2] (see Figure 3.1). This model defined the strategic complexity faced by an MNC in terms of two dimensions: the number of products sold internationally ('foreign product diversity', shown on the figure's vertical axis) and the importance of international sales to the company ('foreign sales as a percentage of total sales', shown on the horizontal axis). Stopford and Wells suggested that at the early stage of foreign expansion, when both foreign sales and the diversity of products sold abroad were limited, worldwide companies typically managed their international operations through an international division. Subsequently, some companies expanded their sales abroad without significantly increasing foreign product diversity; they typically adopted an area structure. Companies facing substantial increases in foreign product diversity tended to adopt the worldwide product division structure. Finally, when both foreign sales and foreign product diversity were high, companies resorted to the global matrix.

Over the two decades since Stopford and Wells presented this simple, descriptive model, academic research on MNCs has developed a far more elaborate understanding of MNC organizations. It is increasingly clear, for example, that the formal macrostructure described in the stages model is only a partial representation of a worldwide organization. To use a biological metaphor suggested by Christopher Bartlett, organizations have

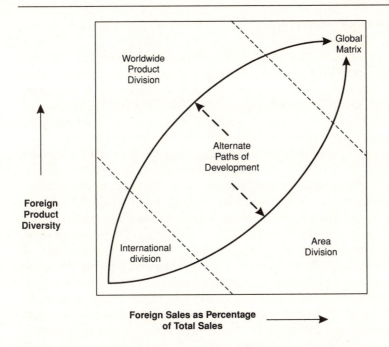

Figure 3.1 The Stopford and Wells model of MNC organizations

an anatomy (formal structure), but they also have a physiology (core management processes) and a psychology (the mind-sets of their managers). To analyze the organizational capabilities a company needs, one must look not only to the anatomy but also to the physiology and psychology.[3]

Further, the prescription of matching organizational characteristics to environmental and strategic demands is also under challenge. Environments do not stand still for organizations to catch up, and organizations themselves, as organic entities, are in a continuous state of flux. Instead of a mechanistic and static view of fit, one needs to recognize the fluid, multidimensional, and changing nature of both environments and organizations. What is needed is not just fit but fit and flexibility.[4]

Unfortunately, academic research and conclusions are inevitably simplified and stripped of nuances. Just as the earlier stages model was converted into a set of simplistic prescriptions, so has this new research been recast as an orgy of complexity. Bartlett and Ghoshal, for example, have repeatedly argued that companies must simplify wherever possible to protect clarity of responsibility and initiative and that the more complex or 'transnational' integrated network organization should be used only for MNCs operating in highly complex environments.[5] Yet their findings have often been interpreted as an all-or-nothing call for this 'transnational' structure in all companies.[6]

In this chapter we wish to make the following two points. First, although the Stopford and Wells model has its deficiencies, it does not follow that MNCs are organizationally too complex for any meaningful yet simple classification. Managers need simple organizational models and classification schemes as a starting-point for thinking about the core attributes of their organizational needs. Similarly, academics need them in order to build theory and develop analytical and testable propositions. Therefore, we will propose here a useful classification scheme for MNC organizations, one that is not defined in terms of traditional structural forms (e.g. area, product, matrix, etc.), but that is based on the company's internal pattern of headquarters-subsidiary relations. Any organizational model or classification scheme is built on simplifications and, therefore, suffers from some deficiencies. Our scheme is no exception. However, in this chapter we will demonstrate its usefulness for both managers and academics.

Second, although flexibility is important, so is fit. Organizational complexity is costly and difficult to manage, and simplicity, wherever possible, is a virtue. Just as a company can suffer from too simple an organization if it is operating in a complex and turbulent environment, so can it also pay an efficiency penalty for adopting an organization too complex for its environmental demands. Although insensitive to the reality of constant flux in both environments and organizations and, therefore, somewhat unfashionable in current organization research, the concept of fit remains one of the relatively few simple and robust findings in organization theory.[7] We will demonstrate here the continued validity of this concept of environment-organization fit and of the positive relationship of such fit with firm performance.

THE EMPIRICAL DATABASE

Our empirical analysis is based primarily on a database that has been described fully elsewhere.[8] This database consists of information on all wholly-owned subsidiaries of sixty-six large MNCs in ten prespecified countries. It was obtained from a mailed questionnaire survey completed by one correspondent from each firm, typically a senior headquarters manager with responsibility for the firm's international operations. These managers assigned values, on a scale of 1 (low) to 5 (high), to a number of variables indicative of the local context (competitive intensity in the local market, technological dynamism of the local environment, extent of local government regulations, and local resources available to the subsidiary) and the structure of the headquarters-subsidiary relation (extent to which its governance is based on centralization, formalization, and normative integration). Although each variable was measured through a single indicator, the reliability and validity of the measures were tested through a multiple-indicator, multiple-respondent survey administered at the head-quarters and subsidiary levels in three large MNCs.[9] In the following analysis, we rely wholly on this database to measure structural attributes of MNCs.

We obtained additional measures, following the framework proposed by Prahalad and Doz, to classify MNC environments in terms of the twin demands of global integration and national responsiveness.[10] To measure global integration, we use Kobrin's 'index of integration,' which we consider a theoretically well-grounded and empirically precise measure of this complex construct.[11] To measure national responsiveness, we use two indicators. The first, extent of government regulations, comes from our questionnaire data. The second, advertising intensity, is computed from the industry averages published in *Advertising Age*.

Finally, we use three different economic indicators – average annual return on net assets, average revenue growth, and average annual growth in return on net assets to measure company performance. Specifically, we compute average values of these three variables for the period 1982 to 1986 as they appear in the relevant annual reports (the company survey was conducted in 1986). Corporate performance can be measured in different ways corresponding to the firms' different goals, but we employ these three economic measures because our purpose is to explore performance difference across a broad sample of firms and because these measures are recognized as both fairly comprehensive and highly important to the companies themselves.[12]

We have complete data (including Kobrin's index) for only forty-one of the sixty-six companies in the database. Accordingly, data on only these forty-one companies are used in the empirical analysis reported in this paper. Table 3.1 lists these companies and their principal businesses.

The chapter is organized as follows. First, we draw on the existing literature to classify the environments of the forty-one companies into four categories. These categories reflect firms' varying needs to respond to distinct local conditions and to integrate across national boundaries. Second, we use Lawrence and Lorsch's dimensions of structural differentiation and integration to classify the forty-one companies into four structural categories. Finally, we hypothesize a one-to-one fit between the environmental and structural categories and test this hypothesis against the information in our database.

CLASSIFYING THE ENVIRONMENTS OF MNCS

Each MNC subsidiary operates in a different national environment. In each country the local subsidiary must be responsive to local customers, governments, and regulatory agencies for its ongoing institutional legitimacy and economic success. To some extent, then, the MNC must respond

Table 3.1 The companies surveyed and their principal businesses

Name of company	Home country	Principal industry
1 Air Products and Chemicals	USA	Industrial chemicals
2 Alcan	Canada	Nonferrous metals
3 Baker International	USA	Machinery
4 Bertelsmann	Germany	Printing and publishing
5 Blue Bell	USA	Textiles
6 British-American Tobacco (BAT)	UK	Tobacco
7 BSN Groupe	France	Food
8 Caterpillar	USA	Construction and mining machinery
9 Colgate-Palmolive	USA	Drugs and pharmaceuticals
10 Continental Group	USA	Metals
11 Cummins	USA	Engines
12 Deere & Co.	USA	Construction and mining machinery
13 Digital Equipment Corp.	USA	Computers
14 DuPont	USA	Chemicals
15 Electrolux	Sweden	Household appliances
16 Emhart Corporation	USA	Machinery
17 Firestone	USA	Rubber
18 Freuhauf Corporation	USA	Automobiles
19 Friedrich Krupp	Germany	Metals
20 General Foods	USA	Food
21 General Motors	USA	Automobiles
22 Glaxo	UK	Drugs and pharmaceuticals
23 Hoechst AG	Germany	Chemicals
24 Honeywell	USA	Scientific measuring instruments
25 ICI	UK	Chemicals
26 Jacobs Suchard	Switzerland	Food
27 Kodak	USA	Photographic equipment
28 Mannesmann	Germany	Metals
29 Norsk Hydro	Norway	Chemicals
30 Norton	USA	Machinery
31 R.J. Reynolds	USA	Tobacco
32 Reckitt & Colman	UK	Drugs and pharmaceuticals
33 Rio Tinto-Zinc	UK	Metals
34 Schneider	France	Machinery
35 Seagram	Canada	Beverages
36 Siemens	Germany	Machinery
37 Solvay & Cie	Belgium	Chemicals
38 Swedish Match	Sweden	Paper and forestry
39 Timken	USA	Machinery
40 United Biscuits	UK	Food
41 Volvo	Sweden	Automobiles

to the different contingencies presented by the multiple environments in which it operates. Such contingencies have been categorized in the multinational management literature as 'forces for national responsiveness'.[13]

These different local environments may also be linked to each other – because there are common customer preferences across countries; because economies of scale, scope, and national comparative advantage create incentives for specialization and interdependence; because knowledge developed in one environment is transferable or adaptable in another; or because key players in the MNC's environment are transnational, such as its multinational clients, suppliers, competitors, and even regulatory agencies (such as the EEC). These linkages across national boundaries pressure the subsidiaries to coordinate their activities; they have been described as 'forces for global integration'.[14]

These two forces – for national responsiveness and for global integration – are not opposite ends of a spectrum. Although they are related, we can consider them as separate dimensions. Thus, a company with a weak force for national responsiveness does not automatically have a strong force for global integration and vice versa. For instance, businesses such as pharmaceuticals, telecommunications, and computers may simultaneously face strong demands for both global integration and local responsiveness. In computers, the growing commoditization of hardware combined with high capital intensity and scale economics constitute powerful forces for global integration. At the same time, the increasing market demands for integration of hardware from diverse sources with software and services to provide 'solutions' to customer problems create equally strong needs for local responsiveness.

The weak-weak combination is also possible. The business of producing and marketing cement is an example. Cement products are highly standardized, and marketing and distribution systems are similar across countries. Thus demands for local responsiveness are weak. However, the trade-offs between the economics of cement production and transport costs are such that global integration is not attractive.

Of course, weak-strong combinations of both sorts are possible as well. Semiconductors and airplane engines confront strong forces for global integration, given their high capital intensities and significant scale economies, but relatively weak forces for national responsiveness because product standardization is relatively high and customer demands are relatively uniform in different geographic markets. In contrast, businesses such as legal services or non-branded foods are likely to face weak forces for global integration and strong demands for national responsiveness.

Four types of MNC environments

The environmental contingencies faced by the MNC as a whole can, therefore, be conceived in terms of the extent to which it must respond to strong and unique national environments and the extent to which it must respond to the linkages across these national environments. Adopting the terms used by Bartlett and Ghoshal, we broadly distinguish among four environmental conditions faced by MNCs:

1 a global environment in which the forces for global integration are strong and for local responsiveness weak;
2 a multinational environment in which the forces for national responsiveness are strong and for global integration weak;
3 a transnational environment in which both contingencies are strong;
4 a placid international environment in which both contingencies are weak (see Figure 3.2).[15]

We adopted the following procedure to classify the environment of each of the forty-one MNCs in our sample as one of these four types. Kobrin's

	Global Environment	**Transnational Environment**
Strong	• Construction and mining machinery • Nonferrous metals • Industrial chemicals • Scientific measuring instruments • Engines	• Drugs and pharmaceuticals • Photographic equipment • Computers • Automobiles
Forces for Global Integration	**International Environment**	**Multinational Environment**
Weak	• Metals (other than nonferrous) • Machinery • Paper • Textiles • Printing and publishing	• Beverages • Food • Rubber • Household appliances • Tobacco

Weak   Strong

Forces for Local Responsiveness

Figure 3.2 The environment of MNCs: classification of businesses

index of integration, which we use to measure the forces of global integration in different business environments, is the ratio of the total intrafirm trade (the sum of affiliate-to-affiliate, affiliate-to-parent, and parent-to-affiliate sales) to the total international sales (sum of total sales of parent and of all affiliates) of all the MNCs in an industry. As Kobrin argues, global integration cannot be measured simply on the basis of bilateral flows. One must consider the overall system of interdependencies: 'Transnational integration implies more than interdependence in the sense that events in one business environment significantly influence those in another; it implies dependence of subsidiaries on the multinational system.' According to Kobrin, cross flows of products within the total MNC system, aggregated to all MNCs in the industry, is one of the most effective ways to measure the forces of global integration. It allows for a systematic and data-driven specification of global industries and avoids the pitfalls of anecdotal and descriptive evidence. Also, the actual measures correlate highly with industry research and development (R&D) intensity – another widely used proxy for the forces of global integration – and are 'certainly in accord with an intuitive, case-study-based concept of global integration'. Kobrin's index is a continuous variable and, as he notes, any particular cut-off point to delineate 'high' and 'low' categories is bound to be somewhat arbitrary. We use 20 per cent (intrafirm trade as a percentage of total sales) as our cut-off point; we classify businesses such as automobiles (44 per cent), computers (38 per cent), photographic equipment (32 per cent), engines (30 per cent), scientific measuring instruments (29 per cent), industrial chemicals (26 per cent), nonferrous metals (23 per cent), pharmaceuticals (21 per cent), and construction and mining machinery (21 per cent) as confronting strong forces of global integration. The remaining businesses confront weak forces for global integration.

We use two indicators to distinguish between businesses facing strong and those facing weak forces of national responsiveness. The first is the advertising-to-sales ratio of the industry, as published in *Advertising Age*. The second is an average of the values we received on our questionnaire for the extent of local regulation, by industry (for example, we averaged the rating given by computer companies on the extent of local regulations to come up with the computer industry average). The two measures are only weakly correlated (rank correlation 0.32, $\varnothing = 0.11$). Given that both regulations and customer preferences can act as powerful forces for local responsiveness, we categorize any business that falls above the sample mean on either of these two indicators as facing strong forces of national responsiveness and one that falls below on either indicator as facing relatively weak forces of national responsiveness.

Figure 3.2 shows how juxtaposition of these two indicators leads to the categorization of the different business environments into international multinational, global, and transnational.

STRUCTURE CLASSIFICATIONS

The main criticism of models that define MNC structure in terms of function, geography, product division, or as a matrix has been that the formal organization chart is a poor representation of how an organization really functions. Organizations represent a set of relationships among individuals, groups, and units, and very different relationship patterns can flourish within the same formal structure. To understand, describe, or categorize organizations, therefore, one must focus on the pattern of these relationships. Accordingly, we suggest that an MNC's structure may be conceived more fruitfully as a nexus of the relationships between its different national subsidiaries and its headquarters.

The nature of each headquarters–subsidiary relationship is the basic unit in this conceptualization. These relationships can be described in terms of the three basic governance mechanisms that underlie them. The first of these is centralization, which concerns the role of formal authority and hierarchical mechanisms in the company's decision-making processes. The second is formalization, which represents decision-making through bureaucratic mechanisms such as formal systems, established rules, and prescribed procedures. The third is normative integration, which relies neither on direct headquarters involvement nor on impersonal rules but on the socialization of managers into a set of shared goals, values, and beliefs that they shape their perspectives and behavior. We believe that centralization, formalization, and normative integration, collectively, constitute a fairly comprehensive characterization of the mechanisms by which corporate–division relations may be governed in multi-unit organizations such as MNCs.[16]

Analyses of MNC organizations have often assumed that headquarters–subsidiary relationships are identical for all subsidiaries throughout the company. There is growing evidence, however, that each headquarters–subsidiary relation can be governed by a different combination of the above-mentioned three mechanisms.[17] Therefore, we conceptualize the MNC's overall structure in terms of the pattern of variation in its different headquarters-subsidiary relationships.

Four structural patterns

Using Lawrence and Lorsch's dimensions of differentiation and integration, we envision MNC structures in terms of four patterns. In the first structure – structural uniformity – there is little variance in how the different subsidiaries are managed, and a common 'company way' is adopted for the governance of all headquarters-subsidiary relationships. The emphasis may be on one of the three governance types or a combination. Of central importance is a strong and uniform governance mechanism for the whole company; overall integration is high, and there is little attention to differentiation.

A second structure – differentiated fit – represents companies that adopt different governance modes to fit each subsidiary's local context. The local context can vary in a number of ways. Two of the most important ways are environmental complexity (the level of technological dynamism and competitive intensity) and the amount of local resources available to the subsidiary.[18] When a company recognizes these differences, it can explicitly differentiate its headquarters–subsidiary relationships to ensure that the management processes fit each local context. We have previously developed a scheme that matches structures to subsidiary contexts.[19] Briefly, this scheme is as follows:

1 Low environment complexity and low levels of local resources dictate a high level of centralization and low levels of formalization and normative integration.
2 Low environment complexity and high levels of resources dictate a low level of centralization and high levels of formalization and normative integration.
3 High environment complexity and low resource levels indicate a moderate level of centralization, a low level of formalization, and a high level of normative integration.
4 High environment complexity and high resource levels indicate a low level of centralization, a moderate level of formalization, and a high level of normative integration.

Based on the theoretical justification and empirical support provided for this scheme, we use this logic to describe and identify companies adopting the differentiated fit structure. Note that differentiation is the dominant characteristic of this structure and that it lacks a strong firmwide integrative mechanism.

A third structural pattern is when a firm adopts the logic of differentiated fit but overlays the distinctly structured relationships with a dominant overall integrative mechanism – whether through strong centralization, formalization, or normative integration. We call such structures integrated variety.

Finally, a fourth pattern is one in which there is neither a dominant integrative mechanism nor an explicit pattern of differentiation to match local contexts. We call this pattern ad hoc variation.

We adopted the following procedure to classify each of the forty-one companies into these four structural categories. We aggregated the measures of centralization, formalization, and normative integration for all of a company's subsidiaries to arrive at a firmwide average of these measures. These averages were used as indicators of the strength of the firm's integrative mechanisms. When a firm's average measure for any of these

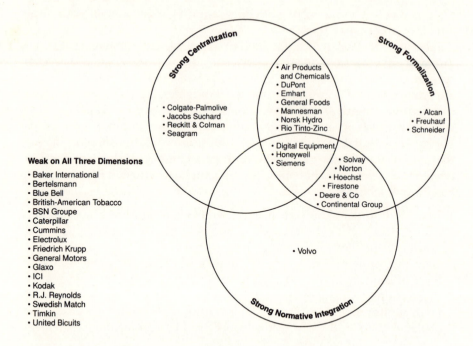

Figure 3.3 Companies with strong integrative mechanisms

three structural variables exceeded the median value across all the firms in the sample, the company was considered to have a strong integrative mechanism along that dimension; otherwise it was considered to have a weak integrative mechanism along that dimension (see Figure 3.3).

Some of the companies appear to have strong integration mechanisms along a single dimension.[20] For example, Seagram, Jacobs Suchard, Reckitt & Colman, and Colgate-Palmolive appear to have a high level of centralization; Alcan, Freuhauf, and Schneider demonstrate a high level of formalization; whereas Volvo appears to have strong normative integration throughout the company. We do not have detailed case studies on all of the companies to cross-check these survey findings, but the results are consistent with some widely known management systems in these firms. Seagram, for example, is well known for its extremely strong and highly centralized financial control system; all sales proceeds deposited in its subsidiaries' bank accounts are transferred daily to a central account managed by corporate headquarters while the central account remits to each local bank account the amounts required to cover specific operating expenses. Alcan's worldwide planning systems are well known, as are Volvo's decade-long efforts to pioneer a new work style and corporate culture that have often been hailed as unique among Western automobile companies.

Other firms appear to have strong integrative mechanisms along multiple dimensions. DuPont, Air Products and Chemicals, Mannesmann, General Foods, Emhart, Norsk Hydro, and Rio Tinto-Zinc appear to have strong levels of both centralization and formalization; Deere & Co., Firestone, Continental Group, Hoechst, Norton, and Solvay & Cie appear to combine formalization with strong firmwide normative integration. Others like Digital Equipment Corporation, Siemens, and Honeywell appear to have high levels of all three mechanisms. Again, the findings are consistent with what little we know about some these companies. Digital, for example, has long had highly centralized engineering, product development, and base product marketing functions; has built elaborate formal rules and systems for revenue and profit planning, pricing and discounts, and manufacturing; and has enjoyed a strong set of shared values concerning management of people, commitment to individual initiatives, and working through consensus.

The remaining companies in the sample appear to lack strong, firmwide integration along any of the three dimensions. They do not have uniform, centralized control over their worldwide activities to any significant extent. They appear to lack institutionalized rules and procedures as well as the glue of any strongly shared norms, values, and culture.

We measured the extent of structural differentiation by comparing the fit between each subsidiary's local context and the type of relationship it had with headquarters. For each company, each subsidiary was classified as high or low on the measures of environmental complexity and local resources. Each subsidiary was then classified as high, moderate, or low on the levels of centralization, formalization, and socialization that characterized its relationship with headquarters. If the headquarters–subsidiary relationship was suited to the subsidiary context (as described above), we considered the subsidiary to represent appropriate differentiation and counted the case as a 'fit'. If not, we counted the case as a 'misfit.' For each company, the extent of differentiation was measured as the ratio of the number of its 'fit' to its 'misfit' subsidiaries. When this ratio for a company exceeded the median value for the sample, it was classified as strongly differentiated in its structure; otherwise, the company was classified as weakly differentiated.

Figure 3.4 shows the results of this analysis, superimposed on the preceding analysis of integrative mechanisms. Some of the companies in the sample, such as Caterpillar, Cummins, Baker International, Bertelsmann, Blue Bell, Friedrich Krupp, Kodak, Timken, and Electrolux appear to lack systematic differentiation and, at the same time, do not have any strong integrative mechanism. These, then, correspond to the overall category we have characterized as ad hoc variation. Others, such as General Motors, Glaxo, BSN Groupe, British-American Tobacco, ICI, R.J. Reynolds, Swedish Match, and United Biscuits appear to have strong and

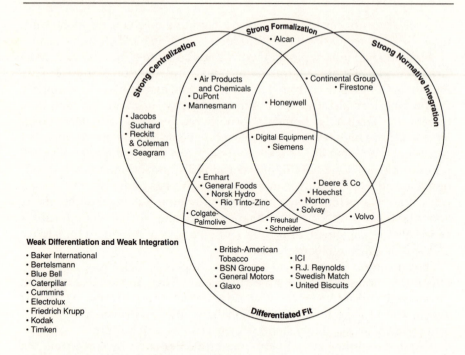

Figure 3.4 Mapping integration and differentiation

systematic internal differentiation but lack strong firmwide integration; these correspond to our differentiated fit category. Firms such as Digital, Siemens, General Foods, Enhart, Norsk Hydro, Rio Tino-Zinc, Colgate-Palmolive, Freuhauf, Schneider, Deere & Co., Hoechst, Norton, and Solvay have strong differentiation as well as strong integration (through one or more of the three integration mechanisms); these we place in the integrated variety category. Finally, the remaining companies demonstrate high integration through one mechanism or a combination of the three mechanisms but are not systematically differentiated internally. These firms belong to the category we have described as structural uniformity.

Figure 3.5 summarizes these findings, showing how the forty-one companies distribute among the four structural categories we have proposed.

ORGANIZATION-ENVIRONMENT FIT

Our basic argument is that for effective performance, the MNC's organizational structure should fit its overall environmental contingencies. We hypothesize that structural uniformity is best suited to global environmental conditions, differentiated fit to multinational environments, integrated variety to transnational environments, and *ad hoc* variety to international environments.

Structural Uniformity	Integrated Variety
• Air Products and Chemicals • Alcan • Continental Group • DuPont • Firestone • Honeywell • Jacobs Suchard • Mannesmann • Reckitt & Colman • Seagram	• Colgate-Palmolive • Deere & Co. • Digital Equipment • Emhart • Freuhauf • General Foods • Hoechst • Norsk Hydro • Norton • Rio Tinto-Zinc • Schneider • Siemens • Solvay • Volvo
Ad Hoc Variation	**Differentiated Fit**
• Baker International • Bertelsmann • Bell Bar • Caterpillar • Cummins • Electrolux • Friedrich Krupp • Kodak • Timken	• British-American Tobacco • BSN Groupe • General Motors • Glaxo • ICI • R.J. Reynolds • Swedish Match • United Biscuits

High — Low: **Structural Integration**

Low — High: **Structrual Differentiation**

Figure 3.5 The structure of MNCs: classification of companies

The logic underlying these hypotheses is straightforward. In global environments, the cross-national linkages create forces for firmwide coordination that predominate over the local environmental forces. Having a common integrative structure in these situations not only enables the MNC to respond to these linkages across these environments, it also economizes on the administrative burden that managing a highly differentiated system imposes.

In multinational environments, in contrast, the MNC must respond to the local environments to be competitive. The most effective structures are likely to be those that are differentiated to respond to the local environments' needs. Here, the administrative burden of a complex differentiated system is almost a cost of doing business, but the MNC must avoid the additional administrative complexity of a strong overlying integrative mechanism.

In transnational environments, it is important for the MNC to be responsive not only to local contingencies but also to cross-national linkages. As such it needs a structure of requisite differentiation overlaid with a strong companywide integrative mechanism. Here the administrative costs of such a complex system are both necessary and justified.

In contrast, placid international environments have neither strong forces of differentiation nor strong forces of integration, and a company in such a situation might derive little benefit from systematic organizational design. Such a firm can probably avoid the costs of both differentiation and integration.

It is important to note that it is the competing costs and benefits of differentiation and integration that underlie these issues of fit. In principle, if there were no administrative costs associated with organizational complexity, one might always recommend a structure of integrated variety, because such a structure would be best able to respond to minor variations in environments as well as to a great variety of linkages. But the costs associated with administrative complexity are significant and thus lead us to the idea of requisite complexity.

To test these hypotheses, we juxtaposed the environmental (Figure 3.2) and structural (Figure 3.5) classifications of the forty-one companies, as shown in Figure 3.6. Each cell in this figure represents a particular environment-structure combination. Cell 1, for example, identifies those companies that, during the study period, confronted an environment of relatively weak forces of both global integration and local responsiveness and whose organizations were neither strongly differentiated internally nor strongly integrated through firmwide mechanisms. Such a combination – an international environment and an ad-hoc variation organization – represents a good fit and, according to our theory, should on average outperform firms in Cells 2, 3, and 4, which operate with the same relatively simple organizational approach but face the more complex multinational, global, or transnational environments. Similarly, the firms in Cell 1 should also outperform, on average, firms in Cells 5, 9, and 13 because these companies adopt the more complex organizational approaches, thereby expending effort and resources on organizational integration and differentiation that are not necessary for responding to the demands of their relatively simple international environment.

Following this logic, it becomes clear that the seventeen companies in the four diagonal cells (1, 6, 11, and 16) – all of which represent good environment-structure fits – should, on average, outperform the twenty-four companies in the other twelve cells, all of which represent misfits. As shown in Table 3.2, actual performances of these forty-one companies conform to our prediction. On all three dimensions of performance –

		International	Multinational	Global	Transnational
Structure	Integrated Variety	• Emhart • Norton • Rio Tinto-Zinc • Schneider • Siemens (Cell 13)	• General Foods (Cell 14)	• Deere & Co • Hoechst • Norsk Hydro • Solvay (Cell 15)	• Colgate-Palmolive • Digital Equipment • Freuhauf • Volvo (Cell 16)
	Structural Uniformity	• Continental Group • Mannesmann (Cell 9)	• Firestone • Jacobs Suchard • Seagram (Cell 10)	• Air Products and Chemicals • Alcan • DuPont • Honeywell (Cell 11)	• Reckitt & Colman (Cell 12)
	Differentiated Fit	• Swedish Match (Cell 5)	• British-American Tobacco • BSN Groupe • R.J. Reynolds • United Biscuits (Cell 6)	• ICI (Cell 7)	• General Motors • Glaxo (Cell 8)
	Ad Hoc Variation	• Baker International • Bertelsmann • Blue Bell • Friedrich Krupp • Timken (Cell 1)	• Electrolux (Cell 2)	• Caterpillar • Cummins (Cell 3)	• Kodak (Cell 4)

Environment

Figure 3.6 Mapping of environment and structure

Table 3.2 Performance of companies with environment-structure fit and misfit

Performance Measures	Companies in cells 1, 6, 11 & 16 (diagonal = fit)	Companies in cells 2, 3, 4, 5, 6, 7, 8, 9 10, 12, 13, 14, & 15 (others = misfit)	p-Value difference
1 Average RONA (1982–1986)	5.72	3.69	<0.001
2 RONA Growth (1982–1986)	6.41	2.32	<0.001
3 Revenue Growth (1982–1986)	7.19	4.98	<0.001

average return on net assets, growth in these returns, and revenue growth – the seventeen companies representing good environment-structure fit outperform by statistically significant margins the twenty-four companies that lack such fit.

CONCLUSION

Empirical results from a correlational analysis do not provide proof of a causal argument. In this case, our ability to draw any conclusive inferences from the findings is additionally constrained because of the small and non-random sample of companies we have considered and because of our relatively simple and coarse-grained measurement procedure. Despite these limitations, we do believe that we have provided some preliminary evidence for our proposition that the appropriate level of organizational complexity leads to effective performance in multi-unit organizations like MNCs. In this process, we have also suggested a useful way to classify the environment and structure of MNCs. Our findings, we believe, provide some justification for the approach we have advocated.

In the recent past, MNC managers have been at the receiving end of a diverse and often conflicting set of organizational prescriptions. On the one hand, influential academics and consultants have been urging them to abandon simplistic structures and processes and instead to build multidimensional network organizations with distributed management roles and tasks, overlapping responsibilities and relationships, and built-in ambiguity and redundancy.[21] On the other hand, equally strong voices have been arguing that the performance problems faced by many large MNCs are often attributable to the complexities of their organizations and that managers must have the courage to reestablish organizational simplicity by reverting to direct decision-making and unambiguous accountability.[22] Admittedly, these prescriptions are more complex than we are painting them. Nevertheless, the intense advocacy accompanying these arguments has made it difficult for managers to get a perspective on such diverse prescriptions.

We believe that the issues we have raised in this chapter will be useful to these managers, if only to structure internal debate and discussions on organizational choices. To reiterate, managers need a detailed understanding of their companies' environmental demands to evaluate the kind of organizational capabilities they need to build. Unnecessary organizational complexity in a relatively simple business environment can be just as unproductive as unresponsive simplicity in a complex business environment. To return to the title of this chapter, companies require different organizational horses to manage superior performance in different environmental courses. What we have proposed here is a method for analyzing these environmental courses and for selecting the appropriate organizational horses.

We need to point out that the part of our study reported in this chapter took a static picture of these companies. In reality, environmental demands evolve over time and managers need to adopt a dynamic view about organizational capabilities. Even though we have not carried out detailed case research on how the different industries covered in this study have been evolving, the limited information we have suggests that the environmental demands in at least some of them may be becoming more complex. In the food and beverages businesses, for example, the forces of global integration appear to be getting stronger, driven, among other factors, by the growing proliferation of regional and global brands. In the scientific measuring instrument business, on the other hand, the need for local responsiveness is increasing as stand-alone products are giving way to integrated systems consisting of packages of hardware, software, and related services. As a result, these and many other businesses may be evolving to the more complex transnational category, and companies competing in these businesses may need to build the kind of organizational form we have described as 'integrated variety'. Managers need to be sensitive to such changes in environmental demands – indeed, they should drive such changes when appropriate – and must develop the ability to differentiate and integrate their organizations to lead or respond to such evolving business conditions.

We focused here on the MNC. Our argument can easily be extended, however, to any multidivisional firm. Consider, for instance, the case of a firm in which each division operates in a different market or business segment. Once again, the overall environmental contingencies faced by such a firm can be characterized in terms of the extent to which each of its business segments have unique and strong forces for local responsiveness and the extent to which these businesses are linked. In a sense, this is similar to identifying the nature of the firm's diversification, whether it is in related or unrelated business segments. Similarly the firm's overall structure can be conceived in terms of the pattern of variation in the governance of the different corporate-division relationships. Again the same four structural patterns may be identified, and we would expect the environment-structure fit to follow the logic of requisite complexity. In this situation, then, all we have done is change the source of environmental variation from geography, in the case of MNCs, to different business segments, in the case of the multiproduct firm. Of course, in some situations, the source of environmental variation in the firm's different units may well be driven by both geography and product markets. Though operationally more complex, this situation can just as easily be accommodated under the same general theoretical rubric.

Finally, let us emphasize once again that in reiterating the two-decade-old notion of environment-organization fit, we do not wish to detract from the much more sophisticated analysis of organization-environment interactions that is the focus of current research on the topic. The perspectives in these studies add richness to our understanding of the underlying processes of influence and adaptation and of the limits of those processes. However, in focusing on those processes and in highlighting the second-order benefits from characteristics such as deliberate misfit and organizational ambiguity, what we often tend to overlook are the first-order benefits of fit and organizational simplicity. We take them for granted, perhaps, but an occasional reminder of these taken-for-granted aspects of organizational analysis may help in placing the rest in proper perspective.

NOTES AND REFERENCES

1 This contingency theory had two separate roots. Lawrence and Lorsch stated it as a set of environment-organization contingencies, as did Thompson. See: P.R. Lawrence and J.W. Lorsch, *Organization and Environment* (Boston: Graduate School of Business Administration, Harvard University, 1967); J.D. Thompson, *Organizations in Action* (New York: McGraw-Hill, 1967).

    Alfred Chandler, on the other hand, suggested the need for a match between strategy and organization as he described the rationale for and process of evolution of the multidivisional organization in corporate America. See: A. Chandler, *Strategy and Structure: Chapters in the History of the American Industrial Enterprise* (Cambridge, Massachusetts: MIT Press, 1962). The subsequent literature on contingency theory adopted one or both sets of views, building in this process a model of environment-strategy-organization linkages.

2 See J. Stopford and L.T. Wells, Jr., *Managing the Multinational Enterprise* (New York: Basic Books, 1972). This research followed the work of Chandler, focusing on strategy-organization contingencies.

3 See C.A. Bartlett, 'Building and Managing the Transnational: The New Organizational Challenge', *Competition in Global Industries*, ed. M.E. Porter (Boston: Harvard Business School Press, 1986).

4 See Bartlett (1986); C.A. Bartlett and S. Ghoshal, *Managing across Borders: The Transnational Solution* (Boston: Harvard Business School Press, 1989).

5 See Bartlett and Ghoshal (1989).

6 This interpretation is manifest, for example, in: W.G. Egelhoff, 'Exploring the Limits of Transnationalism' (Paper presented at the annual meeting, Academy of International Business, Toronto, 11–14 October 1990).

7 For a comprehensive review and a spirited defense of the concept of fit and the contingency perspective that underlies it, see: L. Donaldson, *In Defense of Organization Theory* (Cambridge: Cambridge University Press, 1985).

8 This database was developed in the course of the first author's doctoral dissertation work and is fully described in his unpublished thesis: 'The Innovative Multinational: A Differentiated Network of Roles and Relationships' (Boston: Harvard Business School, 1986).

    Parts of the database relevant to the analysis presented in this paper have also been described in: S. Ghoshal and N. Nohria, 'International Differentiation within Multinational Corporations', *Strategic Management Journal* 10 (1989): 323–337.

9 The 438 companies in the database are those that responded to the questionnaire we sent to the 438 North American and European MNCs listed in: J. Stopford, *World Directory of Multinational Enterprises* (Detroit, New Jersey: Gale Research Company, 1983).

    While we are not aware of any specific bias in the sample that would *a priori* invalidate any of our findings, the generalizability of our conclusions remains constrained because of the small size and potential non-representativeness of the sample. For a detailed description of the sample and of the reliability and validity of our measures, see: Ghoshal and Nohria (1989).

10 See C.K. Prahalad and Y.L. Doz, *The Multinational Mission: Balancing Local Demands and Global Vision* (New York: The Free Press, 1987).

11 See S.J. Kobrin, 'An Empirical Analysis of the Determinants of Global Integration', Special Issue, *Strategic Management Journal* 12 (1991): 17–31.

12 Steers describes some of the different performance measures and their relevance and implication. See: R.M. Steers, 'Problems in the Measurement

of Organizational Effectiveness', *Administrative Science Quarterly* 20 (1975): 546–558.

Venkatraman argues for the appropriateness of the measures we adopt. See: N. Venkatraman, 'A Concept of Fit in Strategy Research: Toward Verbal and Statistical Correspondence', *Academy of Management Review* 14 (1989): 423–444.

13 See Prahalad and Doz (1987).

14 For one of the earliest descriptions of MNC environments in these terms, see: J. Fayerweather, *International Business Strategy and Administration* (Cambridge, Massachusetts: Ballinger Press, 1978).

For one of the most recent and comprehensive elaborations, see: Prahalad and Doz (1987).

For a discussion of the factors that drive the needs for global integration and national responsiveness, see: G.S. Yip, 'Global Strategy. . . In a World of Nations?', *Sloan Management Review*, Fall 1989, pp. 29–41.

15 Our characterization and terminology need some clarifications. Bartlett and Ghoshal (1989) considered three sets of environmental forces: those of global integration, national responsiveness, and worldwide learning. Strong demands along each of these dimensions were characterized as 'global', 'multinational', and 'international' industries, respectively, whereas 'transnational' industries were defined as those facing strong demands simultaneously along all three dimensions. In this paper, we use the relatively simpler two-dimensional conceptualization proposed by Prahalad and Doz (1987). In our framework, global and multinational industries are defined the same way as in Bartlett and Ghoshal (1989), but international and transnational industries are defined as those facing weak-weak and strong-strong combinations of the forces of global integration and national responsiveness. This characterization is consistent with the use of the terminology in Bartlett (1986), except that he did not define the 'international' industry environment explicitly in that paper.

16 There is well-established support for these mechanisms in organization theory. Since the landmark studies of the Aston Group, centralization and formalization have been central constructs in analyzing the structure of complex organizations. See: D.S. Pugh, D.J. Hickson, C.R. Hinings, and C. Turner, 'The Dimensions of Organization Structure', *Administrative Science Quarterly* 13 (1968): 65–105.

Van Maanen and Schein have since argued that normative integration should be considered as another primary element in the structure of organizational relations. See: J. Van Maanen and E.H. Schein, 'Toward a Theory of Organizational Socialization' in *Research in Organizational Behavior*, ed. B.M. Staw (Greenwich, Connecticut: JAI Press, 1979).

17 For a recent review of the evidence and arguments for internal differentiation in headquarters-subsidiary relationships, see: A.K. Gupta and V. Govindarajan, 'Knowledge Flows and the Structure of Control within Multinational Corporations', *Academy of Management Review* 16 (1991): 768–792.

18 See Ghoshal and Nohria (1989).

For alternative conceptualizations of subsidiary context, see: T.A. Poynter and A.M. Rugman. 'World Product Mandates: How Will Multinationals Respond?', *Business Quarterly* 47 (1982): 54–61; and: Gupta and Govindarajan (1991).

19 See Ghoshal and Nohria (1989).

20 It is interesting to observe that there is one null set in this analysis: none of the companies combines high levels of centralization and socialization while lacking formalized systems. Perhaps this is merely an artifact of the sample or a reflection of measurement error. Or perhaps this combination is administratively

infeasible. At this stage we can only speculate on this issue, but it may be a starting point for an interesting future study.

21 For the most provocative and articulate statement of this view, see: G. Hedlund, 'The Hypermodern MNC: A Helterarchy?', *Human Resource Management* 25 (1986): 9–35.
22 See N. Tichy and R. Charan, 'Speed, Simplicity, and Self-Confidence: An Interview with Jack Welch', *Harvard Business Review*, September–October 1989, pp. 112–120.

Chapter 4

Thinking globally, acting locally

Anthony G. Eames

The media call the battle for market share in my industry 'the cola wars' and that is probably not a bad way to characterize it. There is certainly all of the intensity of war.

Fortunately, the cola wars are non-violent, although they are not exactly a summer's day at the cottage either. The soft drink industry, after all, is the most competitive business in the world – and the most international. The stakes are enormous. Our high growth industry already has world-wide revenues in excess of $100 billion.

The cola wars are being fought in over 160 countries, across every time zone, and literally on land, sea and air. The battlefield might be a push cart in Jakarta, the QE2 steaming across the Atlantic or the Concorde, en route to Paris at twice the speed of sound. In each case, we are competing for more than share of market and share of stomach. What we are really fighting for is share of heart – a special place in the hearts and minds of our consumers – the creation of a special bond between our products and those who consume them.

But while war may be hell, the cola wars are fun – and productive fun as well. That is because competition brings out the best in everyone; it demands excellence in everything we do and is undoubtedly why there is so much interest in the cola wars. After all it is a battle for the attention of the five billion inhabitants of planet earth, each of whom is going to be thirsty on numerous occasions each day.

THE AIR WAR STRATEGY

Our 'air war' strategy – promotion and advertising through radio and television – is one of consistency and believability. We try to convey a sense of long-term commitment to a product, building on our rich heritage, and highlighting the extent to which our product is part of the lives of millions of people around the globe.

Perhaps the most famous sortie in the 'air wars' was the Pepsi Challenge back in 1972. As a distant number two in the cola market, Pepsi introduced an in-store public relations and advertisement campaign – taste-testing Coke vs. Pepsi. This program taught us two very important lessons. First, don't be reactive – build your own media and marketing programs for the long haul and then, keep your eye on the fundamentals of your own business.

Second, temporary superiority in the air does not mean much if the other side controls the ground. To keep control of the ground you have won, you have to get the product into the hands of the consumer. You have to make it totally available, highly visible and very affordable. Throughout North America, consumers expect to get the products they want, where and when they want them; that has not always been an easy task in some parts of the world.

THE GROUND WAR

Wherever you go in the world nowadays, you must excel in production, distribution, pricing and merchandizing – the ground war – or you will surely fail. The air war may be more glamorous, but the cola wars, and most marketing wars, are really won or lost on the ground. Winston Churchill, writing of winning a war, put it this way, 'Victory is the beautiful, bright coloured flower. Transport is the stem without which it could never have blossomed.' By transport, of course, Churchill meant all of the logistics of war, those mundane details that capture few headlines but eventually turn the tide of battle.

We have found that the way to win the cola wars worldwide is country by country, market by market, case by case and bottle by bottle, living by our company's simple code: 'Think globally, but act locally.'

One thing you learn quickly in international business is that in reality each country requires its own textbook; there is no magic head-office marketing cookbook with foolproof recipes. Nor can you accept conventional wisdom. For example, soft drinks sell best in warm climates. Right? Wrong! Per capita consumption of Coca-Cola products in Iceland in 1988 was the highest in the world. Indeed, consumption in all of the Nordic countries is high, even in the areas above the Artic circle. In Lapland retailers actually sell Coke warmers instead of Coke coolers, and when people say 'things go better with Coke' up there, they probably mean reindeer, rather than hamburgers or chicken.

Getting product to customers is the constant, the fundamental component that makes all else possible. You can go almost anywhere in the world and see the same elements of this system in place.

Staying close to customers and understanding their needs and wants is also crucial to our business. I can illustrate this principle by our adventure with new Coke back in 1985. Today, five years later, virtually everyone seems convinced that new Coke, and the subsequent return of traditional

Coke as Coca-Cola Classic, was a well-planned, orchestrated marketing ploy. After all, we got tons of free publicity and ended up with two solid products and increased market share.

The truth is, we had had all sorts of survey and demographic information that seemed to tell us that new Coke was the way to go. So we bit the bullet and realized we had live ammunition in our mouths! We quickly had the general public telling us that they had not been part of our survey and that they wanted 'their' product back.

There was a simple lesson to be learned. We do not own our products – the consumer does – and you mess with their product at your peril. Fortunately the end result was a happy one for Coca-Cola, although the flap put quite a strain on our mail room and phone system for the fifity-four days before Coca-Cola Classic returned to the shelves.

FORECASTING CONSUMPTION

My first assignment with the company, back in 1966, was to predict soft drink consumption for Australia ten years out. So I modelled the statistical relationship between historic soft drink consumption and various demand factors, such as population and real income, extrapolated future demand and then did the same for competing beverages such as coffee, tea, milk, beer and juices.

I attempted to judge whether our share of total beverage consumption was going to rise, given the experience of more mature markets such as the United States. My conclusion: that Australian per capita soft drink consumption would double by the year 1980, to the level of US soft drink consumption in 1966. The fact is that Australian per capita consumption doubled, not in 1980 as I had projected, but four years earlier, in 1976. And the much more interesting fact, the really amazing fact that makes the cola wars what they are, is that US per capita consumption increased from 16 imperial gallons in 1966 to more than 36 gallons in 1986, and it is still climbing. We have a market where literally no one knows how high is up.

A couple of quick examples will illustrate how this market growth can be fuelled. Start with Diet Coke. In the early 1980s, in what was at the time seen as a risky move, we introduced a diet soft drink bearing the Coca-Cola name. People thought we would hurt the brand, or simply cannibalize our own sales. Instead, we grew the market, enlarging the soft drink pie. Today Diet Coke is within a few points of displacing our nearest competitor in North America as the number two soft drink.

Market growth can also come from finding innovative ways of getting product to customers. This search for new channels is one of the most exciting developments in the soft drink business. For example, many video stores are selling our products, as are delivered food franchises. Domino's Pizza came out of nowhere to become a billion dollar business in North

American and they did it in part by delivering soft drinks, along with their pizza, in under thirty minutes.

Brazil, China, the Soviet Union and Saudi Arabia are all exciting, high-growth potential markets. But so are Canada and the United States.

Probably the most significant strategic move we have made in Canada involves our bottlers. In 1987 we restructured our Canadian bottling system to enhance our customer focus. Over 80 per cent of our volume is now produced by one bottler, Coca-Cola Beverages, which was previously called T.C.C. This restructuring has produced economies of scale and allowed our bottlers to concentrate on what they know best – production, sales distribution and operating efficiencies. That allows Coca-Cola Ltd., the Canadian parent company, to concentrate on what we do best – marketing, producing advertising and promotions programs that are second to none. And if you take a look at our advertising and promotional events, you can see that we work to develop a consistent set of messages that build on our products' universal appeal.

We expect the soft drink market to continue to grow while other major beverages such as coffee, tea, milk and beer will continue to show zero or negative growth.

In the final analysis, in the cola wars it is not 'to the victor goes the spoils,' but 'to the one who spoils the customer goes the victory'. The cola wars, perhaps more than any other phenomenon in recent memory, demonstrates the full range of those activities called 'marketing'.

We have a secret formula for our syrup but no magic, foolproof marketing plan. In fact, our president and chief operating officer, Don Keough, was once asked to explain 'what makes a winner?' Don, who does not admit defeat easily, said he had no idea. But he said he did know what makes a loser. He called it his 'Commandments for Losing'. He says they are guaranteed to work.

COMMANDMENTS FOR LOSING

1 Quit taking risks.

A young person's attitude, after achieving modest success with a company, can too quickly become, 'Let someone else stick his neck out; I've done okay'.

2 Be content.

Be content with what you have and where you are. Mr Robert W. Woodruff, the late patriarch of the Coca-Cola Company, at 94 years of age said, 'the world belongs to the discontented'. Everlasting dissatisfaction is part of this spirit of winning. Blissful contentment is part of the spirit of losing.

3 Before making any move always ask yourself, 'What would the founder have done?'

Believe it or not, after visonary business leader Walter P. Chrysler died, his successors actually held seances to get in touch with his spirit to find out what Walter would have done to improve performance at his auto company. What he probably would have done was fire them for holding seances in the first place! The simple fact is that no one knows what any leader, no matter how great, would do in a new set of circumstances. The only thing you know is that they would not pick a strategy so sure to lose.

4 Rely totally on your search and experts to make decisions for you.

Our 'experts' said it would be a mistake to introduce Diet Coke. They were afraid we would harm the Coke name, weaken our Tab entry and confuse the marketplace. Well, Roberto Goizueta, our then new CEO, believed otherwise and Diet Coke has become highly successful.

5 Once you have a formula for success never change it.

A corollary to that is to respond to everything that happens and change your formula every day. In truth, winners are the people who have the vision to see around corners; losers never can. The difference is the ability to recognize the fine line between a fad and a genuine trend and that means staying so close to your customer that you think as he or she does.

6 Hide your mistakes.

Even better, make sure that you so diffuse responsibility that no one can be criticized or held responsible when you screw up.

7 Be more concerned with status than with service.

And while you are at it, make sure you are well-positioned at the country club and well-respected at prestigious business and trade organizations. But never have enough time to visit your outlets, shake hands with your employees or thank your customers.

8 Concentrate on your competitor instead of your customer.

'Me too' is the name of the game – imitation instead of innovation. If you spend enough time on your competitors, you will not have to worry about your customers. They will have gone someplace else.

9 Put yourself first.

Punish your suppliers, let your vendors gouge your retailers and despoil the environment; care little about the consumer.

10 Simply memorize the formula T-G-E.

T-G-E stands for 'that's good enough', and if you say 'that's good enough' often enough, I can categorically guarantee loss and failure.

And then there is an eleventh commandment for losing, which I would like to add.

11 To lose you have to find a way to rationalize the slowing of growth.

If you are in Iceland, you have to rationalize it is too cold to sell Coca-Cola. It is not hard. You just blame something – the weather, the system, the phase of the moon.

THE LESSON

The real lesson of these Commandments for Losing is that winners believe deep down, that they can maintain momentum no matter the odds. Losers, on the other hand, are always ready to bet against themselves. Because when you look behind these 'commandments' or strip away marketing jargon, the demographics and the hype, there are some very fundamental truths that come out. One is that you must make the customer the focus of everything you do. *Business Week* editor, Lew Young, once said, 'In too many companies the customer has become a nuisance whose unpredictable behavior damages carefully made strategic plans.'

To win the cola wars, or to win in any enterprise in the decade ahead, we will need to go beyond just satisfying customers; we must learn to think like them as well. We must become aware of their needs and concerns. In one instance, understanding our customers' concerns actually led to a rare truce in the cola wars. I am talking about concern for the environment and about an effort initiated by us called the Blue Box Program. This recycling effort has been supported by all members of the soft drink industry, not because anyone was going to gain market share, but because it was the right thing to do.

The second truth is that you have to believe in your product and your company. Without faith, you cannot win.

Chapter 5

The internationalization of the firm

Four Swedish cases[1]

Jan Johanson and Finn Wiedersheim-Paul

INTRODUCTION

The widespread interest in multinational firms has given rise to many articles and books on various aspects of the international strategies of firms. Research has been concentrated on the large corporations, particularly the American.

Many firms, however, start international operations when they are still comparatively small and gradually develop their operations abroad. From our studies of international business at the University of Uppsala we have several observations indicating that this gradual internationalization, rather than large, spectacular foreign investments, is characteristic of the internationalization of most Swedish firms. It seems reasonable to believe that the same holds true for many firms from other countries with small domestic markets. A related observation is that the type of development during the early stages is of importance for the following pattern. Similar observations have also been made about US firms and have been used as an argument in discussions of foreign investments and international marketing.[2]

In this article we describe and analyse the internationalization of four Swedish firms – Sandvik, Atlas Copco, Facit and Volvo. All of them sell more than two-thirds of their turnover abroad and have production facilities in more than one foreign country. In Sweden[3] they are often used as examples and patterns in discussions of international operations. Usually such discussions only treat the operations of the firms during later years when they have already become large and international. Here we adopt a more longitudinal approach, describing and discussing the whole development which has led to their present international position.

Before the case descriptions we give an account of our view of the internationalization process, on which these descriptions are based, and discuss some patterns which follow from this view. In the concluding section we discuss some similarities and differences between the firms with respect to internationalization.

The term international usually refers either to an attitude of the firm towards foreign activities or to the actual carrying out of activities abroad.[4] Of course there is a close relationship between attitudes and actual behaviour. The attitudes are the basis for decisions to undertake international ventures and the experiences from international activities influence these attitudes. In the case descriptions we have to concentrate on those aspects of the internationalization that are easy to observe, that is, the international activities. We consider, however, these attitudes as interesting and important and the discussion of the internationalization process is basically an account of the interaction between attitudes and actual behaviour.

Our basic assumption is that the firm first develops in the domestic market[5] and that the internationalization is the consequence of a series of incremental decisions. We also assume that the most important obstacles to internationalization are lack of knowledge and resources. These obstacles are reduced through incremental decision-making and learning about the foreign markets and operations. The perceived risk of market investments decreases and the continued internationalization is stimulated by the increased need to control sales and the increased exposure to offers and demands to extend the operations. We are not trying to explain why firms start exporting[6] but assume that, because of lack of knowledge about foreign countries and a propensity to avoid uncertainty, the firm starts exporting to neighbouring countries or countries that are comparatively well-known and similar with regard to business practices. We also believe that the firm starts selling abroad via independent representatives, as this means a smaller resource commitment than the establishment of a sales subsidiary.[7]

Considering the development of operations in individual countries we expect a stepwise extension of operations. Of course is it possible to identify different types of steps and a different number of stages. We have chosen to distinguish between four different stages. They are:

1 no regular export activities;
2 export via independent representatives (agent);
3 sales subsidiary;
4 production/manufacturing.

We think these stages are important because:

(a) They are diferent with regard to the degree of involvement of the firm in the market.
(b) They are often referred to by people in business.

There are two aspects about the degree of involvement. The four stages mean successively larger resource commitments and they also lead to quite different market experiences and information for the firm. The first means that the firm has made no commitment of resources to the market and that it lacks any regular information channel to and from the market. The second means that the firm has a channel to the market through which it gets fairly regular information about sales influencing factors. It also means a certain commitment to the market. The third means a controlled information channel to the market, giving the firm ability to direct the type and amount of information flowing from the market to the firm. During this stage the firm also gets direct experience of resource influencing factors. The fourth stage means a still larger resource commitment.

We call the sequence of stages mentioned above the establishment chain.[8] We have, of course, simplified the matter somewhat by exaggerating the differences between the four steps. It is not always obvious whether a firm has established relations with an agent or not, while a joint venture with an earlier representative can be placed in the second or the third stage.

Of course we do not expect the development always to follow the whole chain. First, several markets are not large enough for the resource demanding stages. Second, we could expect jumps in the establishment chain in firms with extensive experience from other foreign markets.

Considering the extension of activities to new markets, it is possible that the concept of psychic distance may prove useful.[9] This concept is defined as factors preventing or disturbing the flows of information between firms and market. Examples of such factors are differences in language, culture, political systems, level of education, level of industrial development. For obvious reasons, psychic distance is correlated with geographic distance, but exceptions are easy to find. Some countries in the British Commonwealth are far apart geographically (e.g. England and Australia), but for different reasons they are near to each other in terms of psychic distance. The USA and Cuba are near to each other geographically, but, for political reasons, far apart with regard to psychic distance. As these examples indicate, psychic distance is not constant. It changes because of the development of the communication system, trade and other kinds of social exchange. In general we expect most changes to take place rather slowly.[10]

Psychic distance, however, is of course not the only important factor for international operations. In most textbooks about international business the size of the potential market is considered the most important factor for international operations: 'The first activity phase of export planning then, is identifying and measuring market opportunity.'[11] Thus we should expect that market size influences decisions in the internationalization process. We could expect either that the firm first starts operations in countries with large markets or that they prefer to start in smaller markets. In the latter case the argument may be that small markets are more similar to the domestic Swedish market and require a smaller initial resource commitment or have less competitive domestic industries.

But there are reasons to expect that the patterns of agency establishment differ from those of sales subsidiary establishments with respect to the two factors. The agency establishments, according to our view, are made primarily during the early stages of internationalization, which means that they could be expected to be more closely related to psychic distance than to the size of the market. The sales subsidiary establishments – and still more production – could be expected to be influenced primarily by the market size as it generally requires a larger minimum resource commitment than an independent representative. The production establishments are influenced by different forces; on one hand, by psychic distance, on the other, by factors such as tariffs, non-tariff barriers and transport costs. As a result it is hard to observe any correlation between psychic distance and production establishments.

A third pattern which could be expected is that after the establishment of the first agency a phase follows when agencies are established in several markets. In the same way we could expect a separate phase dominated by the establishment of sales subsidiaries in several markets. Last, a phase with the establishment of production in several markets will follow. We assume that the three different phases in the internationalization of the firm are dependent on the development of the activity knowledge and the organizational structure of the firm. During the agent phase the firm builds an export department with the capability and responsibility for the establishment and maintenance of agencies. Establishment of sales subsidiaries means that units for the control of subsidiaries are organized. In the last phase, units for coordination of production and marketing in different countries are developed.

It should be noted that the discussion so far has dealt exclusively with the development of the marketing side of the firm. We do not regard this as a serious limitation. Marketing operations in this sense are predominant among the international activities of at least the Swedish firms.[12] Furthermore it has been shown that the marketing side is often a determining factor in the development of the firm.[13] Last, a similar development is likely when internationalization takes place on the purchasing side of the firm.[14]

THE INTERNATIONALIZATION PROCESS – FOUR CASES

Here we describe the internationalization of the four firms Sandvik, Atlas Copco, Facit and Volvo. The descriptions are based on various types of published data[15] about the firms which have been checked and supplemented by interviews with the firms. As we said before, we have chosen to use the moments when a firm establishes agencies, a sales subsidiary and production facilities as key factors in the process of internationalization. It has been possible to identify these moments with fairly high accuracy in most cases.

In order to help the reader we have constructed diagrams illustrating the 'establishment profiles' of the firms. These profiles show when the firm has started operations in twenty national markets. To standardize the case descriptions the countries are the same for all cases.

The analysis of the establishment patterns is based on a ranking of countries according to psychic distance.[16] As mentioned above, we believe that the psychic distance changes very slowly. Thus the rank order of countries according to the present psychic distance from Sweden, which is given in the 'establishment profiles' with a few exceptions, reflects the psychic distance fairly accurately even when the internationalization has taken a long time, as in our cases.

In order to compare the relations between establishments and the two kinds of market characteristics, we used a very crude indicator of market size, GNP 1960. As it is only used for the ranking of countries we do not think this crudeness is of much importance. Most market size indicators are fairly well correlated with GNP which also changes rather slowly.

Sandvik AB

Steel production in Sandviken started in 1862 in order to exploit the Bessemer process. During the first years the product line consisted mainly of industrial raw material: pig iron, ingot and blanks. These products became successively less important and were replaced by more manufactured special steel products, like cold-rolled strips, wire, tubes and saws – product groups that are still very important for Sandvik. In 1910 production of steel conveyors was started and in the 1940s hard metal products were introduced. The latter have been of great significance for the development of the firm during the last decades. At present about 40 per cent of the turnover comes from this product group and Sandvik is one of the biggest producers of hard metal products in the world. Another type of product which was introduced during the 1960s is alloys used in nuclear reactors.

Of the four firms described Sandvik is the oldest and also the one which first started its internationalization course. The first contacts with representatives were established in the 1860s. Sandvik's early start with representatives in foreign countries was an innovation at that time. Until then the Swedish iron and steel exporting had mainly been undertaken by trading firms. A probable explanation of these early foreign representatives is that the founder of Sandvik, G. F. Göransson, had earlier been general manager in a trading firm with extensive connections abroad. See Figure 5.1.

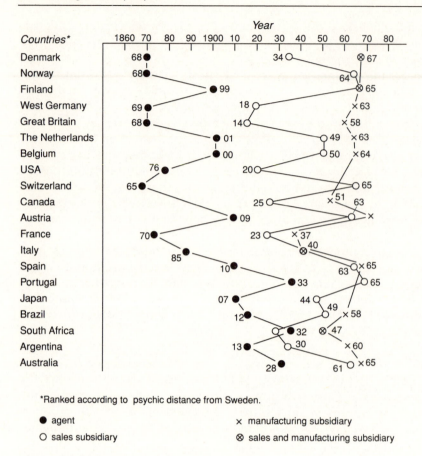

*Ranked according to psychic distance from Sweden.

● agent   × manufacturing subsidiary
○ sales subsidiary   ⊗ sales and manufacturing subsidiary

Figure 5.1 Profiles of establishments, Sandvik

As can be seen from the profile for agency establishments in Figure 5.1 they were set up in successively more distant markets. We computed the Spearman rank correlation coefficient between the time order of establishments and the order of psychic distance and market size respectively (see Table 5.1). Obviously there is a high correlation between the order of agency establishments and distance. The coefficient of the market size factor should be interpreted with care as most of the establishments took place a long time ago, but it is remarkably low.

The same distance-related behaviour, as for the agencies, cannot be observed in the establishments of sales subsidiaries. As the profile shows, Sandvik did not establish the first subsidiaries in the nearest markets, the Nordic countries, but in the large industrial markets like Germany, Great Britain and the USA.

The reason for not establishing trading links in the Nordic countries and the big import markets like Switzerland and the Netherlands was probably that Sandvik had access to efficient representatives, in these markets, with well developed channels to the customers.

Establishments after 1940 have mainly been made in important markets where Sandvik until then lacked sales subsidiaries (e.g. the Nordic countries and EEC countries). During the 1950s Sandvik developed a policy to use subsidiaries in foreign marketing and, when entering new markets during the 1960s, sales subsidiaries were used from the beginning.

Table 5.1 also shows that the sales subsidiary establishments do not follow the same time pattern as the agency establishments. In this case the market size factor's highest correlation is with the order of establishments. This is in accordance with our expectations.

Table 5.1 Rank correlation (Spearman) between the order of Sandvik foreign establishments and psychic distance and market size

	Psychic distance [b]	Market size [b]
Agents	0.79 (0.001)[a]	0.24 (0.181)
Sales subsidiaries	0.16 (0.227)	0.66 (0.002)
Production	−0.01 (0.496)	0.06 (0.386)

[a] In this and all tables that follow, the probability of getting the coefficient or a more extreme value is shown in brackets after each coefficient. It is done in order to give the reader an indication of the 'strength' of the coefficients.
[b] The correlation between the measures of distance and size is only 0.06.

The patterns for the manufacturing subsidiaries is quite different from the other kinds of establishment. The first production establishments were made in distant markets. They were saw production in France, Finland and Italy and drill production in South Africa and Canada. There is no correlation at all between the order of production establishments and the factors of distance and size.

According to the establishment chain, described above, firms first make contacts with an independent representative in the foreign market. Later they set up sales subsidiaries and after that, in some cases, production. At the same time there is also a broadening to other markets. The internationalization course of Sandvik is well in accordance with this picture. On practically all markets, independent representatives have been the first connections. Then, after a considerable period of time, they have been replaced by sales subsidiaries. Canada is the only country where a subsidiary was not preceded by a representative. The reason was that Sandvik's representative in the USA and, later, the subsidiary there, performed the marketing in Canada as well.

In 1971, 85 per cent of the total turnover of around 1800 million Swedish kroner came from abroad. The main part of sales is made by the subsidiaries and the independent representatives are nowadays of little significance. The number of independent representatives reached its maximum about 1950 but, since then, has radically diminished.

Two new patterns can be seen in Sandvik's establishments during the last few years. First, Sandvik has developed a new organization of subsidiaries, especially intended to handle the marketing of conveyor bands. The head office of this group is situated in Stuttgart in Germany and the manufacturing units are in the USA and Germany. Second, several establishments during the last five years have been made as joint ventures. The products involved are those used in the nuclear industry in France, the USA and Germany. One reason for these joint ventures is that a 'national connection' is very important as projects in this area are often characterized by 'buy national' behaviour. Another reason is that Sandvik alone cannot afford the heavy investments needed.

Atlas Copco

The firm started in 1873 with the production of railway material of various kinds. Soon, other products were added: steam engines for ships and machine tools. Production of pneumatic tools started in the 1890s and already at the turn of the century the marketing of rock drills was started. In 1905 Atlas produced the first air compressor of their own design. In 1917 the company was merged with another firm, producing diesel engines.

As early as 1880 exports were substantial. Diesel engines were the dominant export products until some years after 1930, while the compressed air products were sold mostly on the domestic market. After the Second World War the selling of pneumatic products soon dominated and the diesel motor production was sold in 1948.

During the first years after the war the selling efforts were concentrated on 'the Swedish method' – lightweight rock drill equipment combined with Sandvik's rock drills. At the end of the 1950s the production and selling were changed towards heavier equipment, stationary compressors and pneumatic tools.

Atlas Copco is five years younger than Sandvik but started the internationalization process considerably later. The successive establishment of contacts with representatives on more and more distant markets, which the model predicts, is evident also for Atlas Copco but less clear than for Sandvik (see Figure 5.2).

The establishment of sales and production subsidiaries was not common until after the Second World War, when Atlas Copco sold off its production of diesel motors and concentrated on pneumatic products. During the first few years of the 1950s twenty-three sales subsidiaries were on 'the Swedish method', Atlas Copco also concentrated on an active

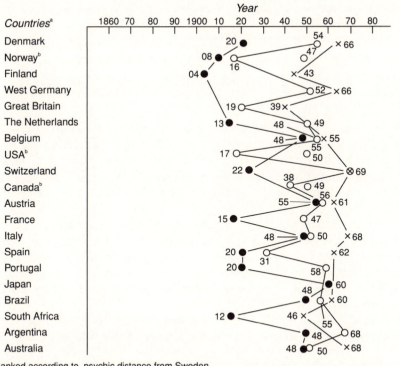

Figure 5.2 Profiles of establishments, Atlas Copco

[a]Ranked according to psychic distance from Sweden.
[b]In Norway, USA and Canada we have marked two sales subsidiary establishments. The first one sold diesel products, the second pneumatic equipment.

● agent   × manufacturing subsidiary
○ sales subsidiary   ⊗ sales and manufacturing subsidiary

marketing strategy, including well-developed sales organizations, storing and technical service in the local markets. Sales subsidiaries were considered necessary for this strategy.

The first manufacturing subsidiary abroad was started in Great Britain in 1939. Most important was the acquisition of Arpic in Belgium. This firm was an important competitor of Atlas Copco. During the 1960s several establishments were made in more distant countries. The reasons for this expansion were mostly to overcome various barriers to trade.

The pattern of establishment is similar to Sandvik's but less pronounced (see Table 5.2). The agency establishments are correlated with the distance factor and the sales subsidiary establishments with the market size factor. The production establishments are correlated with neither.

The development in individual markets is illustrated in Figure 5.2. In most cases representatives have been used before subsidiaries. But many

Table 5.2 Rank correlation (Spearman) between the order of Atlas Copco foreign establishments and psychic distance and market size

	Psychic distance	Market size
Agents	0.40 (0.041)	−0.26 (0.123)
Sales subsidiaries	0.33 (0.072)	0.48 (0.018)
Production	0.16 (0.242)	−0.11 (0.312)

of these representatives were used in the marketing of diesel products. The selling of pneumatic products, being more method- than product-oriented, was from the start performed by subsidiaries in the important markets. Four of the sales subsidiaries were not preceded by representatives. Two of these were failures in so far as they soon had to close down (the USA and Canada).

One of them was not established until 1952 (West Germany). The late establishment in the German market was due to the fact that Atlas Copco met its strongest competition in this market, and it was considered too tough for selling. The first regular export to Germany did not occur until 1951, when the selling of the recently developed pneumatic equipment for mines started.

Selling abroad as a ratio of total turnover 1922 (1900 million Swedish kronor) was nearly 90 per cent. The majority of this selling is made by about thirty-five foreign subsidiaries, but Atlas Copco has representatives in more than 100 countries. There are manufacturing units in ten countries.

Facit

This firm was formed in a reconstruction in 1922. The new enterprise took over the production of a calculating machine from a bankrupt firm, AB Facit. In the beginning of the 1930s a new version of this machine was developed. The new product started Facit's expansion on foreign markets. Some figures of turnover illustrate this. During the period 1923–33 the turnover was constant, 2.5 million Swedish kronor. Until 1939 there was an increase to 10 million Swedish kronor. In 1939 the export ratio was 80–85 per cent and the number of export markets was about seventy.

The expansion also continued with the buying of other firms: for example, in 1939 a manufacturer of typing machines, in 1942 a manufacturer of calculating machines and in 1966 a manufacturer of accounting and calculating machines. In 1972, after a financial crisis, Facit merged with a well-known Swedish multinational firm, Electrolux.

The internationalization process in Facit is unlike Sandvik's and Atlas Copco's. About ten years after the reconstruction in 1922, contacts were established with independent representatives on a large number of markets at the same time. There was no tendency to start on neighbouring markets.

Table 5.3 Rank correlation (Spearman) between the order of Facit foreign establishments and psychic distance and market size

	Psychic distance		Market size	
Agents	0.25[a]	(0.200)	−0.53[a]	(0.040)
Sales subsidiaries	0.60	(0.004)	0.21	(0.179)

[a] Only fourteen observations were used due to difficulties in dating some agent establishments.

There was, however, a high negative correlation with the market size, indicating that Facit first established agency relations in small countries (see Table 5.3).

The establishment of subsidiaries, which started at the end of the 1940s, is less confined to a certain time period. They are highly correlated with the distance factor but not with market size. The reasons for substituting subsidiaries for representatives are numerous. For one thing, it became a policy for Facit to use sales subsidiaries. For specific markets reasons, such as better control, the reinforcement of the selling organization and dissatisfaction with the representative were mentioned.

The motives for setting up manufacturing subsidiaries abroad have been mostly defensive in character. The foremost reasons for these establishments have been barriers to exporting to the markets concerned. This is also the case of those markets where licensing has been used. The general policy of Facit has not been to decentralize production geographically, but to export from Sweden.

In one case Facit has sold a sales subsidiary to the former representative on the market. This is the only example of a backward move in the 'establishment chain'. In all other cases the establishments have followed the 'chain' pattern. See Figure 5.3.

In 1971 the turnover was about 950 million Swedish kronor, of which 47 per cent was sold through subsidiaries, 17 per cent through independent foreign representatives. The total export ratio was 66 per cent. The number of foreign subsidiaries was twenty, distributed among fourteen countries. Three of these were manufacturing units, two both manufacturing and sales and fifteen sales.

A new development, considered of great importance, is various agreements with foreign companies, often Japanese, on development and production of new products.

Volvo[17]

The company started its activities in 1927, but the first product, a car, was already finished the year before. The production of cars appeared to be rather sensitive to seasonal variations and in 1928 Volvo started producing

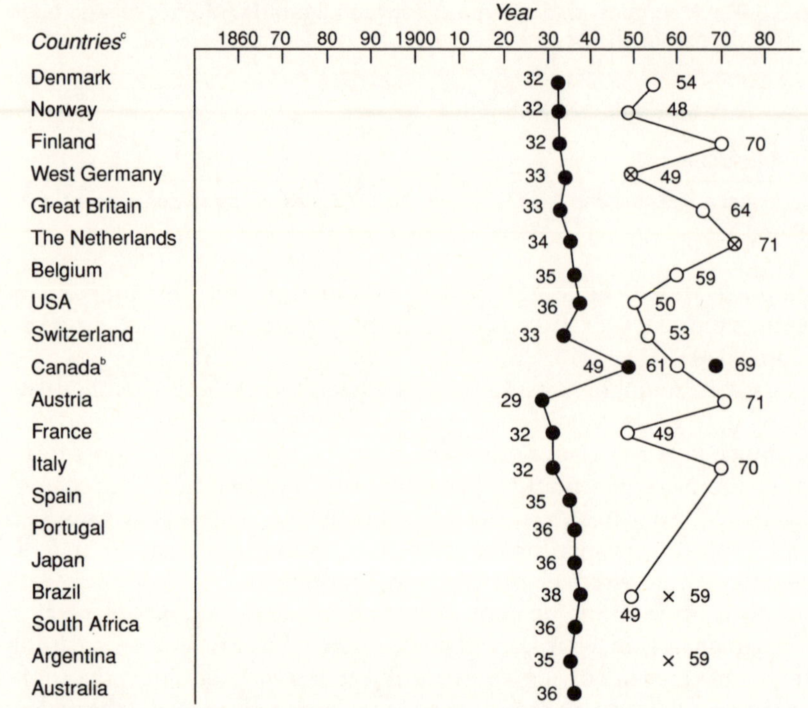

Year

| Countries[c] | 1860 70 | 80 | 90 | 1900 | 10 | 20 | 30 | 40 | 50 | 60 | 70 | 80 |

Denmark   32 ●   ○ 54
Norway   32 ●   ○ 48
Finland   32 ●   ○ 70
West Germany   33 ●   ⊗ 49
Great Britain 33 ●   ○ 64
The Netherlands 34 ●   ⊗ 71
Belgium   35 ●   ○ 59
USA   36 ●   ○ 50
Switzerland   33 ●   ○ 53
Canada[b]   49 ● 61○   ● 69
Austria   29 ●   ○ 71
France   32 ●   ○ 49
Italy   32 ●   ○ 70
Spain   35 ●
Portugal   36 ●
Japan   36 ●
Brazil   38 ●   ○ × 59
                           49
South Africa   36 ●
Argentina   35 ●   × 59
Australia   36 ●

[a]Establishments of manufacturing subsidiaries are so few that they cannot be connected by a line.
[b]The subsidiary started in 1961, but in 1968 was sold to the former agent on the market.
[c]Ranked according to psychic distance from Sweden.

● agent   × manufacturing subsidiary
○ sales subsidiary   ⊗ sales and manufacturing subsidiary

Figure 5.3 Profiles of establishments, Facit[a]

trucks as well, the sales of which were more evenly distributed throughout the year.

Export selling was a part of the first production plans and shortly after the start Volvo began establishing representatives abroad.

This was first done on neighbouring markets, Denmark and Norway, and on less industrialized distant ones like Argentina, Brazil, Spain and Portugal. No attempt was made to sell to the large European markets until the 1950s. One reason for this behaviour was the hard competition from the domestic industries on these markets. From the start Volvo's policy was to not use its own affiliates or subsidiaries. However, early on Volvo had to break with its policy and establish selling subsidiaries in Finland and Norway, due to difficulties in finding retailers on these markets. A wave of establishments followed in the 1950s when Volvo started up new selling subsidiaries in most European countries, and in the USA and Canada.

This establishment pattern is very similar to Facit's with a high correlation between subsidiary establishments and distance and a negative correlation between agent establishments and market size.

The establishment of manufacturing units on most markets has not occurred before that of sales subsidiaries and the strategy has been to keep production in Sweden as long as possible. Establishments are said to be caused mainly by barriers to trade. Volvo has in such cases used assembly plants to avoid tariffs, import fees and other barriers. In Canada and Australia those plants were preceded by sales subsidiaries. This was not the case in Belgium. This plant was intended to produce for the EEC market. Besides the markets studied, Volvo also has its own assembly plants in Peru and Malaysia. As can be seen, assembly plants are often situated in distant countries.

The model's assumption that a firm starts selling to markets through representatives is correct for all countries except Finland. The two other very early establishments, in Norway and Argentina, were soon shut down, in Norway due to the Second World War and in Argentina because of barriers to import. A number of years thereafter the distribution was run by agents. When the markets again became important Volvo established new subsidiaries.

Special circumstances existed in the USA, West Germany and Switzerland. In the USA Volvo had an agent for part of the market before establishing a subsidiary for the other parts. For a couple of years an agency and a subsidiary were used side by side. Volvo thereafter took over and used a single subsidiary for the whole market. In Switzerland an agent was also first used. After some years a subsidiary took over part of the market, but an agency is still used for the other parts. In West Germany two different local agents appeared, but their sales were of minor importance. Volvo therefore started a subsidiary in order to cover the whole market. See Figure 5.4.

In 1973 Volvo had more than 100 export markets and the export ratio exceeded 70 per cent of the total turnover of about 7,000 million Swedish kronor. In 1973 Volvo had manufacturing subsidiaries in five countries and sales subsidiaries in twelve. A new tendency in Volvo's international development in the last few years is a number of cooperation agreements and 'joint ventures' with various foreign companies regarding the construction and production of engines and gear boxes. See Table 5.4.

THE INTERNATIONALIZATION COURSE – SOME CONCLUDING REMARKS

First, compared to their present sizes the four firms were small when they started internationalization. Of course we have to be careful comparing

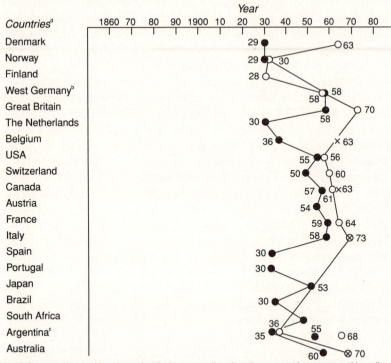

ᵃEstablishments of manufacturing subsidiaries are so few that they cannot be connected by a line.
ᵇEstablishment of agent and subsidiary in the same year.

ᶜThe subsidiary, which started in 1936, was closed down and substituted by an agent in 1955.
ᵈRanked according to psychic distance from Sweden.

● agent   × manufacturing subsidiary

○ sales subsidiary   ⊗ sales and manufacturing subsidiary

Figure 5.4 Profiles of establishments, Volvoᵃ

Table 5.4 Rank correlation (Spearman) between the order of Volvo foreign establishments and psychic distance and market size

	Psychic distance		Market size	
Agents	0.23	(0.076)	−0.70	(0.001)
Sales subsidiaries	0.47	(0.021)	0.06	(0.386)

sizes over so long a time period. However, they were not small in comparison with other Swedish firms in their respective industries at that time. Sandvik had 300 employees and a sales value of 1 million Swedish kronor in 1870. Atlas Copco was of similar size when it started exporting in the 1880s. Facit and Volvo had sales values of 2–3 million Swedish kronor when they started exporting forty years later.

Two of the firms – Sandvik and Volvo – had export in mind when they were established. It is interesting to note that the founders of both these firms – Göransson and Gabrielsson – had long experience of selling abroad. Göransson had been general manager of a trading firm. Gabrielsson was a sales manager in SKF and had been employed at the SKF subsidiary in Paris.

The internationalization process was much faster in the firms that started latest. Sandvik, which established its first agency contact in 1868, needed sixty-five years to get agents in all twenty markets investigated. Atlas Copco, that established its first contact in 1904, needed fifty-five years, Volvo started in 1929 and needed thirty years and Facit, finally, with its first contacts in 1929 needed twenty years.

We expected to find a negative relationship between psychic distance and the establishments. At least we expected that agency relations should be established first in neighbouring and similar countries. To a certain extent we expected the establishment of sales subsidiaries to occur in the same order. Both kinds of establishments were expected to be influenced by the size of the market. In that case, however, we expected the relationship to be stronger with the sales subsidiary establishments.

To a certain extent the establishments have followed this course. However, there are obvious differences between the firms as shown in Table 5.5.

Table 5.5 Rank correlation (Spearman) between agency establishments and psychic distance and respective market size

	Sandvik	Atlas Copco	Facit	Volvo
Psychic distance	0.79 (0.001)	0.40 (0.041)	0.25[a] (0.200)	0.23 (0.076)
Size	0.24 (0.181)	–0.26 (0.123)	–0.53[a] (0.040)	–0.70 (0.001)

[a]Based on only fourteen observations due to lack of information on establishing years of agents.

All the coefficients of distance have the expected sign and some of them are significant at the 0.05 level. But the differences between the firms are so large that there is reason to believe that they have followed different strategies of internationalization. This impression is strengthened when looking at the size of the coefficients which are rather low, with the exception of Volvo and Facit, which have significant negative coefficients. Whereas Sandvik and, to a certain extent, Atlas Copco could be described as having followed a course of establishing agency contracts in successively more distant countries, Volvo and Facit have started in the smaller countries and later extended to large countries. Atlas Copco has not followed any pronounced course with respect to the two country characteristics. This is not surprising as the product on which Atlas Copco based its main internationalization, drill equipment, has markets in countries with certain resources which need not be correlated with any of the above mentioned characteristics.

Looking at the sales subsidiary establishments the pattern is quite different (Table 5.6). It should be noted that the correlations between agency and sales subsidiary establishments are all lower than 0.30. The distance factor seems to have influenced Facit's and possibly Volvo's subsidiary establishments, whereas Sandvik's and Atlas Copco's are correlated with the market size. It seems reasonable to draw the conclusion that the firms have followed different internationalization strategies with respect to the two variables.

Table 5.6 Rank correlation (Spearman) between subsidiary establishments and psychic distance and respective market size

	Sandvik	Atlas Copco	Facit	Volvo
Psychic distance	0.16 (0.227)	0.33 (0.072)	0.60 (0.004)	0.47 (0.021)
Size	0.66 (0.002)	0.48 (0.018)	0.21 (0.179)	0.06 (0.386)

To a certain extent the establishing behaviour is similar within two groups, Sandvik and Atlas Copco in one and Facit and Volvo in the other. A possible explanation of the difference between the two groups is that the members of the first group had started their internationalization process already at the end of the nineteenth century, while the two other firms did not start establishing until the late 1920s and the effects of the two factors may very well have changed during this long time period.

Another possible explanation of the difference between the two groups is that Sandvik and Atlas Copco manufacture and market more unique products than Facit and Volvo. The latter firms, according to that explanation, have had to avoid the domestic competitive situation in the big industrial countries, whereas the former have found gaps in those markets.

We may conclude that in order to be able to understand the patterns of different firms we have to develop some conditional model of internationalization. At the present stage we cannot formulate any such model, but we consider this a primary objective of our future research.

It should also be noted that the manufacturing establishments of Sandvik and Atlas Copco – the others have set up so few of such establishments – are not at all correlated with the two factors (−0.01 and 0.06 for Sandvik and 0.16 and −0.11 for Atlas Copco).

The establishment chain – no regular export, independent representative (an agent), sales subsidiary, manufacturing – seems to be a correct description of the order of the development of operations of the firms in individual countries. This is illustrated in Table 5.7. Of sixty-three sales subsidiaries, fifty-six were preceded by agents and this pattern is the same for all the firms. With regard to the manufacturing establishments there

Table 5.7 Establishment patterns for the investigated firms

Firm	Sales subsidiary		Production subsidiary		
	n ↓ s	a ↓ s	n ↓ p	a ↓ p	s ↓ p
Sandvik	2	18	0	2	13
Atlas Copco	3	14	0	3	9
Facit	0	14	0	2	3
Volvo	2	10	0	2	3
Total	7	56	0	9	28

n no regular export activity
a export via an agent
s sales subsidiary
p production subsidiary
An arrow denotes change from one state to another.

is a difference between Sandvik and Atlas Copco on one hand, where twenty-two out of twenty-seven establishments were preceded by sales subsidiaries, and Facit and Volvo on the other, where five out of seven occurred without the firm having any sales subsidiary in the country. However, in no case has a firm started production in a country without having sold in the country via an agency or sales subsidiary before.

In all firms there have been periods of agency establishments, sales subsidiary establishments and, in the case of Sandvik and Atlas Copco, of manufacturing establishments. In two of the firms – Sandvik and Volvo – there has followed a period of international joint ventures for special purposes.

Considering the first establishment of sales subsidiaries it does not seem to have been a step in a conscious and goal directed strategy of internationalization – at least not in the case of Sandvik, Atlas Copco and Volvo. For various reasons they had to take over representatives or start subsidiaries. Gradually, when they had gained experience of setting up and managing subsidiaries they developed policies of marketing through subsidiaries in some of the firms. It should be noted that the firm Atlas Copco, which most consistently used subsidiaries for export marketing, did so when it appointed a new general manager, the former manager of a department store.

The manufacturing subsidiaries almost all manufacture for local or, in some cases, regional markets. They have finishing, assembly or component production which could be called marketing production. The only exception is Atlas Copco's factory in Belgium making stationary pneumatic equipment.

Generally the development of the firms seems to be in accordance with the incremental internationalization view discussed. In a few cases, notably Atlas Copco after the Second World War and Facit's agency establishments, the direction and velocity of internationalization has, however, been influenced heavily by strategic decisions.[18]

NOTES AND REFERENCES

1 This study has been financially supported by the Swedish Council for Social Science Research and the Svenska Handelsbanken Foundation for Social Science Research. Appreciation is expressed to our colleagues in the international business research programme for their valuable comments.
2 See Gruber, W., Mehta, R. and Vernon, R., 'The R and D Factor in International Trade and International Investment of the United States', *Journal of Political Economy*, Vol. 75, No. 1, February 1967, pp. 20–37; Caves, R. E., 'International Corporations: The Industrial Economics of Foreign Investment', *Economica*, Vol. 38, No. 149, 1971, pp. 1–27, in discussions of foreign direct investments; also Terpstra, V., *International Marketing*, New York: McGraw-Hill, 1972.
3 Since its crisis in 1971, Facit is not quoted as an example any longer.
4 These two aspects of the international process are discussed in Kindleberger, C. P., *American Business Abroad*, Boston: Yale University Press, 1969.
5 Cf. Vernon, R., 'International Investment and International Trade in the Product Cycle', *Quarterly Journal of Economics*, Vol. 80, pp. 190–207, 1966; May and Burenstam-Linder, S., *An Essay on Trade and Transformation*, Stockholm: Almqvist & Wicksell, 1961. Market and country are used interchangeably in this paper.
6 This question is investigated in a research project by F. Wiedersheim-Paul entitled 'Export Propensity of the Firm'.
7 A more detailed discussion of the internationalization process is given in Johanson, J. and Vahlne, J. E., 'The Internationalization Process of the Firm', *Mimeographed Working Paper*, Department of Business Administration, Uppsala, 1974.
8 Similar discussions of a stepwise extension of activities in individual countries can be found in, for example, Gruber, W., Mehta, R., Vernon, R., op. cit., and Caves, R. E., op. cit.
9 'Psychic distance' has been used by, for example Beckermann, W., 'Distance and the Pattern of IntraEuropean Trade', *Review of Economics and Statistics*, Vol. 28, 1956; Linnemann, H., *An Econometric Study of International Trade Flows*, Amsterdam: North-Holland, 1966; Wiedersheim-Paul, F., *Uncertainty and Economic Distance – Studies in International Business*, Uppsala: Almqvist and Wicksell, 1972. Here we use the concept with the same meaning as Widersheim-Paul, op. cit., 1972.
10 Of course, changes due to political decisions can be very fast (e.g. USA–Cuba).
11 Root, F. R., *Strategic Planning for Export Marketing*, Copenhagen: Elhar Hareks Forlag, 1964, p. 11.
12 See information from 'A File of Swedish Subsidiaries Abroad', Centre for International Business Studies, Department of Business Administration, University of Uppsala.
13 Chandler, A. D., *Strategy and Structure*, Cambridge, Mass.: MIT Press, 1962.
14 Håkansson, H. and Wootz, B., 'Internationalization of the Purchasing Function of the Firm', *Mimeographed Working Paper*, Department of Business Administration, Uppsala, 1974.

15 Carlson, S., *Ett Halvsekels* Affärer, in *Ett Svenskt Jernverk* (*A Swedish Steel Mill*), Sandviken, 1937; Gärlund, T., Janelid, I. and Ramström, D., *Atlas Copco, 1873–1973*, Stockholm: 1973; *Mimeographed Research Papers* by students at the Department of Business Administration, Uppsala.
16 The ranking, with minor modifications, is taken from Hörnell, E., Vahlne, J.-E. and Widersheim-Paul, F., *Export och Utlands Etableringar (Export and Foreign Establishment*), Stockholm, 1973.
17 The discussion below relates exclusively to the automobile manufacturing part of the company.
18 Three of the firms, after a period of international operation, changed their names to adapt to the international market. The only exception is Volvo.

Chapter 6

Business environment assessment

Daniel A. Sharp

INTRODUCTION

This article analyzes the various ways in which US multinational corporations structure their assessments of the external business environment.

By external business environment, I mean primarily government policies and practices plus the economy, but also other external influences, such as labor unions, consumer groups, the media, and public opinion. Increasingly, government policies include international and regional government organizations such as the European Economic Community and the UN. I exclude from this article those aspects of the business environment which cover competitive activity, customer needs, and technological developments (i.e. those more normal aspects of the business environment which have been covered traditionally).

Many of my colleagues use the term political risk instead of business environment, even when they really mean the total environment for their business activities. Political risk analysis is really the province of government (more particularly the State Department and CIA), while we in business must carefully monitor government policies concerning business in general, and our industry and company in particular – and must be clearly understood by our host governments to be doing nothing more. I believe that our primary concern is not political, since many significant political changes have far less importance for foreign investors than do less dramatic economic or even administrative policy changes. Consider whether a political change of government is always more crucial for a corporation than the freezing of exchange and repatriation auithority or the selection of one nationalized company as the exclusive supplier of equipment to the government.

The other problem with the term political risk is the word risk, which implies that environmental issues all tend to be constraints. This can lead to an essentially negative management attitude toward environmental assessment. The real business of environmental analysis is to identify issues and trends, recognize both potential constraints and opportunities, and find ways to convert the constraints into opportunities. After all, in many situations, 'one person's risk is another's opportunity'.

HOW AND WHY CORPORATIONS ORGANIZE DIFFERENTLY TO ASSESS THEIR BUSINESS ENVIRONMENT

In my experience, there are five different models of organization that corporations have adopted for dealing with external government policies.

Model R: Reactive without formal structure

The most common approach is to have no formal structure at all. This model can be easily understood both historically and functionally. Historically, for most corporations, the host government was seldom very important when they started their operations in a given country. As companies grew in size, many became significant economic forces in the local economy at the same time that host governments grew increasingly concerned with unemployment and balance of trade and payments pressures. Some companies moved into product areas of increasing government interest at the same time that government industrial strategies were giving increased importance and support to strategic local enterprises, much to the detriment of foreign investors.

As the importance of government to business increased gradually in most cases, there was often a time lag at corporate headquarters in recognizing the significance of external pressures, particularly those concerning medium- and long-term planning.

There are also significant functional reasons that further delayed recognition of the need to make a serious effort to track and incorporate into planning the newly important external pressures. The education and experience of most US executives in traditional management functions predisposes them against each of the major characteristics of the external business environment. For example, while traditional management activities (such as finance, personnel, manufacturing) are relatively controllable, tangible and short-term, the external environment involves factors that are more uncontrollable, intangible and longer term. (Many are also uncomfortably short term.) Besides, the importance of the internal traditional factors is well known to US managers, while the importance of the external forces is less clear. US management is therefore less experienced and consequently less comfortable in dealing with external environmental issues. And as a further complication, even to the extent that they may know the US government, few US executives know how foreign governments work.

For these reasons, among others, management has been slow to structure a formal process. The majority of corporations, which have no structure and little systematic analysis of their external environment, tend to be more reactive than anticipatory, so I call their approach Model R, for Reactive.

Those corporations that have some structure can be divided into four additional categories that I label as follows, for reasons that will become apparent.

Model K: Consisting primarily of an international advisory board

For a while, a popular approach was to set up advisory boards of prominent former government officials and outside experts from various major countries. The board would meet one or twice a year with top management to discuss political and economic developments. Seldom was the process institutionalized, so almost nothing entered directly into corporate planning or decision making. Ex-ministers could not advise on new government thinking, nor about the nuts and bolts kinds of decisions of immediate impact on the overseas subsidiaries – policies such as remittance controls, licensing practices, or emerging trends in legislative or administrative control over foreign investors. Top management received the benefit of very highly priced advice on macro-economic and macro-political trends – and could drop big names with their friends and colleagues – but little specific, relevant information found its way into the mainstream of the organization.

Because Henry Kissinger was among the most sought after members for such boards, I have called this approach Model K.

Model S: Centralized responsibility, with some decentralized consultation

Most companies that have some kind of organized approach use a small corporate staff of specialists in economic and political affairs, who are often academics or have government experience in the State Department or CIA. These are usually Americans, with little or no business experience. Model S has the advantage of devoting careful attention to external relations by analysts who are often very talented. However, this approach reveals the suspicion that some corporations tend to harbor toward the foreign citizens whom they have hired for overseas management positions. Analysis takes place primarily at headquarters, not in the field, and it is usually not based on systematic formal reporting from overseas subsidiaries or, in any event, places greater reliance on the judgments of the headquarters staff than of the field management.

Because it depends on the staff as helpers to the corporate management at the top, and assumes that contacts at the highest level are the best, I have called this Model S, for Summit.

Model B: Decentralized responsibility, but centralized management

I call it Model B, for 'Bottom-up'. As this is the general approach I recommend, and as Xerox fits within this model, I will describe it in much greater detail after listing the final model.

Model C: Containing some combination of Models S, B, and/or K

MODEL B APPROACH TO MANAGING BUSINESS ENVIRONMENT ASSESSMENT

I would now like to describe in detail the model which I favor, Model B. It is based on an actual operation in a major US multinational corporation, which I will call Corporation B. Its main instrument is called the Issues Monitoring System (IMS). (Issues Monitoring is a more limited approach than a full Issues Management System, towards which it should be evolving in the near future.)

Corporation B believes that relations with its host government determine not only its level of profit or loss, but also its ability to continue doing business as a guest in another country. For this reason government relations has been institutionalized as a distinct and valued professional function like marketing, finance, personnel, or manufacturing. In some overseas operating companies, government relations is among the most important aspects on which general managers are evaluated.

Corporation B's approach to the assessment of their business environment is based on three major principles:

1 Rely primarily on local management (and partner, where one exists).
2 Institutionalize their participation through ongoing line management systems. This provides: (a) motivation (by demonstrating trust and reliance); (b) links directly to planning and decision-making through existing management systems; (c) early warning and continuous updates; (d) focusing of local management attention.
3 Headquarter's role is coordination, support and verification. This provides for: (a) professionalization and cross fertilization; (b) regional perspectives; (c) objective perspectives for management; (d) worldwide trends; (e) validation by outside consultants and experts.

Sources

Corporation B relies first on its local country management. Each managing director, usually working closely with his staff, prepares a one-page list of up to ten topics, in priority order, based on their importance to the corporation and urgency for attention. For those issues at the top of his list, he provides a one-page analysis that describes the issue, its impact on the company, and his presently planned or recommended actions.

Country reports are sent directly to the regional government relations officer. These reports are then consolidated at regional headquarters. Each regional report takes the same simple form, but presents the issues in terms of their regional priority, implications, and action plans. This report may include regional issues not identified by the individual countries, including regional trends.

The six regional reports are then sent to the Director of International Relations at corporate headquarters, along with the individual country reports. From these reports he prepares a global consolidation, which also incorporates information obtained from headquarters staff reporting in the same manner and from many outside sources, including consultants, reading materials, and personal involvement in international business organizations.

When so many other companies are relying on professional risk analysis in corporate headquarters, why is Corporation B's first principle to rely primarily on its local management and partner? First of all, because they are there. I am not facetiously adapting a quotation from the first team to climb Mount Everest. Rather, I am referring to the fact that economic and political events in each country are changing so rapidly and in such complex ways that someone who is not living there would be severely handicapped in providing accurate analysis, timely warnings or forecasts. Of course, the company is fortunate that its local management and partners are broadly educated in the economic, social and political factors in their own societies, and are generally well connected with their colleagues in business, government, and universities, often as a result of school and social friendships.

In the past, local management's views on their external business environment were often solicited, but not in a structured way that demonstrated reliance on their input, nor did it show trust. By establishing regular links with the planning process, and by negotiating specific objectives for government relations (just as for marketing, service, or manufacturing), with a percentage of annual salary increase based on performance against those objectives, appropriate attention is encouraged by reinforcing their message of reliance and importance. The information base for planning and decisions is also improved by providing an earlier, continuous, and more accurate picture of the external business environment.

Some have criticized reliance on host country personnel on the grounds of national bias, lack of corporate perspective, or lack of appropriate training. Frankly, this has not been a real problem for Corporation B. However, to reassure management, and themselves, they follow their third principle of headquarters coordination, support and verification. Of course such coordination is necessary in any event to prepare regional summaries and recommendations to management, to provide a useful cross-fertilizing exchange of ideas among countries and regions, to help spot emerging trends before they reach other countries, and to encourage discipline and professionalism.

This process, and its requirement to be aware of major developments in all major parts of the world, places a considerable responsibility on headquarters. It means active personal involvement in major organizations such as the Council of the Americas, the Japan Society, the National Foreign Trade Council, the US Council for International Business, the Council on Foreign Relations, and chambers of commerce, among others. It also means a great deal of reading of newsletters, magazines, specific issues papers from specialized consultants, and books on major countries and issues such as industrial strategy, protectionism, transborder data flows and other technology developments of importance to business. It requires maintaining an extensive network of personal contacts around the world for additional exchanges of information, insights, and judgments.

In addition to the above activities, the IMS approach places a heavy demand for coordination and support on headquarters to make it work. There is a constant flow of paper and phone calls, following up on missing reports, asking for clarification or additional information, updates on fast-moving issues on which the corporation is about to make decisions, and the essential maintenance of an internal corporate network. This includes helping in the selection, training and support of colleagues in the regions and in the major individual countries. It also involves a very substantial amount of effort to assure the product is well and appropriately used.

USE OF THE IMS SYSTEM

Although the system was originally created for use primarily by the Government Relations functions, it has become increasingly important to the other departments. I will treat their use of the IMS in the order listed below, which corresponds roughly to the order of their most important usage.

1 The Corporate Strategy Office (CSO).
2 The Chief Executive Officer (CEO) and his direct reports.
3 Operations.
4 Strategic Business Units.
5 Finance and Treasury.
6 Personnel and Training.
7 Government Relations and Corporate Affairs.

The Corporate Strategy Office (CSO)

When the IMS process began, there was no corporate strategy office. In fact, the corporate officer responsible for strategy expressed a preference for having the Director of International Relations work more with the operating companies in each country than with him.

However, when corporate headquarters was reorganized, the major staff office created was a new Corporate Strategy Office. It has become a major user of IMS in several ways. Most important was its use in the development of a ten-year 'strategic reconnaissance,' called 'Corporation B '92'. in which the portions concerning government policies were produced by the IMS process. The messages to the field requesting their input were signed jointly by the Senior Vice President of CSO and by the Director of International Relations.

A second new use was the preparation of the Critical Planning Assumptions (CPAs) for their worldwide Strategic Business Units (SBUs) to use in their annual planning cycle. When the Director of International Relations was asked by the corporate officer to whom the SBUs report to prepare his CPAs, he asked the head of the CSO to prepare them jointly with him, in order to assure a fully integrated political economic, and social perspective. The third use is on a routine basis, twice-a-year, in which the CSO and International Relations functions review the regular IMS reports together, identifying those issues of relevance to planning. They are considering that, as a follow-on to the 'Corporation B '92' project, they may interject into the standard IMS checklist some additional questions for CSO use.

The Chief Executive Officer (CEO) and his direct reports

The results of the IMS process are presented to the senior management committee chaired by the CEO, called the Corporate Management Committee (CMC), and consisting of the top few officers of the corporation. When this was first done last year, the International Relations Director made a series of recommendations concerning how the corporation should alter its approaches and responses to host governments, all of which were approved. One of the major recommendations was turned over to the CSO by the CMC for implementation as part of its normal planning process.

Operations

Operations in Corporation B refers to the management of the marketing affiliates and units which operate in about 100 countries throughout the world. From the beginning, IMS reports were taken to the head of operations for his information and advice. The present Senior Vice-President of Operations, for whom the system was originally developed five years ago when he headed only the Latin American region, has continued his strong support. In fact, now that his responsibilities have grown to cover the whole world, his needs for this kind of information have grown commensurately; he has sent messages supporting the IMS process to the field groups, which has helped immeasurably in continuing to improve the quality and timeliness of Corporation B's inputs.

Strategic Business Units

As mentioned above, these SBUs, created during the recent reorganization, now use the IMS system to create their critical planning assumptions. In addition, following the completion of each worldwide report, the Director of International Relations visits them to review in detail those issues of direct relevance.

Finance and Treasury

As with most headquarters staff functions, the International Relations Director meets with the Senior Finance Officer every six months to present the results of the latest IMS, highlighting those issues of greatest relevance to their areas of responsibility. On his last visit, the Treasurer requested an expansion of the IMS checklist and reporting to include an evaluation of 'political risk', by which he meant the risk to the company's assets in each country and the necessity of considering risk insurance or other options to minimize risk. Discussion continues concerning how to provide that service within the limits of staff, budget, and the capacity of the present IMS system.

Personnel and Training

Among the gratifying uses of IMS reports is their recent inclusion in the opening day of the new course that will be required for the top few hundred executives of the corporation. The reports are also being integrated into all other executive training courses.

In addition, IMS materials are being included in the training of salespeople, in the realization that an understanding of their host country's objectives and policies concerning business and our industry, and of how Corporation B is contributing towards those objectives, is an essential part of their preparation for selling of products in each country. For Corporation B, at least, many of their sales personnel must first be able to 'sell the company' before they will obtain a hearing to sell the product.

Government Relations and Corporate Affairs

The original purpose was to develop IMS as a management tool for government affairs personnel around the world. It continues to be actively used in that way. A major value of IMS continues to be that it prompts local management, with the cooperation of the local government affairs staff, to focus at least twice a year on the major external pressures on the company. It also creates a checklist for conversations with the managing director by his immediate supervisor, as well as the regional government relations staff, and for use by other corporate staff for their occasional visits.

During its first few years, meetings were held by the major government relations staff directors from around the world. This group, called the Corporate Affairs International Advisory Board (CAIAB), would meet twice a year, just after each IMS cycle, to review the major issues raised, compare one region's issues with the rest, and try to identify worldwide trends of importance to the company. Corporation B is now considering a reconstituted CAIAB, which would include non-government relations line and staff, to move more towards action planning than analysis, and more towards issues management than issues monitoring.

EXAMPLES OF PRIORITY ISSUES SURFACED BY IMS, AND THEIR PLANNING AND MANAGEMENT TREATMENT

As examples I would like to discuss several different kinds of issues raised by IMS reports: Protectionism and a European Strategy, Transborder Data Flows, and Industrial Strategy.

Protectionism and a European Strategy

From the first reports several years ago protectionism was identified as among the most serious global issues for the corporation. In response to IMS recommendations, it was soon acknowledged by management that they really did not have a strategy to respond to the increasing trend of protectionism. Colleagues in the European headquarters set up an action plan to produce an approach towards a European strategy in coordination with the management of the major operating companies. Their thoughtful document was presented to senior corporate management, discussed in person in Europe by the Corporate President and by senior staff officers, and, as a direct result, a new and different approach was undertaken towards joint ventures, valued added, and how to negotiate with host governments.

As a result of the increasing importance of the issue, as identified in subsequent IMS report, an ongoing task force has now been created in European Headquarters to maintain senior management focus.

The coordination of this issue through corporate headquarters highlighted the fact that the company has different interests and experiences in various countries. In some countries, a company may benefit from protection by meeting host country objectives for local activities. In most, it does not benefit. Corporation B is carefully developing a corporate position to maximize corporate short- and long-term interest with respect to protectionism.

Transborder Data Flows (TBDF)

A very different kind of issue than protectionism, TBDF required a different kind of structural approach. Transborder Data Flows are important to all MNCs, but especially to Corporation B, which is in the information industry. Since this was a new and technically complex issue when first raised about four years ago, the first problem was to increase awareness, and the second was to establish some formal structure to maintain awareness, develop corporate positions for participation in government advisory bodies, trade associations, etc., and to provide input to the planning process.

To accomplish those objectives, International Relations first made a series of presentations around the company to explain the issue and then developed a briefer presentation for a smaller, higher level group, and to recommend the designation of an issue control officer. After two years of such efforts, a senior manager with appropriate technical background, interests, and present responsibility, was named. He maintains an active network of contacts throughout the company, overseas and in HQ staff, both to receive and to send up-to-date policy information. He represents the corporation in a full range of private sector and government committees dealing with the issue which have had a useful impact on policy. He also prepares the IMS update each cycle.

Industrial Strategy

A third kind of issue, Industrial Strategy, is a newly emerging topic of vital importance to any US corporation in an industry chosen as a high national priority by major foreign governments, in part because the USA does not have a developed industrial strategy, and in part because many countries do have industrial policies upon which considerable importance is placed. Corporation B is in a high-technology industry usually targeted by such policies. IMS' role was, first, to alert the corporation to the trend of industrial policies around the world and to describe the seriousness of the direct impact on it. Second, the International Relations function is thinking through with corporate management how they can participate in the US dialogue and in the efforts of various trade associations to develop recommendations to the US government.

Because this is a key strategic planning issue for the corporation, International Relations works very closely with the CSO on its implications for the future.

HOW THE IMS PROCESS IS MANAGED

One of the most effective ways to manage the process is to institutionalize it. By this I mean to find all of the existing mechanisms within the present organization and value systems and to move this function directly into them. Corporation B developed a management structure that included Management By Objectives (MBO), annual performance appraisals, and quarterly management review meetings in some of the international regions. They therefore built IMS directly into those existing processes. When the program started in the Latin American region, they worked with the regional VPs and the managing directors for each of the major countries on developing explicit objectives concerning the management of the IMS process and also specific government relations objectives that were linked directly to the overall business targets (e.g. pricing, import licensing, and the establishment of an effective network of communications with government). These MBO targets became a factor for annual performance reviews and for the awarding of annual merit increases and bonuses. They built into each of the regional meetings of the managing directors a reporting requirement for each managing director to summarize his IMS issues in front of his colleagues and headquarters personnel. This procedure was both reinforcing and motivating, and also facilitated the achievement of another objective (i.e. the exchange of information about emerging trends so as to identify regional implications). Finally, IMS was the direct link into planning through headquarters functions. Corporation B also established a procedure in which the IMS system generated planning assumptions; the operating plans began by commenting on the priority IMS issues as a foundation of planning assumptions.

You will find in your own organization the management procedures and culture that will allow you most effectively to institutionalize the process.

USE OF CONSULTANTS

Specific uses of consultants and other outside experts will obviously vary from company to company depending on internal circumstances. Consultants are particularly useful:

- to complement in-house strengths and fill gaps where the local capability is lacking or missing (particularly in small or new subsidiaries);
- to provide validation of information inputs, bringing an independent, external perspective, which can be shared and discussed with local management;
- to assist with analyses of international issues, which transcend countries and regions and are, therefore, the rightful responsibility of the international headquarters (this includes serving as an 'early warning system' for local and regional management);

- to assist in analyzing IMS reports in order to develop overall corporate summary for top management and for feedback to the field;
- to assist with the development of the IMS process itself.

Another important role is for a consultant with sufficient expertise and experience in multinational company organization and related international issue management systems to provide creative support in the continuous improvement and development of the process. There are very few who have been in the business long enough and who have worked with a sufficient range of companies to go beyond general platitudes in what, in my estimation, is one of the more complex areas of management. The international system is not a simple extension of a domestic system; the number of variables is greater and the organizational dimension more complicated.

Finally, in addition to regular consultants, from time to time I find it useful to bring in one or more recognized experts on an issue or country for a discussion with top management. Such experts may not always offer anything very new or different, beyond the IMS analysis, but they can provide important validation and their reputation can often get the message across more easily to top management. Such experts can be an expensive waste of time and undermine one's credibility, unless they are carefully briefed in advance to ensure that their inputs are relevant to top management concerns.

EVALUATION – STRENGTHS AND WEAKNESSES

I will try to give an objective and balanced evaluation of the strengths and weaknesses of the Issues Monitoring System by commenting on a number of factors.

Reliability

Although the decentralized approach can occasionally be criticized for 'national bias', it generally tends to increase the level of trust between headquarters and the field. If appropriately institutionalized with reinforcing mechanisms, it actually will yield greater reliability than other systems. The requirement of a formal written IMS analysis tends to decrease local bias. This IMS approach may take longer to implement, but its results are better.

Cost

IMS is probably the cheapest approach because it works through existing management structures and requires the fewest specialized professionals.

(For headquarters validation, it is desirable to maintain a very active network of outside contacts with some specialized consultants.)

Management structure

The more decentralized the process, the more there is a requirement for very strong staff coordination, both to install and to maintain the system effectively. This requires a particularly persistent, yet sensitive management, and a system that is built on the existing management structure and communications channels and values (what is now called management 'culture'). It will require much more management follow-up than the other more centralized systems. Probably its single most important strength is that it integrates external business environment assessment into the mainstream of decision-making and planning.

Continuity and quality of coverage

IMS depends on local people, some of whom, obviously, may be untrained, inexperienced, lacking in interest concerning political economic and social analysis and/or likely to be distracted by other or higher priorities, or at least by those functions for which they have been trained. On the other hand, the system relies on people who are living in the country, most of whom have extensive and excellent contacts throughout the business, academic and government communities, are rather well educated concerning their own environment and are involved on a day-to-day basis with these issues. They are also the ones most likely to understand the impact of our corporation of developments that others may not perceive so clearly. For companies that have more expatriate managers, or high turnover, IMS might not be so effective.

Workload

There is a small additional workload imposed on local management, which is always over-burdened. In that sense, it may be seen as 'another report'. On the other hand, the external business environment is increasingly becoming one of the most important elements in any general manager's responsibility; IMS, more than other systems, makes the monitoring and action planning in response to outside pressures an intrinsic element of general management.

Sensitivity to and in the host country

There is always the risk of misinterpreting the 'reporting role' of local management by host country government officials or citizens. They have not yet run into that problem, but one should be aware of the possibility.

Sensitivity within the country

A very real anticipated risk on the part of local management was the fact that, by reporting more thoroughly their local external pressures, head-quarters would be encouraged to meddle in sensitive local affairs. I do not believe they have found this to be the case, although there has been some reticence to report fully – mostly at regional headquarters, rather than on the country level.

Validation

Senior management was mildly apprehensive that, because of relying essentially on untrained observers of the external environment, they might be misinformed. For this reason, the IMS has relied also on outside networks of colleagues and consultants and on direct personal involve-ment in a number of international organizations.

Usefulness and simplicity

There is a legitimate concern that local management may not look sufficiently far ahead for planning purposes to anticipate the important medium- and longer-term trends, nor would they report in sufficient detail. On the other hand, there is no more effective way of identifying the company-specific issues. The IMS, appropriately reinforced from head-quarters, certainly heightens the ongoing attention of management. Over time they are developing increased sensitivity to the medium- and long-term implications of current developments. The system certainly helps line management to keep track of the vital but less time urgent issues. It also provides essential staff support to the Operations Vice-President to whom each country manager reports. It has the great advantage of simplicity, being among the briefest reports required of any management personnel. It gets management's attention at least twice a year – at times selected to immediately precede their annual planning cycles.

Impact on thought process

By forcing the primary responsibility down to the country management, there is an increased tendency to start business strategy by analyzing, first, the host country environment and its government policy objectives, and only then to plan the company objectives, fitting them into that context. This is preferable to doing a corporate business plan and then adjusting for country environment. As one senior executive overseas said to me, 'Through IMS, we start by understanding the reality, rather than, later on, fighting against it. This reduces friction and misunderstanding, and leads to better business plans.'

CONTRIBUTION TO MANAGEMENT PROCESS

Corporation B is quite pleased with the contribution the IMS process has already made, both to corporate decision-making and to the planning process. However, it is certainly hard to evaluate the effectiveness of an early warning system. A crisis averted never happened. How do you know what might have happened if it were not for the issues identified and dealt with?

Important improvements can be observed in the quality and frequency of attention to environmental issues, both at the country and headquarters management level. One can see the creation in some major countries of a separate department of government external relations reporting directly to the managing director. Generally the people who have been chosen to direct the function come from among the more experienced company business people, rather than from government and academia. This works very well.

Senior management is increasingly paying attention to IMS and placing demands on it for dealing with specific problems. On balance, they have found, after several years of experience, that it pays to trust local employees with the primary responsibility for assessing their external environment, especially if that process is institutionalized in a system that rewards the effective management of the process.

COMPARISON OF THE PRINCIPLE ALTERNATIVES

I would now like to summarize and contrast the various models discussed:

Principles (and myths?) of Model S

The principles can be summarized as:

1 Build international business environment assessment expertise at corporate headquarters.
2 Provide full scenarios for senior management.
3 Provide interpretations to senior management which differ from the field's, since the host country management view is often biased.
4 Provide specific forecasts of key events, especially political risks of change of government.
5 Help management to understand that the international business climate is deteriorating, and that they should adjust their profit targets downward.

Among the myths of Model S are the following:

1 Headquarters knows best. The corollary is: You can't trust the locals to see the corporate interest.

2 Give management the full picture.
3 Forecast specific political risks of events. (This results in a definition of competence in our field as the ability to forecast what is going to happen, and then, afterwards, being able to explain why it did not happen.)
4 The Corporate president or CEO should have direct contact with the most senior host country officials possible – ideally, the president of the country.
5 The future is ominous and full of threats to the business. Planning targets should be reduced accordingly.

Principles (and myths?) of Model B (Bottom-up)

By contrast, the following are the principles (or myths?) of Model B:

1 The field knows best (about the local business environment). This is because they are there. Therefore, expertise on the external business environment should be primarily at the country level. (If management cannot trust them to protect their company's interests concerning local government policies, then it should find management that it can trust.)
2 Give management the priority issues only, not the full scenario. Regional and global management cannot deal with the information overload that results from excessive data. Answer only the following three questions for management concerning only the top priority issues, and briefly at that:

   1 What is the issue? (usually irrespective of the company implications).
   2 How does the issue hurt, or help, the company?
   3 What can the company do about it, or what is it now doing about it?

3 Build contacts at the senior civil servant level, not only at the top political levels. The senior civil servants are more likely to be in place over time, and they are often the ones who really develop and implement most of the policies and regulations of greatest importance to most companies.
4 Identify trends and key issues of importance to your company, rather than forecasting specific events or political risk. This will offer management a continuous moving picture out to the future, rather than merely a snapshot.
5 The future is full of threats that can be converted into opportunities. Our job is to develop a strategy and exploit any possible competitive advantage, since most external problems will have similar impacts on most competitors, other than the local 'national champion'. In fact, one can become, or at least become a partner with, the local firm.
6 Hold local management responsible for the accuracy and timeliness of the identification of the major issues – not specific events – that are important to your company.

7 Use outside consultants and organizations to increase your own perception and for validation of what comes to you from within the company.

8 The primary role of the headquarters manager of the business environment assessment is to manage the process rather than to be the resident expert. He must be sufficiently aware of the major global trends concerning the issues of importance to the corporation, to reconcile diverse views coming from different parts of the world and interpret those views effectively to his management.

Principles (and myths?) of Model K

1 Famous former high-level government officials know best.
2 Management wants the macro picture.
3 The environment trends of most importance to management are those at the highest level.
4 The top management of the company should be in touch only with the highest level of government.
5 A global business strategy can be built on this kind of global trend analysis.

Principles of Model C

1 Take one from column S and one from column B, in other words, it is better to adapt from the various models to the particular requirements of each company.
2 Give management either the macro or the micro picture that is most relevant for their needs.
3 Local option – that is, identify trends of importance to the company and/or forecast those specific events, political or otherwise, which may be of particular relevance.
4 Decide at which level it is best for your various company levels to make their contacts (i.e. take your pick).
5 The future is uncertain and offers both risks and opportunities to your company as well as to its competitors.

Obviously, the only universal model is Model C, to be adapted to the particular management culture, and the circumstances of its international operations.

CONCLUSION

In this article I have attempted to present descriptions and comparisons of the principal approaches being used by corporations to assess their external business environment. I have described in some detail one approach, the Issues Monitoring System (IMS), which has been successfully developed and implemented in a large, multinational manufacturing firm. Up to now IMS has been primarily a monitoring system, although several of the highest priority issues identified by the system have already been moved into the action/management mode. The next step is to extend IMS to include company-wide procedures for issues management.

My message has been that each organization must draw from alternative models those components that most effectively build on their own organizations' internal management structure, communications channels, and value systems. It must also respond to the nature of the company in each country, and must attempt, to the extent possible, to institutionalize the process so that it becomes an ongoing priority concern of general management.

ANNEX I

Table 6.1 Model S and Model B compared

	Model S 'Summit' centralized conventional wisdom	Model B 'Bottom-up' decentralized unconventional wisdom
Corporate Expertise	*HQ*	*Field*
Output	Detailed scenarios • forecast events • especially political risks • snapshots	Brief MIS 1 Identify priority issues and trends 2 Identify impact on company 3 Identify alternative actions
Primary contact level	Summit Our CEO/president with host country president/cabinet	Local management with senior civil servants

Attitude	Change is bad for the company
	• Lobby for change in government policy
	• Help company adjust its plans and targets downward
		Change = opportunity as
		  risk
		Look for competitive advantage
		Seek occasional participation in
		  policy process

Primary purpose	External communication
	  Present best picture of the Corporation to host government
		Internal adaptation
		  Assure Corporation is adapting
		  • to changing external
		    environment
		  • to its maximum advantage
		Therefore early warning, time to adapt

Primary role	Advise management (internal)
	Handle top-level government relations (external)
		Manage process and insure
		  effective advice from the field
		Provide management with results
		  of field
		Work with some outside
		  validation
		Coordinate external
		  communications

Primary audience	Host government
	senior officials
	  (president, cabinet)
		Our own management
		Senior career civil servants and
		  legislative committees

Methodology	Academic analysis • Full picture • Dramatize	Institutionalize (same as any other important management functions) • MBO targets • Annual bonus • Management meetings • Planning process links

ANNEX II

IMS priority worldwide issues (spring 1982)

1 Foreign government policies designed to preserve jobs and control national economy.

- Restructuring of specific industrial sectors

  - with specific emphasis on high technology (e.g. industrial strategy of Japan, France, etc.)

- Accelerating protectionism

  - (blocks foreign products)

- Economic nationalism

  - puts performance requirements on foreign investors (e.g. value added, equity, joint ventures; export; balance of trade/balance of payments)

- Free trade zones, regionalization

2 Increasing government controls on information policy.

- Government monopoly control of telecommunications (PTTs)

  - and marketplace for office automation equipment

- Transborder data flow controls (TBDF)

  - increasing controls of data transmission, with contradictory rules in different countries

3 Increasing government controls on all multinationals.

- re: employee participation, consultation
- re: corporate governance

4 Other threats/opportunities.

- International economic crisis
- Mexico border protection
- Arab boycott

ANNEX III

Checklist and guidelines for completing Fall 1982 IMS and Corporation B 92 Report (sent to six regional headquarters around the world)

Purposes

1 Provide essential background data and analyses of issues and trends for strategy analysis in the CSO, which should also be useful for operating company and group planning.
2 Provide issue analyses for regular IMS reports.

Corporation B 92 defined

Corporation B 92 is the ten-year strategy analysis being conducted by the new Corporate Strategy Office (CSO). They are undertaking a careful analysis of the prospective external environment as the necessary prelude to consideration of corporate strategies for the next decade.

International Relations has been asked to provide the analysis of national and regional government policies and trends. Others have agreed to provide inputs on other aspects of the external environment, including technology, competition, economics and demographics.

Your report and your OPCO reports

Reports will be used here to identify major trends and forces likely to have an impact on Corporation B business in the next ten years.

Please prepare a relatively brief but comprehensive document (perhaps fifteen to twenty-five pages in total) which identifies and summarizes the likely short-term (one to two years), medium-term (five years), and long-term (ten years) trends of each of the topics in the outline below your region, and also on any other topic which in your judgment is likely to be of importance to Corporation B during the next ten years. Include a synthesis of the operating company submissions.

Operating company input is vital. It may be necessary to get back to operating company management several times, as an interactive process. Each individual country report should also be submitted as an attachment to your regional report. You will probably want to communicate the relevant portions of this attachment and cover memo to each of your operating companies immediately.

'Country' reports should be prepared for any relevant intergovern-mental group within your region (e.g. European Economic Community, Latin American Integration Association). Separate reports will be obtained by corporate covering major international organizations such as the UN, OECD, ILO, UNTC, UNCTC so you need not cover them.

In developing forecasts for the USA the CSO has to make certain assumptions about global political, economic and social trends to 1992. In the next week or so we will send you a brief summary of the most likely scenarios to which we are working. Since, obviously, it makes sense for all units to work within a consistent set of these global assumptions, we should like you to use this scenario or, if you disagree, to tell us where your assumptions differ and why.

Sign-off

Each country report should be approved and signed by the country managing director.

Topic list

A Economic and business policies.

1 Overall economic objectives and trends.
2 Industrial policy, with special emphasis on high-technology sectors including office automation, telecommunications (including government grants and other state aids).
3 Trade policy, including approach to GATT, Treaty of Rome, protectionism, etc., with special references to non-tariff barriers as well as tariffs as relevant.
4 Policy towards multinationals, including value added, equity, import/export, local content or other performance requirements, and approach to controls of multinationals in areas such as disclosure and prior consultation, pricing and transfer pricing, repatriation, technology transfer, local equity, corporate governance, price controls, etc.
5 Employment and related social policies, including union policies.
6 Monopoly policy, and policy concerning restrictive business practices.
7 Procurement policy.
8 Policy considerations affecting the nature, structure and size of the market as a whole (e.g. rate of growth in manufacturing vs. services, growth in education sector, policies towards small businesses).
9 Proportion of economy in public sector.

B Information policy

10 Information policy, including regulation of, and tariffs on, transborder data flows, etc.
11 PTT policies and structure, with special emphasis on impact on Corporation B market and Corporation B plans for maintaining effective contacts with relevant PTTs.

12 Information industry – government desires to build/sustain national information industry, R&D.

C Political and social trends

13 Political trends (e.g. nature, composition and stability of government) that could impact Corporation B by influencing other policies.
14 Social trends, including labor/work attitudes, demographic shifts, other relevant attitudinal changes such as attitudes to business/free enterprise, social changes (e.g. working from home, attitudes to new technologies).

D Foreign policy issues

15 Relations with other countries and regions and with relevant international organizations, migration policies, etc.

E Other

16 Please add any other topics not covered above which in your judgment may be relevant to consideration of strategies for Corporation B over the next ten years.

Treatment for each issue numbered on topic list

For each part of the numbered issues there should be a four-part treatment with each of the sub-parts sub-titled as follows, but limited only to those aspects of potential relevance to consideration of Corporation B strategies:

1 Policy. Identify the current direction of national policy and its likely trend over the short, medium and long term. (If this is subject to change because of changes in government, indicate the possible timing and direction of such changes.)
2 Impact. Describe the corporate implications of each policy analysis including, wherever possible, an order of magnitude quantification of the impact (e.g. 10 per cent drop in revenue, reduce share of market by 12 per cent = $X million).
3 Consistency. Describe the extent to which present and planned corporate activities are consistent or inconsistent with government policy and trends. Include specific data on our contribution towards national, regional policies and objectives, and how it is perceived in the country. (Given the time limitations, a conceptual approach may be all that can be done at this time.)

Comment on the extent to which our competition's behavior is consistent or inconsistent with policy trends, now and in the future.

4 Recommendations. To the extent feasible in the short time allowed, please give your recommendations for appropriate plans and action in relation to each issue or groups of issues and give any guidance that should be taken into consideration in examining alternative corporate strategies for the next ten years.

Executive summary

For each regional report submitted there should be an executive summary of the overall report, which also prioritizes the top five or ten issues over the short, medium and long term.

Chapter 7

International economic integration

Progress, prospects and implications

David Henderson

SETTING THE SCENE

Introduction

My concern here is with the changing world economic environment, and under this broad heading, with one aspect of change in particular, one process or phenomenon. This phenomenon goes under various names: internationalization, globalization, increasing international interdependence, and closer international economic integration. Whatever the exact terminology used, what is being referred to is a tendency for the economic significance of political boundaries to diminish.

It is generally agreed that in the world of today such a tendency is clearly apparent: internationalization is seen as a well established and pervasive trend. My task here is to comment on the extent to which this trend has gone, the likelihood that it will go further, the consequences that it has brought and may bring, and the issues of policy that it raises. These questions can be addressed from various perspectives, various orientations if you like. One involves viewing the process of internationalization in relation to business enterprises across the world. From this perspective, it is corporations that are in the limelight: while national states and their governments are also present among the cast, they do not have leading parts. I take the opposite focus. My topic is the integration of economic systems across political boundaries. From this standpoint, corporations are present on the stage, but they are not in the foreground. My concern is with states and governments, and with national economic systems, within the world economy as a whole.

This means that my main single theme is the evolution of government policies. In these matters governments count, and they will continue to count. International economic integration is sometimes presented as a kind of economic tidal wave, an inexorable tendency which is sweeping governments and peoples before it. This view has an element of truth in it, but not much. The world economy of today is far from being a single entity, and it is neither inevitable nor even probable that it will become so. How far and how fast international economic integration proceeds will largely depend in the future, as it has in the past, on what governments and peoples want to establish or are prepared to accept. This is not predetermined.

Before looking at the sequence of events and the evolution of policies, let me sketch out, in this first section, what I mean by economic integration and what the process involves.

The meaning of economic integration

I start with a brief word of definition. The term 'economic integration' is commonly used in two senses. First, it can refer to a process by which economies become more closely integrated, the tendency for the economic significance of political boundaries to diminish. Second, it can also mean the end result, the culmination, of such a process – that is, a situation in which integration is complete, so that political boundaries no longer possess economic significance. I shall use 'economic integration' by itself to refer to the process. The possible end result – to repeat, there is nothing inevitable about it – I shall call 'full international economic integration', or 'full integration' for short.

In this context, all political boundaries may possess or acquire significance, and different levels of government may be involved. Generally speaking, the governments that chiefly count are those of national sovereign states – i.e. of the countries that form the membership of the UN, the IMF, and the World Bank. But other public authorities may also have speaking parts, or even on occasion leading roles: these can be state or local governments within countries, or agencies such as the European Community in which a group of national states is acting in concert. Strictly speaking, it is cross-border rather than international economic integration which is my subject matter.

I define full integration, whether within or across national frontiers, as a state of affairs in which two closely interrelated conditions are satisfied.

Condition one: that there is free movement of products, capital and labour, thus establishing a single unified market for all goods and services, including the services of people.
Condition two: that there is complete non-discrimination with the result that economically speaking, there are no foreigners. In each country (or each region within a country) people or enterprises from outside the area are treated in their capacity as economic agents in precisely the same way as people or enterprises that are viewed as belonging to it.

You may wonder why I bother to spell out my own personal definition of full integration when shorter and better descriptions lie to hand. For example, Richard O'Brien (Amex Bank, London) has subtitled his recent study of financial market developments *The End of Geography*,[1] while Kenichi Ohmae (head of McKinsey, Japan) has written of *The Borderless World*.[2] These are excellent titles, and I would gladly have borrowed one or both of them. But alas, neither is suitable: what they point to is not what I have in mind. I am concerned only with the economic aspects of international integration, and the qualification is important. Even if full international economic integration as I define it were to become permanently established – which is in fact not at all probable – this would not mean the end of geography, nor would it imply a borderless world. Even if political boundaries lost entirely their economic significance, they could still remain important in other ways. I shall return to this theme at the end of my discussion.

Economic integration: two factors, three dimensions and three routes

Two main factors bear on the extent to which national or regional economies become more integrated over time. One is broadly technical, and the other political. Each of them may influence the other.

Under the first heading, the potential for integration increases as and when the costs associated with cross-border transactions fall in relation to the costs of transactions within regions or national states. In large part, though not wholly, this is a matter of transport and communications costs. Let me summarize this aspect in a single phrase, which I borrow from the Australian historian Geoffrey Blainey. In a remarkable book, Blainey has written an account of Australian economic history in terms of a single theme, encapsulated in the title of the book which is *The Tyranny of Distance*.[3] Following this line of thought, one can view the economic history of the world, over the five centuries since Columbus set sail for the Indies, as a process by which the tyranny of distance has been cumulatively eroded by a host of discoveries and innovations. As a result the potential for closer integration, and the incentives for people and businesses to tap this potential for private advantage, have greatly increased down the years. Indeed, one could say that the very notion of what full integration would mean in practice has broadened over time: new dimensions of economic integration have become feasible. Most of this has happened during the last two centuries, and a good deal of it over the past two decades. It is this cumulative process of discovery and innovation which has given meaning the to idea of an economically borderless world.

While technical factors determine what is possible, it is – let me repeat – governments that largely decide how far the potential for closer integration will actually be realized. It is true that in deciding they are not entirely free agents: they may be subject to pressures and constraints of various kinds, internal and external. But the fact remains that it is the actions and policies of governments that determine how far the principle of non-discrimination will apply, and therefore the extent to which particular national economies are an integral part of an open international economic system. The history of international economic integration is in part a story of technical progress, increasing knowledge, and the diffusion across frontiers of ideas, cultures and tastes; but it is also, and predominantly, an aspect of political history – a story of the evolution of official policies in relation to cross-border transactions.

It is normal and useful to group these cross-border transactions into three different categories, namely:

1 International trade in goods and services, the distinction between goods and services being itself of some significance in this connection.
2 International flows of capital (or, if you prefer, transactions in assets), including direct foreign investment flows, lending both short term and long term, and acquisitions of real estate.
3 Movement of people across borders – (i.e. international or interstate migration).

Full economic integration, were it ever to be established, would extend to all three categories: there would be free trade, free capital movements and free migration. Economies would be fully open. In practice, however, governments have viewed some kinds of openness as more acceptable than others. This means that different categories of transactions have to be separately considered.

Three main routes to closer integration can be distinguished: unilateral, where a government decides on liberalization on its own account; pluri-lateral, where two or more countries forming a group are involved, often though not necessarily in some kind of regional arrangement of which the European Community is an outstanding example; and multilateral, when liberalization is arrived at within a larger group, as for example in the General Agreement on Tariffs and Trade (GATT) where in general all the contracting parties have been involved in successive stages of reducing trade barriers.

What happens when you integrate?

So far I have been discussing economic integration in rather abstract and general terms. Before turning to recent developments and their significance, let me make the notion more concrete by drawing on three examples from the last century and two from today.

What happens when you integrate depends on how great a change is implied, on how closed the economy was before the change, how open it

becomes as a result and how abrupt is the transition. In my first example
the change was swift, far-reaching and decisive.

In 1850 Japan was almost wholly isolated from the rest of the world, not
only in economic terms but also politically and culturally. This was the
outcome of deliberate and long established official policy. The channels of
foreign trade were closely restricted, and both the amount and the
composition of this trade were strictly controlled. As part of this system
of control, Japanese were forbidden to build ships with a carrying capacity
of more than 75 tons. The policy of exclusion embraced not only overseas
trade, but also foreign contacts and cultural influences: 'In the early part
of the [Tokugawa] era even translations from European languages were
proscribed; while Japanese were forbidden to leave Japan and foreigners
to settle there'. Despite some weakening in its hold towards the end, 'the
policy of seclusion was on the whole effectively carried out'.[4]

This economic and cultural isolation of Japan was brought to an abrupt
end in the 1850s as a result of foreign coercion. Through what one might
describe in the language of 1992 as a Super Structural Impediments
Initiative, embodied in the 'unequal treaties' of 1858 and 1866, the great
powers of the day constrained the Japanese government to open up the
economy. Under the treaty arrangements, rights of trade were granted to
foreigners; specified Japanese ports were opened to foreign trade and
shipping; export and import duties were restricted, generally speaking to
a 5 per cent *ad valorem* rate; and extraterritorial rights were conferred on
the foreigners who were now legally entitled to residence in Japan. In the
1866 tariff convention, the rights of Japanese merchants and traders to deal
with foreigners without official interference, and of Japanese citizens to
travel abroad for purposes of trade and study, were explicitly recognized.
Thus within a decade or so Japan emerged, under foreign duress, from
being an almost completely isolated economy and society to a condition
not far short of full integration as I have defined it.

The consequences of this transformation were far-reaching, all the more
so because it was to be associated before long with a process of fundamental domestic reform following the Meiji Restoration of 1868. Even
before this programme of reform was set under way, the efforts of opening
the economy to foreign trade had become evident, particularly in the
pattern of relative prices, and therefore incentives, to which economic
activity soon responded. Here is one summary description of events:

There was an enormous rise in the price of raw silk, egg cards, rice, tea
and, in general, articles for which a foreign demand became keen. On
the other hand, imports of cheap cotton textiles, yarn and other products
of machine industry brought about a steep fall in the price of such goods.
The silk weaving trade suffered through the rise in price of its raw
material, and the producers of cotton textiles were damaged by the

influx of foreign goods. Many of the farmers, however, benefited as a result of the expansion of the foreign demand for raw silk and tea. Capital began to flow into Japan from abroad not merely through the [official] loans raised ... but also through the financial activities of foreign merchants who now settled in Japan. This affected the whole organisation of industry.[5]

Thus even before the Meiji reforms came into operation, the effects of freeing cross-border contacts and transactions had begun to be substantial. After 1868 the domestic economy and society of Japan were systematically modernized, and this made possible new modes of adjustment and advance.

An important dimension of reform was that it brought about the internal integration of the Japanese economy. As a result of the changes:

People were free to choose their trade or occupation, and could produce any crop or commodity. Guilds were eliminated. Feudal property relations were terminated and private property established in land which could now be sold freely. State taxes in money replaced old feudal levies in kind, and their incidence was equalised throughout the country. Internal tolls on the movement of goods and passport check-points for movement of people were abolished. Export prohibitions on rice, wheat, copper and raw silk were jettisoned.[6]

Hence Japan effectively became (to introduce again a 1992-vintage term) a Single Market as well as an open economy: domestic and international integration proceeded together. Largely in consequence, the Japanese economy was the first instance, and for several decades the only instance, where modern economic growth became established in a country whose people were neither European nor of predominantly European origin.

Since the economy was now so open, where formerly it had been effectively closed, it was in its foreign trading sectors that growth was conspicuously rapid. A few comparative figures will serve as illustration. Table 7.1 shows annual average growth rates of output (GDP) and the volume of merchandise exports for four countries over the period 1870–1913.[7] For all four countries export growth exceeded the growth of GDP, but in the case of Japan the difference is particularly striking: the volume of merchandise exports rose well over three times as fast as GDP. While the growth of Japanese GDP was somewhat less than that of Germany, the growth of exports was more than twice as high. In 1860 Japanese foreign trade had been negligible. By 1913 merchandise exports were about one-eighth of GDP, which itself had approximately tripled over this period.

My second example of what happens when you integrate is that of present-day Mexico. Here the direction of economic policy changed in a

Table 7.1 Growth of GDP and exports in four countries, 1870–1913 (volume growth, annual average percentage rates of change)

	GDP	*Merchandise exports*
USA	3.9	4.8
Germany	2.9	4.1
Japan	2.5	8.5
UK	1.9	2.8

Note: Figures relate to the areas enclosed by the actual territorial boundaries of the two years.
Source: Angus Maddison, *Dynamic Forces in Capitalist Development* (Oxford and New York: Oxford University Press, 1991).

remarkable way from the mid-1980s. While the Mexican economy of a decade ago was by no means isolated from world markets, as had been the case with Japan 130 years earlier, the trend for some time had been away from rather than towards integration: both imports and exports had fallen in relation to GDP, while both foreign trade and direct foreign investment had become closely regulated. This trend has now been decisively reversed. Partly in response to the debt crisis, the government decided to combine policies for macroeconomic adjustment with a substantial programme of trade liberalization and deregulation of foreign investment. Tariffs have been brought down, quantitative restrictions on imports have been greatly reduced, restrictions on technology licensing have been abolished, restrictive conditions for foreign investment have been eased, and areas of the economy in which such investment had previously been barred were opened up, wholly or partly, to investors from abroad. In 1986 Mexico became a contracting party to the GATT. In July 1992 a Mexican delegation came to Paris to take part in a meeting at OECD at which a draft OECD economic survey of Mexico – the first such survey of a non-member country outside the European continent – was discussed in committee. It has been made clear by the government of Mexico that it hopes in due course to become a full member of the OECD.

All the changes that I have so far listed were decided, and have been carried into effect, unilaterally: until recently, there was no question of joint liberalization, or special forms of regional integration with other countries. But Mexican liberalization has now been extended beyond unilateral measures. In 1990 Mexico opened negotiations with the USA and Canada with a view to transforming the already existing US–Canada Free Trade Agreement into a tripartite arrangement, a North American Free Trade Area. At the same time, membership of the GATT (and later possibly of the OECD) opens up the possibility of Mexican participation in multilateral liberalization.

My third example of an integrating country is likewise drawn from the present day, but from Europe rather than Asia or America. On 1 January

1986 Portugal became a full member of the European Community. The Portuguese situation at the time, however, was very different from that of Mexico a few years earlier. Portugal was already a highly open economy, and had been associated with the liberalization of trade and payments which the countries of Western Europe had effected over the previous four decades: the country's accession to the Community marked the end of a lengthy transition period in Portugal's international economic integration. All the same, accession was a notable event, and it has already had clear and positive effects on the economy and economic prospects of Portugal.

The main effects fall under two headings, only one of which is linked specifically to closer economic integration. First, Portugal is one of the poorest member countries of the Community in terms of income per head, and its infrastructure is less developed than the EC average. It has therefore qualified for financial and technical assistance through the European Structural Fund. Let me stress that this is not the result of or an aspect of integration as such. Arrangements of this kind within a political and economic grouping, by which the better-off member states give aid to the poorer members, go beyond what full economic integration itself brings with it. It is because the European Community is more than a customs union, more even than the Single Market which it is in the course of becoming, that countries such as Portugal, Greece and Ireland benefit from intra-EC redistributive schemes.

In this connection, let me also underline that this assistance for which Portugal now qualifies is not compensation for losses arising from its integration with larger and wealthier countries. It is often asserted that when countries which are small or poor – or both – become more closely linked to the world economy in general, or to a particular group of richer countries, the gains from integration will largely accrue to the latter. There is no basis for this belief. If anything, the reverse is true: it is the small countries, and the poor countries, that need access to the markets of the larger and more prosperous states. The aid to Portugal is given because it is a poor country by EC standards, not because there is reason to think that accession to the Community will have made it poorer in absolute or relative terms.

A second respect in which Portugal has already benefited from accession, even before the actual agreement came into effect in 1986, is the flow of direct foreign investment. Two factors have operated here. First, restrictions on direct investment were further dismantled, as indeed they would have had to be under the terms of EC membership. Second, Portugal became clearly established as a location which gives full and unrestricted access to the EC market, and which will continue to do so. Accession has underlined the Portuguese government's determination to maintain an open economy within the Community. It is evidence of a commitment to integration which investors can see is binding. In the same way, Mexican membership of a North American Free Trade Area would be viewed, and I think rightly viewed, as making it much less likely that recent liberalization measures would at some later stage be reversed. Even OECD membership, though it involves relatively little by way of specific commitments, would serve the same purpose. Portugal has become locked into liberalization, and Mexico is following the same path.

Despite the many differences between Japan in the 1850s and the two other examples I have cited five basic features of the process of international economic integration emerge from all these historical examples:

1 The extent to which integration is taken depends in large part on government policy.
2 Integration changes the balance of profitability and the pattern of incentives within an economy. Those firms and sectors that were previously insulated from competition, by limits or restrictions on the freedom of agents to enter into contracts, will lose from integration, while new opportunities will open up for sectors and firms that are now revealed as competitive.
3 Integration brings with it an increase in the extent not only of competition, but also of exposure to new influences, products, methods and ideas. This is likely to make for faster growth of productivity and output.
4 Integration may be rapid, as it was for Japan in the nineteenth century, or a more gradual, phased process as in the Mexican and Portuguese cases that I have also quoted. But to produce its full effects it must be seen as decisive, irreversible. Investors must perceive it as a firm commitment.
5 Full economic integration is a serious business, since it raises fundamental issues of national autonomy and sovereignty.

Against this background, let me now review both past trends and the current situation with respect to cross-border integration.

PAST TRENDS AND THE PRESENT SITUATION

What is new and what is not

Commentators are apt to tell us that we stand at the dawn of a new era. Various forms of this attention-arousing message are now in circulation, and one of these relates to my subject today. This particular message is that internationalization, or globalization, is a dramatic new development which has already taken the world a long way down the path towards full economic integration. Let me examine critically both parts of this assertion – first, that the pace of integration has recently acquired a new momentum; and second, that this has created, or is in the course of creating, a closely integrated international economy.

First, a long-term historical perspective on what is new and what is not. If economies are becoming more closely integrated, we might expect foreign trade to grow in relation to national product, just as it did in the case of Japan – and other countries too – between 1870 and 1913. This has in fact been the prevalent long-run historical tendency, as is brought out in Table 7.2. The Table presents estimates of the comparative growth of output and of merchandise exports in the world economy over the period 1870–1987. Five separate sub-periods are distinguished, and in four of these the growth of exports exceeded the growth of output, so that in this respect economies were becoming more interdependent. The exception is the period 1913–50, which is clearly unrepresentative since it covers two world wars and a devastating international depression. This evidence suggests that, viewed in historical perspective, closer economic integration is not at all a dramatic novelty. Rather, it is a well-established, long-run tendency, which in my judgement can be traced back as far as the end of the Napoleonic Wars in 1815.

Table 7.2 Growth of world GDP and exports, 1870–1987 (volume growth, annual average percentage rates of change)

	(1870–1900)	1900–13	1913–50	1950–73	1973–87
GDP	(2.9)	2.5	2.0	4.8	3.3
Merchandise exports	(3.8)	4.3	0.6	7.6	4.5

Note: From 1900 onwards, data relate to thirty-two countries, comprising (i) sixteen of the twenty-four OECD countries, including the seven largest economies; (ii) the Soviet Union; and (iii) fifteen countries from Asia and Latin America, including China, India, Argentina and Brazil.
  For 1870–1900, the figures relate to fourteen out of the sixteen OECD countries for which information is available, again including the seven largest economies.
Sources: Angus Maddison, The World Economy in the 20th Century (Paris: OECD, 1989) and *Dynamic Forces in Capitalist Development* (Oxford and New York: Oxford University Press, 1991).

From these figures, it is not the most recent phase which stands out as worthy of note. The most striking development is that which took place after the end of the Second World War – the contrast between 1913–50, a period of slow growth in output accompanied by increasing disintegration within the world economy, and 1950–73, when world output grew faster than ever before while the volume of exports increased at an average annual rate over twelve times that of the previous period.

Many factors contributed to this extraordinary (and quite unforeseen) break in trends, but it is clear that one important influence was a far-reaching liberalization of the trade and payments regimes of what are now the OECD countries. For the twenty-four countries taken together, this included very substantial reductions in tariffs, the removal of most quantitative import restrictions, a partial freeing of capital movements including in particular foreign direct investment flows, and the establishment of an effective system of multilateral exchange and payments with full convertibility of currencies. At the same time, the creation and later enlargement of the European Community, and the links established by the Community with the European Free Trade Association (EFTA) countries, led to a remarkable extension of freedom with respect to transactions across national boundaries within Europe. Both individually and in concert, the industrialized countries undertook a range of actions designed to make their economies more open, and more closely integrated not only with each other but also with the rest of the world. Unilateral, plurilateral and multilateral routes were all involved.

In this respect, however, the OECD countries were not typical of the world in general. Apart from them, there were two other main groupings of states, and in neither of these did the cause of economic liberalization flourish after the Second World War. The communist countries – which had by this period become more numerous and more extensive, and from 1949 included the world's most populous country – continued to operate economic systems which were not only tightly regulated but also largely isolated from developments in the world economy. As for the third group, the developing countries, there remained considerable diversity in their external policies and regimes; but in the group as a whole, there was a clear tendency for governments to move in the direction of greater trade protectionism and closer control over international transactions in general. Even within the OECD countries themselves, there remained wide areas of policy which were largely unaffected by liberalization – for example, agriculture, trade in services, public procurement and systems of exchange control. Thus the world economy of the early 1970s, while much more open – as well as more prosperous – than the highly fragmented system which emerged from the Second World War, was very far from being a single market: indeed, it was only in certain regions and in certain areas of policy that there was a decisive trend towards integration.

Since then policies have evolved further, and in some important respects they have moved in a liberal direction. But the trend has not been uniform, and full integration remains a distant prospect.

Looking first at the OECD economies, there are three main developments to note. In two of these, official policies have extended the process of liberalization, and made national economies more open. In a third area of policy, however, the tendency has on balance been the other way: recent measures in many OECD countries have taken the world economy further away from full integration.

Under the heading of liberalization, a significant recent change across the OECD area as a whole has been the freeing of international capital movements. In this process there have been some notable landmark events, such as the day in October 1979 when Her Majesty's Government suspended all forms of exchange control in the UK. But more broadly there has been a continuing movement towards both deregulation and inter-nationalization, in which two main interacting influences have been at work. One is the remarkable change – some would say, the revolution – in communications and computer technologies, which has opened up new dimensions in cross-border financial transactions. The second influence has been the general tendency in all OECD countries for economic policies to evolve in a market-oriented direction: deregulation of financial markets has been part of a wider trend towards economic liberalism. The technical changes have given greater impetus to official liberalization, by making it more difficult to enforce regulations and by exposing national govern-ments to the risk that failure to deregulate would make it harder for their own financial service enterprises and financial centres to compete in world markets. All this has brought closer integration of financial markets, and with it more intense competition, both within national economies and across their borders. The process is still continuing, and in some cases it has now extended also to financial markets in developing countries.

A second respect in which most though not all OECD countries have recently moved towards closer integration is that new regional arrange-ments have been made or are in prospect. These include the US/Canada Free Trade Agreement, which may well now be extended to include Mexico; the Closer Economic Relations Agreement between Australia and New Zealand; and, most far reaching of all, the completion within the European Community of the Single Market. Since these agreements are regional rather than multilateral, and are of their nature discriminatory, they can also be viewed as a factor making for disintegration, rather than integration, within the world economy as a whole: I shall consider this aspect in a moment. But viewed in themselves, all these arrangements have both the intention and the effect, within the regions that they cover, of reducing further the economic significance of national boundaries.

This, however, is not the whole OECD story. If we set aside these various regional initiatives, and consider the trade policies of the OECD countries more broadly, a different picture emerges. In the majority of these countries, and most conspicuously in the world's two largest trading entities, the USA and the European Community, there has for some time been a clear trend towards greater reliance on forms of trade intervention which are highly discriminatory. The main types of measure involved are three:

1 So-called, voluntary export restraint agreements (VERs), the scope of which has widened over time.
2 Procedural protection, most notably in the form of anti-dumping actions.
3 Specific subsidies, both to exports and to goods and services competing with imports.

Under all these three headings, the evolution of policies has been gradual and undramatic. But the cumulative effect over the years has been substantial. Managed trade is now established as an integral and accepted feature of economic policies in the OECD area. Because the various instruments of managed trade are inherently discriminatory – as between different countries, industries, products, and even in some cases individual enterprises – they constitute within the world economy a continuing element of disintegration.

In the rest of the world, by contrast, the last few years have seen a remarkable tendency for trade regimes to evolve in a liberal direction. This trend has now become apparent in Central and Eastern Europe as well as in the developing countries. I was impressed to read not long ago, in a consultant's report prepared for an OECD meeting, that 'protection in the Czech and Slovak Federal Republic and Poland is now lower, more uniform and (being based largely on tariffs) more transparent than that accorded to domestic producers in most OECD countries'. A similar statement could now be made, I believe, about Chile and Mexico, while a substantial number of other non-OECD countries either are or may soon be on the same liberalizing path. For the first time in economic history the main impulse to more liberal trade policies is now coming, not from the industrial countries which profess to accept liberal norms, but from countries whose past tradition has been to question or reject them.

But it is not only in relation to trade in goods and services that liberalization has been going ahead in a growing number of developing countries. A parallel and equally striking development has been the change in attitudes towards, and in the regulations affecting, foreign direct investment. I need say little about this, except to refer you to an article in *Finance and Development* by Guy Pfeffermann. The article was summarized in an issue of *World Bank News* under the headline, 'Developing Countries Reverse Policies That Discouraged Foreign Investment'.[8] In this important area, many developing countries have been taking steps, largely via a unilateral route, towards closer integration with the world economy.

In this case very similar developments have been taking place in the OECD countries also. Let me quote from an OECD publication, which a Secretariat colleague kindly sent me after reading a first draft of this article.

If the 1980s, especially the latter half of the decade, were among the most remarkable periods since World War II for the expansion of international flows of direct investment among Member countries, the way in which policies and attitudes towards direct investments evolved during the period is perhaps especially remarkable. No one can fail to be astonished by the extent of Member countries' progress since the beginning of the decade towards greater liberalisation and the removal of restrictions and obstacles to direct investment flows to and from other countries; and most significantly still in their broader regulatory approaches to such investment.[9]

The same colleague also made the point that (here I quote from an OECD memo): 'Liberalising cross-border services is more difficult, but real progress has been made, and more is on the way regardless of the outcome of the Uruguay Round.'

At the same time, I have the feeling that in almost every country liberalization still has quite a long way to go in relation to direct foreign investment. Even in countries where strict regulations and screening procedures have been swept away, there is often a tendency by governments to pursue special deals, involving for example

• specific subsidies or tax concessions;
• local content requirements;
• export performance clauses;
• indigenization targets or conditions of various kinds;
• commitments to further local processing.

In so far as these involve discrimination between firms, they are not consistent with full integration.

The present extent of integration: May 1992 and May 1914

Just as recent integrationist tendencies across the world have been both less novel and less pervasive than is often suggested, so their results up to now have been in many respects, and not surprisingly, rather limited. The present extent of cross-border integration is far from complete. There are even now many national states in which full economic integration does not prevail, and several within which elements of disintegration may actually be growing in strength. As for the integration of national economies, despite all that has happened since 1945, including those recent developments that have given rise to all the talk about globalization, the world economy in May 1992 is further away from full integration than it was in May 1914.

If we compare the situation now and that which existed just before the First World War:

• Trade regimes are generally speaking less liberal, even in the OECD countries and those others that have recently liberalized, and still more in the rest of the world (with the striking exceptions of Hong Kong and Singapore).
• It is true that major financial markets have recently become almost as free as in 1913, thanks to the liberalizations of recent years; but with a few exceptions this applies to the OECD area only. Moreover, in almost

all countries private direct investment is still some way from being treated on a fully non discriminatory basis.
• International migration is heavily controlled almost everywhere, and indeed there are countries in which internal migration is not free.

Thus a borderless world economy, far from being close to realization, would require far-reaching changes in the policy regime of virtually every country in the world.

There is another difference between 1992 and 1914, which results not from current restrictions on the free movement of goods and services, capital and labour, but from the legacy of past restrictions. Because of their long isolation – though it was less complete than in the case of Tokugawa Japan – the countries of Central and Eastern Europe, and some of the developing countries which have long kept their economies substantially isolated from world markets, have economically speaking the status of recently discovered continents. Integration would bring profound changes in these economies; and though in a number of cases such a process is already well under way, it is far from being either general or complete.

Hence the world economy of 1992, despite the remarkable changes that have taken place since the end of the Second World War, is further away from full economic integration than it was on the eve of the First. From this a simple conclusion follows. The scope for further moves towards integration, both within and (still more) across national boundaries, is still very great – if this is what peoples and governments would like, are prepared to accept, or find themselves unable to prevent.

So much for past history and the present state of affairs. I have now to consider the form which future developments might take.

FUTURE PROSPECTS AND OPTIONS

The uneasy trend towards closer integration

It seems probable that the trend towards closer international economic integration will continue, both in the OECD member countries and more generally. As I have argued, not only is there a lot of scope still for movement in this direction, but there is also, for the time being at least, considerable momentum behind liberalized tendencies of various kinds. On the other hand, the trend will not I think either be universal or consistent; there are strong elements of disintegration on the world scene, some of which are new with obvious potential for growth.

Let me give three examples of ways in which disintegration is continuing, or is even extending its range.

• First, we may note the incapacity so far of the EC and the USA, despite their often repeated statements of intention, to arrive at an agreement which would enable the GATT Uruguay Round negotiations to be brought to a productive conclusion. There is a depressing failure of leadership here.

- Second, disintegration may become more of a problem, in some countries at least, within existing national boundaries. There are signs of this in the USA; and in a recent conference that I attended, an American professor referred to what he called 'a growing thicket of sub-federal regulations', bringing with it major problems for multinational corporations.
- Third, it is sadly evident that catastrophic disintegration is now taking place within the borders of what used to be Yugoslavia, while there are obvious signs and risks of disintegration within the former USSR.

On the other side of the balance, what is particularly striking at the moment is the continuing trend towards regional integration. This is most marked in Europe: the Community is in the course of completing the Single Market, and has laid plans for achieving economic and monetary union later in the decade; it will be joining with the seven EFTA countries in 1993 to form the European Economic Area (EEA); three of the EFTA countries (Austria, Finland and Sweden) have applied for membership of the Community, and are expected to join it by 1995; three other European countries – Cyprus, Malta and Turkey – have applied for membership (though in these cases the outcome is less certain). The Community has signed Association Agreements with Poland, Hungary and the Czech and Slovak Federal Republic, while similar links with other countries in Central and Eastern Europe are likely in due course to be established.

General de Gaulle, in a memorable phrase, once referred to Europe as extending from the Atlantic to the Urals. With the collapse of the old division between east and west, an even wider association is in prospect, stretching from the eastern Atlantic to the western Pacific – from Limerick to Vladivostok. Moreover, a recent press report has referred to the possible creation of a free trade area embracing the Community (or more probably, the EEA) and the Maghreb countries of North Africa.

Looking further west, it now seems likely that the North Atlantic Free Trade Area will be established, though no doubt some problems still lie ahead; while a recent press report carried the news that Chile may become a candidate for entry into this arrangement. The possibility of a pan-American free trade area, though still distant, can no longer be ruled out.

Regional arrangements of this kind are often viewed with suspicion, as a source of disintegration and friction within the world economy. Let me explain why my own view is more positive.

'Trade blocs': reality or illusion?

Contrary to what is often asserted, regional arrangements do not necessarily, or even probably, involve a move away from closer integration in the world as a whole. 'Trade blocs' (so-called) are not with us now, nor on present evidence are they the wave of the future. By way of amplifying and reinforcing this statement, let me make three observations relating to it.

My first observation is that closer regional integration does not necessarily give rise to discriminatory trading blocs, and it may even further the cause of trade liberalization in the world as a whole. I think the early history of the European Community lends support to this view; but the simplest way to make the point is to consider a single sovereign state. Take Canada as an example. A few years ago, in a country economic survey of Canada, the OECD Secretariat made the point that:

> Paradoxically, while the Free Trade Agreement liberalises trade between [Canada and the United States], signficant trade barriers between Canadian provinces remain. Provincial procurement policies are a major barrier. . . . Other restrictions include transport regulations, marketing boards, agricultural policies, product standards and liquor board policies.[10]

Suppose that in a federal system, such as Canada or Australia, such barriers between the constituent provinces or states are removed – so as to ensure that economically speaking there are no 'foreigners'. The end result of such a process would be very close to what the twelve countries of the European Community are planning to achieve by the end of 1992: in both Canada and Australia, there would be a Single Market. But it is not reasonable to argue that simply by establishing full freedom of transactions across their boundaries the Canadian provinces or the Australian states would be creating a 'trade bloc' where no such thing existed before. Provided that the external trade regime was unaffected in each case, neither the Canadian nor the Australian market would be more closed than before; and in so far as closer integration brought positive effects on economic efficiency and growth, the result would be to widen the market for imports. Moreover, the benefits accruing from the freer internal market would be shared by all businesses operating in these countries, including those that are foreign-owned. the same is true for closer economic integration as between the USA and Canada, or within the European Community. Economic integration within an area comprising several countries is not a qualitatively different process from integration within a single sovereign state in which elements of disintegration exist; and in both cases, closer regional integration in itself does not entail a weakening of the multilateral trading system.

Of course, this may not be the whole story; and this brings me to my second observation under this heading. One could well imagine a case in which closer regional integration went together with a more protectionist trade regime for the country or the group of countries as a whole. More specifically and topically, some important decisions remain to be taken about the future trade regime of the European Community, in the context of completing the Single Market; and I would personally not dismiss as absurd the risk of a 'Fortress Europe'. All the same, such a development is not in the least inevitable, and in my opinion it is not the most likely outcome. In that connection, let me just note:

1 that the governments of the Twelve have clearly stated that they do not intend to move in a more protectionist direction as an accompaniment to completing the Single Market;
2 that a recent – and in many respects quite critical – review of the Community's trade policies by the GATT Secretariat found no evidence of any such tendency or intention.

My third and final observation is that the current widespread talk about (so-called) trade blocs is doubly misplaced. It conjures up a picture of a world trading system which is now reasonably well knit together, and in good shape, within which however a strong impulse towards disintegration has just arisen, as a new and disturbing threat. Both elements in this picture are distorted. New regional arrangements are not bound to have disintegrating effects; and in any case, the world traind system is not all in good shape; disintegration is already endemic within it as a result, not of trade blocs, but of long established features of national trade regimes in each of the three main groupings of countries – the countries of Central and Eastern Europe, the developing countries and the OECD member states.

Options for non-OECD countries

Given the situation and prospect that I have just sketched out, is there anything that can usefully be said about the choices that face the developing countries and the countries of Central and Eastern Europe? Since circumstances vary greatly, and since this is a subject area in which the World Bank and IFC have well recognized expertise, I will make only a few brief and general points.

First, let me quote the response of a well-informed Indian economist whom I recently asked about the direction which trade policies in India should now take. His response was simple: 'India has to liberalize. Whether liberalization is unilateral, bilateral, trilateral, quadrilateral, multilateral or a mix of these is of secondary importance. What matters is liberalization.' There are no doubt many non-OECD countries for which a similar generalization still holds good.

Second, it is not necessary – though it may be useful – for non-OECD countries to form or participate in regional trading arrangements. Provided that existing and future arrangements involving other countries are not accompanied by moves towards higher levels of protection *vis-à-vis* the rest of the world, there need be no threat to the interests of outsiders.

Third, arrangements as between non-OECD countries, though by no means to be ruled out, are no substitute for what matters most, which is access to OECD markets.

Fourth, and contrary to the philosophy and programme which have been long embraced by the developing countries collectively in the Group of 77, the non-OECD countries share with the OECD member states a common interest in the maintenance and strengthening of the open multilateral trading system. It is through freer trade and investment, rather than through an internationally concerted programme of affirmative action by the OECD group, that these countries stand to gain from cross-border transactions. They could well subscribe to one of the goals set out in the original Convention of the OECD (a document which goes back more than thirty years) – namely, 'to contribute to the expansion of world trade on a multilateral, non-discriminatory basis in accordance with international objectives'.

In pursuit of this goal, the non-OECD countries need to act together, more effectively than at present, to try to influence the course of trade negotiations and the policies of the OECD countries. Continuing pressure has to be brought to bear on OECD member states, and in particular on the Big Three – the USA, the EC and Japan – to ensure that their actions in relation to international trade and investment conform more closely to the liberal principles which they profess to hold. This is an area in which international agencies – the IMF, the World Bank, the OECD and the GATT – can play a useful role.

How far to go? Free trade, residence and migration

Up to now I have treated closer international integration as a positive process, which makes for greater and widely shared prosperity. I believe this perspective is correct. The fact is, however, that few countries in the world either practise or propose to achieve free trade, and that the arguments for some forms and degree of protectionism are not necessarily to be set aside. While it is difficult to defend the instruments of discriminatory protection which are most widely practised today – such as the EC's Common Agricultural Policy, or the Multi-Fibre Arrangement – it is arguable that for many countries, and perhaps especially for those in the non-OECD group, cross-border liberalization should for the time being at least stop short of complete free trade.

In this connection, the example of postwar Japan is often quoted as showing that active government policies, within which selective protection for industry forms one element, can contribute, at least at a certain stage of development, to improving a country's economic performance. As you know, there is now an active debate, both in OECD countries and elsewhere, on the merits of industrial policy; and as you also doubtless know, or would have guessed, this is an issue on which economists hold conflicting views. I do not wish to pursue this topic further (though just for the record, let me state my personal view that free trade is the best rule to follow), but I want to note:

1 that full international economic integration, even with respect to trade in goods and services, is not now accepted as an official goal except by one or two individual governments and within the European Community;
2 that in part this is because of differing opinions on the extent to which full integration, as distinct from qualified (though possibly progressive) liberalization, will serve the cause of national prosperity.

Moreover, this is only part of the story, since integration raises issues which go beyond that of greater prosperity. Even in the economic sphere, governments have to take account of the distribution of gains and losses associated with integration. In any case, economic aspects are not the only ones that count. If integration goes at all far, it is likely to raise fundamental issues concerning the extent to which frontiers can and should continue to define areas of sovereignty and national identity. Some major questions of acceptability are likely to arise.

The main single aspect of acceptability is the way in which rights of residence and citizenship are to be defined. Free trade in goods does not normally raise this problem in an acute form: it is the least controversial aspect of non-discrimination. Free trade in services is more likely to do so, in that rights of establishment may be involved. Free trade in assets clearly does: should overseas-based businesses have the unrestricted right to acquire domestically owned firms, and to bring in whoever they may choose, as indefinite residents, to manage their subsidiaries in the home country? Should countries be prepared to grant individuals and countries abroad the unrestricted right to acquire land and property within their borders?

The most controversial issues arise in relation to the last of my three dimensions of integration, the movement of people. A leading economic and political issue of the next century, and increasingly of the present decade, is likely to be that of international migration. We now have a situation which has no precedent in economic history, in that:

1 There are very large and still growing cross-country inequalities in income per head.
2 All over the world people are increasingly well aware of these differences, and of the opportunities that exist in the richer and more open economies.
3 Rates of population growth are highest in the poor countries.

4 Costs of migration are extremely low in relation to the possible gains involved.

All this means that very strong pressures, which are already evident, are likely to grow stronger. It is clear that, given the scale and character of the potential flows, close control over migration will continue: in this respect a borderless world, or even a much more open system such as that which prevailed before the First World War, is not at all in prospect.

In this dimension as in others, a world of closed borders can be viewed as a world of unexploited opportunities: greater freedom of movement would in itself contribute to international prosperity; and the gains thus arising would be widely shared, by recipient countries and countries of origin alike. Judged in this light, 'economic migrants' have a clearly positive role. But general prosperity is only one aspect of the matter, and not necessarily the most important. It is likely that in relation to issues of cross-border migration, far from having reached 'the end of history' the world is now entering into a new and more difficult phase.

Economic integration and national sovereignty

Finally, let me underline the importance in its own right of the political dimension. Even full economic integration does not necessarily imply political integration or loss of sovereignty; nor does it even guarantee peaceful relations between the national states concerned. In 1870, and again in 1914, France and Germany went to war. Both in 1870 and after the peace treaty of the following year, neither country had any serious restrictions on flows of trade or capital movements between them, nor even – so far as I know – on the migration of people across the Franco-German border. Except for some generally moderate tariffs on both sides, which in both cases were largely non-discriminatory, the situation in 1914 was much the same. In this and other instances, history demonstrates that close or even full economic integration need not lead to the end of geography in political terms.

National states can go a long way towards full economic integration while still retaining autonomy – if they choose – in such matters as fiscal policies, defence, foreign policy, cultural affairs, citizenship, voting rights and the status of the national language. Closer economic links may well prove to be the first stage in a broader process of integration: this was the case with the German Zollverein in the last century; and the evolution so far of the European Community, since its establishment in the 1950s, has followed a broadly similar course. But there is nothing inevitable about such a process, and no single sequence or model which is universally applicable. Here as elsewhere, historical outcomes are by no means predetermined.

NOTES AND REFERENCES

1 Richard O'Brien, *Global Financial Integration: The End of Geography* (London: Pinter/Royal Institute of International Affairs, 1992).
2 Kenichi Ohmae, *The Borderless World* (New York: HarperCollins, 1990).
3 Geoffrey Blainey, *The Tyranny of Distance* (Melbourne: Sun Books, 1966; rev. edn 1983).
4 G.C. Allen, *A Short Economic History of Modern Japan, 1867–1937* (London: Allen and Unwin, 1946).
5 G. C. Allen, *A Short Economic History,* pp. 23–4.
6 Angus Maddison, *Economic Growth in Japan and the USSR* (London: Allen and Unwin, 1969), p. 9.
7 Angus Maddison, *Dynamic Forces in Capitalist Development* (Oxford and New York: Oxford University Press, 1991).
8 *World Bank News*, Vol. 11, No. 16 (23 April 1992).
9 *Foreign Direct Investment: Policies and Trends in the OECD Area* (Paris: OECD 1992).
10 *Economic Survey: Canada* (Paris: OECD, 1988), p. 75.

Chapter 8

The cultural relativity of organizational practices and theories

Geert Hofstede

INTRODUCTION

Management and national cultures

A key issue for organization science is the influence of national cultures on management. Twenty or even ten years ago, the existence of a relationship between management and national cultures was far from obvious to many, and it may not be obvious to everyone even now. In the 1950s and 1960s, the dominant belief, at least in Europe and the USA, was that management was something universal. There were principles of sound management, which existed regardless of national environments. If national or local practice deviated from these principles, it was time to change local practice. In the future, the universality of sound management practices would lead to societies becoming more and more alike. This applied even to the poor countries of the Third World, which would become rich as well and would be managed just like the rich countries. Also the differences between management in the First and Second World (capitalist and socialist) would disappear; in fact, under the surface they were thought to be a lot smaller than was officially recognized. This way of thinking, which dominated the 1950s and 1960s, is known as the 'convergence hypothesis'.

During the 1970s the belief in the unavoidable convergence of management practices waned. It was too obviously in conflict with the reality we saw around us. At the same time supranational organizations like the European Common Market, which were founded very much on the convergence belief, had to recognize the stubbornness of national differences. Even within existing nations, regional differences became more rather than less accentuated. The Welsh, the Flemish, the Basques, the Bangladeshi, the Quebecois defended their own identity, and this was difficult to reconcile with a management philosophy of convergence. It slowly became clear that national and even regional cultures do matter for management. The national and regional differences are not disappearing; they are here to stay. In fact, these differences may become one of the most crucial problems for management – in particular for the management of multinational, multicultural organizations, whether public or private.

The importance of nationality

Nationality is important to management for at least three reasons. The first, very obviously, is political. Nations are political units, rooted in history, with their own institutions, forms of government, legal systems, educational systems, labor and employer's association systems. Not only do the formal institutions differ, but even if we could equalize them, the informal ways of using them differ. For example, formal law in France protects the rights of the individual against the state much better than formal law in Great Britain or Holland. However, few French citizens have ever won court cases against the state, whereas this happens quite regularly in Holland or Britain. Such informal political realities are quite resistant to change.

The second reason why nationality is important is sociological. Nationality or regionality has a symbolic value to citizens. We all derive part of our identity from it; it is part of the 'who am I'. The symbolic value of the fact of belonging to a nation or region has been and still is sufficient reason for people to go to war, when they feel their common identity to be threatened. National and regional differences are felt by people to be a reality – and therefore they are a reality.

The third reason why nationality is important is psychological. Our thinking is an effect of early life experiences in the family and later educational experiences in schools and organizations, which are not the same across national borders. In a classroom, I can easily demonstrate the process of conditioning by experience. For this purpose I use an ambiguous picture: one that can be interpreted in two different ways. One such picture represents either an attractive young girl or an ugly old woman, depending on the way you look at it. In order to demonstrate the process of conditioning, I ask one half of the class to close their eyes. To the other half, I show for five seconds a slightly changed version of the picture, in which only the young girl can be seen. Then I ask the other half to close their eyes, and to the first half I show, also for five seconds, a version in which only the old woman can be seen. After this preparation, I show the ambiguous picture to everyone at the same time. The results are amazing: the vast majority of those 'conditioned' by seeing the young girl first, now see only the young girl in the ambiguous picture; and most of those 'conditioned' by seeing the old woman first can see only the old woman afterwards.

Mental programming

This very simple experiment shows that as a teacher I can in five seconds condition a randomly taken half of a class to see something else in a picture than would the other half. If this is so, how much stronger should the differences in perception of the same reality be between people who have been 'conditioned' by different educational and life experiences not for a mere five seconds, but for twenty, thirty, or forty years? Through our experiences we become 'mentally programmed' to interpret new experiences in a certain way. My favorite definition of 'culture' is precisely that its essence is collective mental programming: it is that part of our conditioning that we share with other members of our nation, region, or group but not with members of other nations, regions, or groups.

Examples of differences in mental programming between members of different nations can be observed all around us. One source of difference is, of course, language and all that comes with it, but there is much more. In Europe, British people will form a neat queue whenever they have to wait; not so, the French. Dutch people will as a rule greet strangers when they enter a small, closed space like a railway compartment, doctor's waiting-room, or lift; not so, the Belgians. Austrians will wait at a red pedestrian traffic light even when there is no traffic; not so the Dutch. Swiss tend to become very angry when somebody – say, a foreigner – makes a mistake in traffic; not so the Swedes. All these are part of an invisible set of mental programs which belongs to these countries' national cultures.

Such cultural programs are difficult to change, unless one detaches the individual from his or her culture. Within a nation or a part of it, culture changes only slowly. This is the more so because what is in the minds of the people has also become crystallized in the institutions mentioned earlier: government, legal systems, educational systems, industrial relations systems, family structures, religious organizations, sports clubs, settlement patterns, literature, architecture, and even scientific theories. All these reflect traditions and common ways of thinking, which are rooted in the common culture but may be different for other cultures. The institutions constrain and reinforce the ways of thinking on which they are based. One well known mechanism by which culturally determined ways of thinking perpetuate themselves is the self-fulfilling prophecy. If, for example, the belief is held that people from a certain minority are irresponsible, the institutions in such an environment will not admit these people into positions of responsibility: never being given responsibility, minority people will be unable to learn it, and very likely they will actually behave irresponsibly. So, everyone remains caught in the belief – including, probably, the minority people themselves. Another example of the self-fulfilling prophecy: if the dominant way of thinking in a society is that all people are ultimately motivated by self-interest, those who do not pursue self-interest are considered as deviant. As it is unpleasant to be deviant, most people in such an environment will justify whatever they want to do with some reference to self-interest, thereby reinforcing the dominant way of thinking. People in such a society cannot even imagine motives that cannot be reduced to self-interest.

National character

This article shall be limited to national cultures, excluding cultural differences between groups within nations; such as, those based on regions, social classes, occupations, religion, age, sex, or even families. These differences in culture within nations, of course, do exist, but for most nations we can still distinguish some ways of thinking that most inhabitants share and that we can consider part of their national culture or national character. National characters are more clearly distinguishable to foreigners than to the nationals themselves. When we live within a country, we do not discover what we have in common with our compatriots, only what makes us different from them.

Statements about national culture or national character smell of superficiality and false generalization. There are two reasons for this. First, there is no commonly accepted language to describe such a complex thing as a 'culture'. We meet the same problem if we want to describe someone's 'personality': we risk being subjective and superficial. In the case of 'personality', however, psychology has at least developed terms like intelligence, energy level, introversion-extroversion and emotional stability, to mention a few, which are more or less commonly understood. In the case of 'culture', such a scientific language does not exist. In the second place, statements about national character have often been based on impressions only, not on systematic study. Such statements can indeed be considered false generalizations.

A RESEARCH PROJECT ACROSS FIFTY COUNTRIES

My own research into national cultures was carried out between 1967 and 1978. It has attempted to meet the two objectives I just mentioned: to develop a commonly acceptable, well-defined, and empirically based terminology to describe cultures; and to use systematically collected data about a large number of cultures, rather than just impressions. I obtained these data more or less by accident. From 1967 to 1971 I worked as a psychologist on the international staff of a large multinational corporation. As part of my job I collected data on the employees' attitudes and values, by means of standardized paper-and-pencil questionnaires. Virtually all employees of the corporation were surveyed, from unskilled workers to research scientists in many countries around the globe. Then from 1971 to

1973 the surveys were repeated once more with the same group of employees. All in all the corporation collected over 116,000 questionnaires which were stored in a computerized data bank. For 40 countries, there were sufficient data for systematic analysis.

It soon appeared that those items in the questionnaires that dealt with employee values rather than attitudes showed remarkable and very stable differences between countries. By an attitude I mean the response to a question like 'how do you like your job?' or 'how do you like your boss?' By a value I mean answers to questions of whether people prefer one type of boss over another, or their choice of factors to describe an ideal job. Values indicate their desires, not their perceptions of what actually went on. These values, not the attitudes, reflect differences in mental programming and national character.

These differences, however, were always statistical in nature. Suppose people were asked whether they strongly agreed, agreed, were undecided, disagreed, or strongly disagreed with a certain value statement. In such a case we would not find that all employees in country A agreed and all in country B disagreed; instead we might find that 60 per cent of the employees in country A agreed, while only 40 per cent in country B agreed. Characterizing a national culture does not mean that every individual within that culture is mentally programmed in the same way. The national culture found is a kind of average pattern of beliefs and values, around which individuals in the country vary. For example, I found that, on average, Japanese have a greater desire for a strong authority than English; but some English have a greater desire for a strong authority than quite a few Japanese. In describing national cultures we refer to common elements within each nation, but we should not generalize to every individual within that nation.

In 1971 I went as a teacher to an international business school, where I asked the course participants, who were managers from many different countries, to answer the same values questions we used in the multi-national corporation. The answers revealed the same type of pattern of differences between countries, showing that we were not dealing with a phenomenon particular to this one company. Then in my later research, from 1973 to 1979, at the European Institute for Advanced Studies in Brussels, I looked for other studies comparing aspects of national character across countries. I found about forty such studies comparing five or more countries which showed differences confirming the ones found in the multinational corporation. All this material together forms the basis for my book *Culture's Consequences* (Hofstede 1980). Later, supplementary data became available for another ten countries and three multi-country regions, thereby raising the total number of countries to fifty (Hofstede 1983).

FOUR DIMENSIONS OF NATIONAL CULTURE

My terminology for describing national cultures consists of four different criteria which I call 'dimensions' because they occur in nearly all possible combinations. They are largely independent of each other:

1 Individualism versus Collectivisim;
2 Large or Small Power Distance;
3 Strong or Weak Uncertainty Avoidance;
4 Masculinity versus Femininity.

The research data have allowed me to attribute to each of the forty countries represented in the data bank of the multinational corporation an index value (between 0 and about 100) on each of these four dimensions.

The four dimensions were found through a combination of multivariate statistics (factor analysis) and theoretical reasoning. The cases analysed in the factor analysis were the forty countries; the variables were the mean scores or answer percentages for the different value questions, as produced by the multinational corporation's employees within these countries. This factor analysis showed that 50 per cent of the variance in answer patterns between countries on the value questions could be explained by three factors, corresponding to the dimensions 1 + 2, 3 and 4. Theoretical reasoning led to the further splitting of the first factor into two dimensions. The theoretical reasoning meant that each dimension should be conceptually linkable to some very fundamental problem in human societies, but a problem to which different societies have found different answers. These are the issues studied in primitive, non-literate societies by cultural anthropologists, such as, the distribution of power, or the distribution of roles between the sexes. There is no reason why such issues should be relevant only for primitive societies.

Individualism versus Collectivism

The first dimension is labeled 'Individualism versus Collectivism'. The fundamental issue involved is the relation between an individual and his or her fellow individuals. At one end of the scale we find societies in which the ties between individuals are very loose. Everybody is supposed to look after his or her own self-interest and maybe the interest of his or her immediate family. This is made possible by a large amount of freedom that such a society leaves individuals. At the other end of the scale we find societies in which the ties between individuals are very tight. People are born into collectivities or ingroups which may be their extended family (including grandparents, uncles, aunts, and so on), their tribe, or their village. Everybody is supposed to look after the interest of his or her ingroup and to have no other opinions and beliefs than the opinions and beliefs in their ingroup. In exchange, the ingroup will protect them when they are in trouble. We see that both the Individualist and the Collectivist society are integrated wholes, but the Individualist society is loosely integrated, and the Collectivist society tightly integrated.

All fifty countries can be placed somewhere along the Individualist-Collectivist scale. On the basis of the answers obtained on the questionnaire in the multinational corporation, each country was given an Individualism index score. The score is such that 100 represents a strongly Individualist society, and 0 a strongly Collectivist society: all 50 countries are somewhere between these extremes.

It appears that the degree of Individualism in a country is statistically related to that country's wealth. Table 8.1 shows the list of countries used, and Figure 8.1 shows vertically the individualism index scores of the 50 countries, and horizontally their wealth, expressed in their gross national product per capita at the time the surveys were taken (around 1970). We see evidence that wealthy countries are more Individualist and poor

Table 8.1 The countries and regions

ARA	Arab countries (Egypt, Lebanon, Lybia, Kuwait, Iraq, Saudi Arabia, UAE)	JAM	Jamaica
		JPN	Japan
		KOR	South Korea
ARG	Argentina	MAL	Malaysia
AUL	Australia	MEX	Mexico
AUT	Austria	NET	Netherlands
BEL	Belgium	NOR	Norway
BRA	Brazil	NZL	New Zealand
CAN	Canada	PAK	Pakistan
CHL	Chile	PAN	Panama
COL	Colombia	PER	Peru
COS	Costa Rica	PHI	Philippines
DEN	Denmark	POR	Portugal
EAF	East Africa (Kenya, Ethiopia, Zambia)	SAF	South Africa
		SAL	Salvador
EQA	Equador	SIN	Singapore
FIN	Finland	SPA	Spain
FRA	France	SWE	Sweden
GBR	Great Britain	SWI	Switzerland
GER	Germany	TAI	Taiwan
GRE	Greece	THA	Thailand
GUA	Guatemala	TUR	Turkey
HOK	Hong Kong	URU	Uruguay
IDO	Indonesia	USA	United States of America
IND	India	VEN	Venezuela
IRA	Iran	WAF	West Africa (Nigeria, Ghana, Sierra Leone)
IRE	Ireland		
ISR	Israel	YUG	Yugoslavia
ITA	Italy		

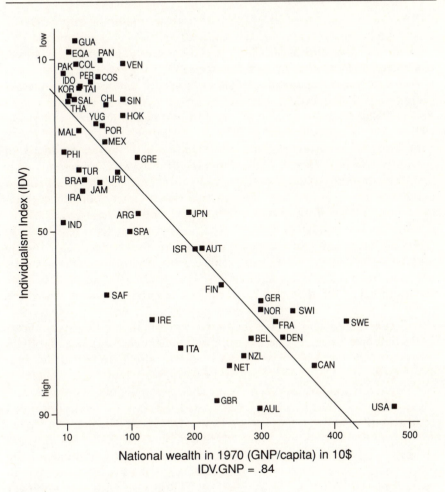

Figure 8.1 The position of the 50 countries on their Individualism Index (IDV) versus their 1970 national wealth (per capita GNP)

countries more Collectivist. Very Individualist countries are the US, Great Britain, the Netherlands; very Collectivist are Colombia, Pakistan, and Taiwan. In the middle we find Japan, India, Austria, and Spain.

Power Distance

The second dimension is labeled 'Power Distance'. The fundamental issue involved is how society deals with the fact that people are unequal. People are unequal in physical and intellectual capacities. Some societies let these inequalities grow over time into inequalities of power and wealth; the latter may become hereditary and no longer related to physical and intellectual capacities at all. Other societies try to play down inequalities in power and wealth as much as possible. Surely, no society has ever reached complete equality, because there are strong forces in society that perpetuate existing inequalities. All societies are unequal, but some are more unequal than others. This degree of inequality is measured by the Power Distance scale, which also runs from 0 (small Power Distance) to 100 (large Power Distance).

In organizations, the level of Power Distance is related to the degree of centralization of authority and the degree of autocratic leadership. This relationship shows that centralization and autocratic leadership are rooted in the 'mental programming' of the members of a society, not only of those in power but also of those at the bottom of the power hierarchy. Societies in which power tends to be distributed unequally can remain so because this situation satisfies the psychological need for dependence of the people without power. We could also say that societies and organizations will be led as autocratically as their members will permit. The autocracy exists just as much in the members as in the leaders: the value systems of the two groups are usually complementary.

In Figure 8.2 Power Distance is plotted horizontally and Individualism-Collectivism vertically. The Philippines, Venezuela, India, and others show large Power Distance index scores, but also France and Belgium score fairly high. Denmark, Israel, and Austria score low. We see that there is a global relationship between Power Distance and Collectivism: Collectivist countries always show large Power Distances, but Individualist countries do not always show small Power Distances. The Latin European countries – France, Belgium, Italy, and Spain, plus marginally South Africa – show a combination of large Power Distances plus Individualism. The other wealthy Western countries all combine smaller Power Distance with Individualism. All poor countries are Collectivist with larger Power Distances.

Uncertainty Avoidance

The third dimension is labeled 'Uncertainty Avoidance'. The fundamental issue involved here is how society deals with the fact that time runs only one way; that is, we are all caught in the reality of past, present and future, and we have to live with uncertainty because the future is unknown and always will be. Some societies socialize their members into accepting this uncertainty and not becoming upset by it. People in such societies will tend to accept each day as it comes. They will take risks rather easily. They will not work as hard. They will be relatively tolerant of behavior and opinions different from their own because they do not feel threatened by them. Such societies can be called 'weak Uncertainty Avoidance' societies;

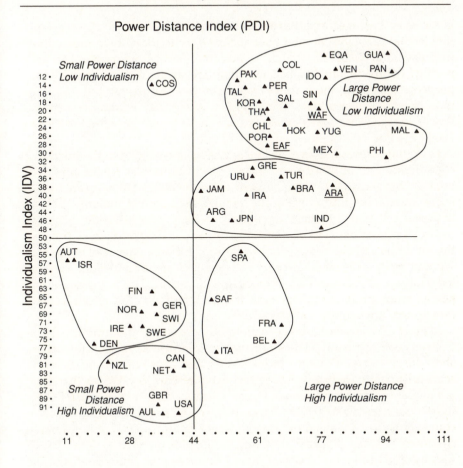

Figure 8.2 The position of the 50 countries on the Power Distance and Individualism scales

they are societies in which people have a natural tendency to feel relatively secure.

Other societies socialize their people into trying to beat the future. Because the future remains essentially unpredictable, in those societies there will be a higher level of anxiety in people, which becomes manifest in greater nervousness, emotionality, and aggressiveness. Such societies, called 'strong Uncertainty Avoidance' societies, also have institutions that try to create security and avoid risk. We can create security in three ways. One is technology, in the broadest sense of the word. Through technology we protect ourselves from the risks of nature and war. We build houses, dikes, power stations, and ICBMs which are meant to give us a feeling of security. The second way of creating security is law, again in the broadest sense of the word. Through laws and all kinds of formal rules

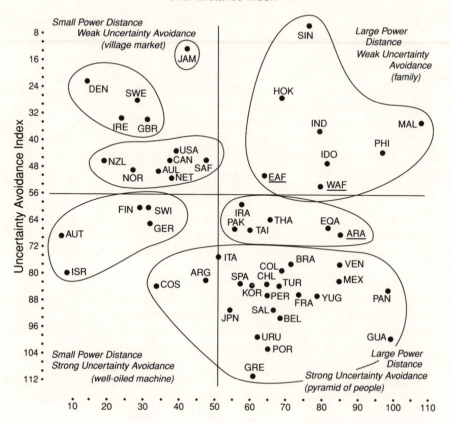

Figure 8.3 The position of the 50 countries on the Power Distance and Uncertainty Avoidance scales

and institutions, we protect ourselves from the unpredictability of human behavior. The proliferation of laws and rules implies an intolerance of deviant behaviours and opinions. Where laws cannot be made because the subject is too fuzzy, we can create a feeling of security by the nomination of experts. Experts are people whose word we accept as a kind of law because we assume them to be beyond uncertainty. The third way of creating a feeling of security is religion, once more in the broadest sense of the word. This sense includes secular religions and ideologies, such as Marxism, dogmatic capitalism, or movements that preach an escape into meditation. Even science is included. All human societies have their religions in some way or another. All religions, in some way, make uncertainty tolerable, because they all contain a message that is beyond uncertainty, that helps us to accept the uncertainty of today because we interpret experiences in terms of something bigger and more powerful that transcends personal reality. In strongly Uncertainty Avoiding societies we find religions which claim absolute truth and which do not tolerate other religions. We also find in such societies a scientific tradition looking for ultimate, absolute truths, as opposed to a more relativist, empiricist tradition in the weak Uncertainty Avoidance societies.

The Uncertainty Avoidance dimension, thus, implies a number of things, from aggressiveness to a need for absolute truth, that we do not usually consider as belonging together. They appear to belong together in the logic of culture patterns, but this logic differs from our own daily logic. Without research we would not have found that, on the level of societies, these things go together.

Figure 8.3 plots the Uncertainty Avoidance index for fifty countries along the vertical axis, against the Power Distance index on the horizontal axis. We find several clusters of countries. There is a large cluster of countries with strong Uncertainty Avoidance and large Power Distance. They are: all the Latin countries, both Latin European and Latin American; Mediterranean countries, such as, Yugoslavia, Greece, and Turkey; and Japan plus Korea.

The Asian countries are found in two clusters with large Power Distance and medium to weak Uncertainty Avoidance. Then we find a cluster of German-speaking countries, including Israel and marginally Finland, combining small Power Distance with medium to strong Uncertainty Avoidance.

Both the small Power Distance and weak Uncertainty Avoidance are found in Denmark, Sweden, Great Britain, and Ireland, while the Netherlands, USA, Norway, and the other Anglo countries are in the middle.

Masculinity versus Femininity

The fourth dimension is labeled 'Masculinity versus Femininity'. The fundamental issue involved is the division of roles between the sexes in society. All societies have to deal with the basic fact that one half of mankind is female and the other male. The only activities that are strictly determined by the sex of a person are those related to procreation. Men cannot have babies. Human societies, however, through the ages and around the globe, have also associated other roles to men only, or to women only. This is called social, rather than biological, sex role division.

All social role divisions are more or less arbitrary, and what is seen as a typical task for men or for women can vary from one society to the other. We can classify societies on whether they try to minimize or to maximize the social sex role division. Some societies allow both men and women to take many different roles. Others make a sharp division between what men should do and what women should do. In this latter case, the distribution is always such that men take the more assertive and dominant roles and women the more service-oriented and caring roles. I have called those societies with a maximized social sex role division 'Masculine' and those with a relatively small social sex role division 'Feminine'. In Masculine societies, the traditional masculine social values permeate the whole society – even the way of thinking of the women. These values include the importance of showing off, of performing, of achieving something visible, of making money, of 'big is beautiful'. In more Feminine societies, the dominant values – for both men and women – are those more traditionally associated with the feminine role: not showing off, putting relationships with people before money, minding the quality of life and the preservation of the environment, helping others, in particular the weak, and 'small is beautiful'. In a Masculine society, the public hero is the successful achiever, the superman. In a more Feminine society, the public sympathy goes to the anti-hero, the underdog. Individual brilliance in a Feminine society is suspect.

Following the procedure used for the other dimensions, each of the fifty countries was given an index score on the Masculinity–Femininity scale: a high score means a more Masculine, a low score a more Feminine country. Figure 8.4 plots the Masculinity index score horizontally and the Uncertainty Avoidance index again vertically. The most Masculine country is Japan; also quite Masculine are the German-speaking countries: Germany, Austria, and Switzerland. Moderately Masculine are a number of Latin countries, such as Venezuela, Mexico, and Italy; also the entire cluster of Anglo countries including some of their former colonies: India and the Philippines.

On the far end towards the Feminine side we find the four Nordic countries and the Netherlands. Some Latin and Mediterranean countries like Yugoslavia, Chile, Portugal, Spain, and France are moderately Feminine.

SOME CONSEQUENCES FOR MANAGEMENT THEORY AND PRACTICE

The naive assumption that management is the same or is becoming the same around the world is not tenable in view of these demonstrated differences in national cultures. Consider a few of the ideas about management which have been popularized in the Western literature in the past fifteen years: in particular, about leadership, about models of organization, and about motivation. These theories were almost without exception made in the USA; in fact, the post-Second-World-War management literature is entirely US dominated. This reflects the economic importance of the USA during this period, but culturally the USA is just one country among all others, with its particular configuration of cultural values which differs from that of most other countries.

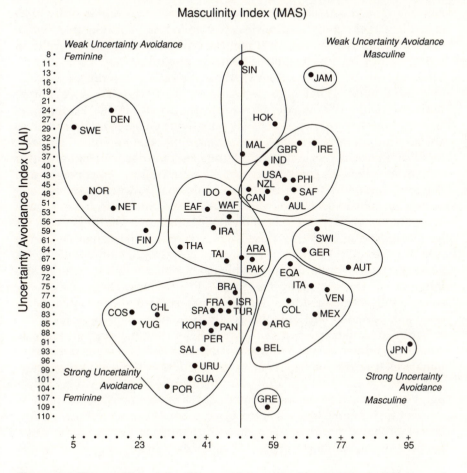

Figure 8.4 The position of the 50 countries on the Uncertainty Avoidance and Masculinity scales

Leadership

The most relevant dimensions for leadership are Individualism and Power Distance. Let us look at Figure 8.2 again. We find the USA in an extreme position on the Individualism scale (50 out of 50) and just below average on the Power Distance scale (16 out of 50). What does the high Individualism score mean? US leadership theories are about leading individuals based on the presumed needs of individuals who seek their ultimate self-interest. For example, the word 'duty', which implies obligations towards others or towards society, does not appear at all in the US leadership theories.

Leadership in a Collectivist society – basically any Third World country – is a group phenomenon. A working group which is not the same as the natural ingroup will have to be made into another ingroup in order to be effective. People in these countries are able to bring considerable loyalty to their job, providing they feel that the employer returns the loyalty in the form of protection, just like their natural ingroup does.

Let us now look at the Power Distance dimension in terms of participative leadership. What does participative leadership US style mean? Individual subordinates are allowed to participate in the leader's decisions; it is the leader who keeps the initiative. Management prerogatives are very important in the USA. Let us remember that on Power Distance, the USA is more or less in the middle zone. In countries with higher Power Distances – such as many Third World countries, but also France and Belgium – individual subordinates as a rule do not want to participate. It is part of their expectations that leaders lead automatically, and such subordinates will, in fact, by their own behavior make it difficult for leaders to lead in any other way. There is very little participative leadership in France and Belgium. If the society is at the same time Collectivist, however, there will be ways by which subordinates in a group can still influence the leader. This applies to all Asian countries. Let us take some countries on the other side, however: Denmark, Sweden, or Israel. In this case, subordinates will not necessarily wait until their boss takes the initiative to let them participate. They will, for example, support forms of employee codetermination in which either individuals or groups can take initiatives towards management. In these cultures there are no management prerogatives that are automatically accepted; anything a boss does may be challenged by the subordinates. Management privileges in particular are much more easily accepted in USA than in some of the very low Power Distance countries. A similar difference is found in the ratios between management compensation and subordinate compensation.

Organization

In organizations the decisive dimensions of culture are Power Distance and Uncertainty Avoidance. Organizations are devices to distribute power, and they also serve to avoid uncertainty, to make things predictable. So let us look at Figure 8.3 again. My former colleague, Professor James Stevens from *INSEAD*, once gave the same description of an organizational problem to separate groups of French, West German, and British management students. The problem described a conflict between two departments. The students were asked to determine what was wrong and what should be done to resolve the problem. The French in majority referred the problem to the next higher authority level. The Germans suggested the setting of rules to resolve such problems in the future. The British wanted to improve communications between the two department heads, perhaps by some kind of human relations training. My colleague concluded that the dominant underlying model of an organization for the French was a pyramid, a hierarchical structure held together by the unity of command (larger Power Distance) as well as by rules (strong Uncertainty Avoidance). The model for the Germans was a well-oiled machine; the exercise of personal command was largely unnecessary because the rules settled everything (strong Uncertainty Avoidance, but smaller Power Distance). The model for the British was a village market; no decisive hierarchy, flexible rules, and a resolution of problems by negotiating (small Power Distance and weak Uncertainty Avoidance). These models left one corner in the diagram of Figure 8.3 unexplained, but a discussion with an Indian colleague led me to believe that the underlying model of an organization for the Indians is the family: undisputed personal authority of the father-leader but few formal rules (large Power Distance and weak Uncertainty Avoidance). This should also apply in the Chinese culture city-states of Hong Kong and Singapore (see Figure 8.3).

The USA is close to the center of Figure 8.3 and so are the Netherlands and Switzerland. This may explain something of the success of US, Dutch, and Swiss multinationals in operating a variety of cultures. In the US literature and practice, all four models of organization – the pyramid, the well-oiled machine, the village market, and the family – can be found, but none of them can be considered dominant.

Motivation

The theories of motivation (what makes people act) and the practices of motivating people can both be related to the Individualism–Collectivism dimension. In the USA, the highest motivation is supposed to stem from the individuals' need to fulfill their obligations towards themselves. We find terms like 'self-actualization' and 'self-respect' on the top of the list of motivators. In a more Collectivist society, however, people will try primarily to fulfill their obligations towards their ingroup. This may be their family, but their collective loyalty may also be directed towards some larger unit: their enterprise, or their country. Such people do not seek self-actualization or self-respect, but they primarily seek 'face' in their relationships with ingroup members. The importance of face as a motivator does not appear in the US motivation literature at all. The distinction between 'face' cultures and 'self-respect' cultures is similar to the distinction between 'shame' and 'guilt' cultures identified by the anthropologist Ruth Benedict (1974).

Other dimensions relevant to motivation are Uncertainty Avoidance and Masculinity–Femininity. Let us look at Figure 8.4 again. The dominant theme of the US literature of the past twenty years is that people are basically motivated by a desire to achieve something. We should, therefore, allow our people to achieve: give them challenge, and enrich their jobs if they do not contain any challenge. The idea of 'achievement' and 'challenge,' US style, implies two things: a willingness to take some risks (weak Uncertainty Avoidance) and a need to perform, to assert oneself (Masculinity). It is therefore no wonder that in Figure 8.4 we find the USA in the weak Uncertainty Avoidance, Masculine corner. It shares this position with the other Anglo countries. Let us take the case of some other countries, however: Japan or Germany. These are also Masculine countries but with stronger Uncertainty Avoidance. This means that in these countries there is less willingness to take risks: security is a powerful motivator. People are very willing to perform if they are offered security in exchange. Interestingly, these security seeking countries seems to have been doing better economically in the past twenty years than the risk-takers; but the management theories that tell us that risk-taking is a good thing were made in the USA or Great Britain, not in Japan or Germany.

If we go to the other corner of Figure 8.4, we find the Netherlands and the Nordic countries combining weak Uncertainty Avoidance with a more Feminine value system. Here, the maintenance of good interpersonal relations is a strong motivator, and people frown at competition for performance. In these countries we meet a powerful interpersonal motivation which is missing in the US theories. There is striking difference in the forms of 'humanization of work' proposed in the USA and in Sweden: a stress in the USA on creating possibilities for individual performance, but a stress in Sweden on creating possibilities for interpersonal solidarity. In the fourth corner of Figure 8.4 we find both security and interpersonal motivation; Yugoslav worker self-management contains both elements. We are far away here from the motivation to achieve according to the US style.

CONCLUSION: THE CULTURAL RELATIVITY OF MANAGEMENT AND ORGANIZATION PRACTICES AND THEORIES

Both management practitioners and management theorists over the past eighty years have been blind to the extent to which activities like 'management' and 'organization' are culturally dependent. They are culturally dependent because managing and organizing do not consist of making or moving tangible objects, but of manipulating symbols which have meaning to the people who are managed or organized. Because the meaning which we associate with symbols is heavily affected by what we have learned in our family, in our school, in our work environment, and in our society, management and organization are penetrated with culture from the beginning to the end. Practice is usually wiser than theory, and if we see what effective organizations in different cultures have done, we recognize that their leaders did adapt foreign management ideas to local cultural conditions. This happened extremely effectively in Japan, where mainly US management theories were taken over but in an adapted form. This adaptation led to entirely new forms of practice which in the Japanese case were highly successful. An example is the Quality Control Circle, originally based on US impulses but adapted to the Japanese uncertainty-avoiding, semicollectivist environment. The Quality Control Circle has been so effective in Japan that now the Americans are bringing it back to the USA, but it is doubtful whether most of its present US protagonists realize the role that Japanese educational and social conditions play in the ability of Japanese workers to function effectively in a Quality Control Circle.

Not all other countries have been as fortunate as Japan in that a successful adaptation of American management theories and practices could take place. In Europe, but even more often in Third World countries, foreign management methods and ideas were indiscriminately imported as part of 'technology transfer'. The evident failure of much of the international development assistance of the 1960s and 1970s is at least partly due to this lack of cultural sensitivity in the transfer of management ideas. It has caused enormous economic losses and human suffering. Free market capitalism as practised in the USA, for example, is an idea which is deeply rooted historically and culturally in Individualism. 'Everybody for himself' is supposed to lead to the highest common good, according to Adam Smith (1970: 1776). If this idea is forced upon a traditionally Collectivist society, it means that work organizations will be created which do not offer to employees the protection which they expect to get in exchange for their loyalty. The system itself in such a society breeds disloyal, irresponsible employees. Japan has not taken over this aspect of capitalism and has maintained a much higher level of protection of employees by their organization. Many US managers and politicians have great problems with recognizing that their type of capitalism is culturally unsuitable for a more Collectivist society. It is for good cultural reasons that various forms of state capitalism or state socialism are tried in Third World countries.

Most present-day management theories are 'ethnocentric', that is, they take the cultural environment of the theorist for granted. What we need is more cultural sensitivity in management theories; we could call the result 'organizational anthropology' or 'management anthropology'. It is unlikely to be the product of one single country's intellectual effort; it needs by definition a synergy between ideas from different sources. The fact that no single country now enjoys a degree of economic dominance as the USA once did will certainly help: economic power is all too often related to intellectual influence. In a world in which economic power is more widely spread, we can more easily hope to recognize truth coming from many sources. In this process, the contribution of Japanese and Chinese scholars, for example, will be vital, because they represent sources of practical wisdom and ideas which complement practices and ideas born in Europe and the USA.

The convergence of management will never come. What we can bring about is an understanding of how the culture in which we grew up and which is dear to us affects our thinking differently from other peoples' thinking, and what this means for the transfer of management practices and theories. What this can also lead to is a better ability to manage intercultural negotiations and multicultural organizations like the United Nations, which are essential for the common survival of us all.

REFERENCES

Benedict, Ruth. *The Chrysanthemum and the Sword: Patterns of Japanese Culture*. New York, NY: New American Library, 1974 (1946), p. 222.
Hofstede, Geert. *Culture's Consequences: International Differences in Work-Related Values*. Beverly Hills/London: SAGE Publications, 1980.
—— 'Dimensions of National Cultures in Fifty Countries and Three Regions.' In *Expiscations in Cross-Cultural Psychology*, edited by J. Deregowski, S. Dziurawiec, and R. C. Annis. Lisse, Netherlands: Swets and Zeitlinger, 1983.
Smith, Adam. *The Wealth of Nations*. Harmondsworth, UK. Penguin, 1970 (1776).

Chapter 9

Developing a 'European' model of human resource management

Chris Brewster

Emphasis will be placed, in the analysis presented below, on a contrast between the situation in the United States of America and in Europe which, it will be argued, has led to different approaches to the notion of human resource management and, hence, to the need for a theory of HRM which encompasses these variations. By its nature, the argument will involve a considerable degree of generalization: conflating differences within the USA and, more tendentiously, within Europe. The analysis is built on the assumption, identified by another commentator on 'the conditions and circumstances within Western Europe', that, although there are differences in HRM in each country, taken as a whole 'they stand out as being distinct from other economic areas like the USA, USSR or Japan' (Remer 1986). The argument is also strained by a lack of hard data available on representative practices in the USA. Indeed, in this area there is a real danger of falling into the mistake identified, more generally, by Legge (1989), of comparing empirical evidence from Europe with normative statements of what should be from the USA. Much of the US literature can be read as a prescriptive indictment of what is not happening rather than a description of what exists. Finally, in this brief list of caveats before the argument, it is worth repeating that the core elements abstracted from the 'American' texts are, precisely, an abstraction. No conception of HRM in the USA or among its adherents in Europe mirrors this version exactly and many have other perspectives. Nevertheless, it is clear that the fundamental core of the HRM concept noted here – autonomy – underlies nearly all the leading texts.

ORGANIZATIONAL AUTONOMY

Central to the concept of HRM as currently propounded is the notion of organizational independence and autonomy. Defining and prescribing HRM strategies makes sense only if the organizations concerned are free to develop their own strategies. The fact that US views of HRM may be culture-bound, particularly in this stress on organizational autonomy, has been recognized by North American authors (Adler and Jelinek 1986). And in the UK Guest (1990) has argued that this view of freedom and autonomy in HRM is peculiar to the USA – related to the US view of their country as the land of opportunity in which any individual, through hard work or self-improvement can be a success, with the ideal model of the 'rugged individualist' or self-reliant small businessman and a vision of the 'frontier mentality'. We can see these ideals reflected in the comparatively low levels of support, subsidy and control provided, or at least commonly understood to be acceptable, from the state. We can see them in the 'private enterprise' culture of the USA. We can see them in the concept of 'the right to manage' and in the antagonism of management towards trade unions.

These factors are untypical of most European countries.[1] Certainly they have some limited acceptability in Great Britain: but each point remains the focus of considerable controversy in Britain. In countries such as Germany and Sweden, by contrast, these assumptions would be held by only a small minority of the population.

In the European system organizations are less autonomous. Their autonomy is constrained at a national level, by culture and legislation; at the organizational level, by patterns of ownership; and, at the HRM level, by trade union involvement and consultative arrangements.

CULTURE AND LEGISLATION

At the most general level the empirical data on national cultural differences, though limited, point clearly to the uniqueness of the USA. 'The US', one of the leading researchers in the field writes, 'is quite untypical of the world as a whole' (Trompenaars 1985). The US culture is more individualistic and more achievement-orientated than most other countries (Hofstede 1980).

These national cultural differences are reflected in legislation. One German authority, Pieper, pointed out that 'the major difference between HRM in the US and Western Europe is the degree to which [HRM] is influenced and determined by state regulations. Companies have a narrower scope of choice in regard to personnel management than in the US' (Pieper 1990: 8).[2] Expanding on this, Pieper included the greater regulation of recruitment and dismissal, the formalization of educational certification and the quasi-legal characteristics of the industrial relations framework in comparison to the USA. This catalogue clearly shows its origins in the German system. Including other European countries it is possible to add legislative requirements on pay, on health and safety, on the working environment and hours of work; and to supplement those with legislation on forms of employment contract, rights to trade union representation, requirements to establish and operate consultation or codetermination arrangements – and a plethora of other legal requirements.

Furthermore, Europe is unique in the world in having twelve of its countries at present (and more soon) committed to a supranational level of legislation on a considerable range of aspects of the employer/employee relationship. The European Community, particularly through the steps associated with its Social Action Programme, is having an increasing legislative influence on HRM (Brewster and Teague 1989; Brewster and Lockhart 1992).

PATTERNS OF OWNERSHIP

State involvement in HRM is not limited to the legislative role. In broad terms, in Europe as compared to the USA the state has a higher involvement in underlying social security provision, a more directly interventionist role in the economy, provides far more personnel and industrial relations services and is a more extensive employer in its own right by virtue of a more extensive government-owned sector.

Patterns of ownership in the private sector also vary from one side of the Atlantic to the other. Although public ownership has decreased to some extent in many European countries in recent years it is still far more widespread than in the USA. Nor should it be assumed that ownership in the private sector implies the same thing. In Germany, for example, most major companies are owned largely by a tight network of a small number of substantial banks. Their interlocking shareholdings and close involvement in the management of these corporations means less pressure to produce short-term profits and a positive disincentive to drive competitors out of the market-place (Randlesome 1993).

TRADE UNION REPRESENTATION

These outside constraints on organizational autonomy are supported by a variety of internal constraints: particularly in the form of employee representation. It has been pointed out (Beaumont 1991a) that studies of HRM in the USA have tended to take place in the non-union sector. A constant thread in research programmes in the USA has been the link between HRM practices and non-unionism (see, for example, Kochan *et al.* 1984; Kochan *et al.* 1986). 'In the US a number of . . . academics have argued that HRM [the concept and the practice] is anti-union and anti-collective bargaining' (Beaumont 1991b: 300).

The definition, meaning and reliability of union membership figures vary across countries (Walsh 1985; Blanchflower and Freeman 1990). However, it is quite clear that, in general, the European countries are more heavily unionized than the United States. Some, such as Germany, France and the Benelux countries, have legislation requiring employers over a certain size to recognize unions for consultative purposes. In France,

Greece and Portugal employers have to negotiate with a union if it can show that it has any members in the workplace.

Europe is a highly unionized continent (OECD 1991). Trade union membership and influence varies considerably by country, of course, but is always significant. Sweden has union membership of 85 per cent of the working population, the UK around 40 per cent and even in the less unionized countries such as France union membership at 12 per cent remains double that in the USA. In many European countries union recognition for collective bargaining purposes is required by law wherever there are trade unions and even in the UK, where there is no legal mechanism for enforcing recognition, there are still 72 per cent of organizations with more than 200 employees recognizing the trade unions (Gunnigle *et al.* 1993).

Trade unionism remains widespread and important in Europe, with an importance that current EC approaches will certainly not diminish, and may well enhance. Furthermore, in most European countries most of the union functions in such areas as pay bargaining, for example, are exercised at industrial or national level, outside the direct involvement of organizational managers (Hegewisch 1991; Gunnigle *et al.* 1993).

EMPLOYEE INVOLVEMENT

Beyond the immediate issue of trade union membership lies the European practice of employee involvement. In countries such as France and Germany the establishment of workers' councils is required by law.

In Germany, Italy and Portugal employers have to deal with workplace (and often company-wide) works councils wherever the employees request it. In Greece the unions can insist on the establishment of a works council only where the organization is larger than twenty employees; there have to be thirty-five or more employees in the Netherlands; fifty or more in Spain and France and 100 in Belgium. These various forms of works council have differing degrees of power, but most would shock American managers brought up on the theories of 'management's right to manage'. In Germany and the Netherlands, for example, employee representatives can resort to the courts to prevent or to delay managerial decisions in areas (recruitment, termination, changing working practices) which in the USA would be areas for almost unfettered managerial prerogative.

Beyond the workplace, legislation in the Netherlands, Denmark and, most famously, Germany requires organizations to have two-tier management boards, with employees having the right to be represented on the more senior supervisory board. Employee representation can, depending on country, size and sector, range up to 50 per cent of the board.

These arrangements give considerable (legally backed) power to the employee representatives and unlike the American position, for example, they tend to supplement rather than supplant the union position. In relatively highly unionized countries it is unsurprising that many of the representatives of the workforce are, in practice, trade union officials. In Germany, as one instance, the majority of them are union representatives.

At the supranational, European Communities level it is clear that the EC is committed to maintaining the role of the 'social partners' as it calls them: employers and trade unions. In particular, the latest proposals from the European Commission on the subject of employee involvement offer a series of options for the member states. These are, in effect, an attempt to draw on the best practice available in all the Community countries rather than to impose the system which exists in one state on the others.

ALTERNATIVE APPROACHES TO HRM

So far as this article has argued that the concept (or perhaps bundle of concepts) of HRM that have come to Europeans from the USA have as a key component the notion of organizational autonomy. It has also argued that such autonomy looks very different from this side of the Atlantic. This final section attempts to pull together these differing threads; to argue that, despite differences within Europe, a European approach to HRM is discernible; and to use that to build on available theories to propose a more internationally applicable model of HRM.

Such an ambitious programme would be more daunting if much of the groundwork had not already been laid. Europeans are increasingly critical of the American model. Looking at the UK, Guest sees 'signs that . . . the American model is losing its appeal as attention focuses to a greater extent on developments in Europe' (Guest 1990: 377) and the same author is elsewhere sceptical of the feasibility of transferring the American model to Britain. However, the elements of a model that could serve as the basis for comparative international research are not made explicit.

The inapplicability of American models in Europe has also been noted in Germany. 'An international comparison of HR practices clearly indicates that the basic functions of HR management are given different weights in different countries and that they are carried out differently' (Gaugler 1988: 26). Another German, Pieper, surveying European personnel management similarly concludes that 'a single universal model of HRM does not exist' (1990: 11). Critiques of any simplistic attempts to 'universalize' the American models have also come from France (see, for example, Bournois, 1991a, 1991b).

It is valuable to point out weaknesses in theory but it is not sufficient. There is a need to move beyond that to proposing at least tentatively, improvements to the models. This is more important in the light of two very different developments: the increasing interest in the linkage between HRM and economic success; and the drive towards Europeanization.

THE HRM–ECONOMIC SUCCESS EQUATION

It is frequently argued that there is a direct correlation between strategic HRM and economic success. Porter (1985) believed that HRM can help a firm obtain competitive advantage. Schuler and Macmillan (1984: 242) make a similar point, that 'effectively managing human resources' gives benefits which 'include greater profitability'. Other authors make the point explicitly that 'firms that engage in a strategy formulation process that systematically and reciprocally considers human resources and competitive strategy will perform better . . . over the long term' (Lengnick-Hall and Lengnick-Hall 1988: 468). HRM has even been propounded as 'the only truly important determinant of success' (Beyer, 1991: 1). Salaman(1991) comments 'this is an obvious but important point'. Pieper builds on this to argue that 'since HRM is seen as a strategic factor strongly influencing the economic success of a single company one can argue that it is also a strategic factor for the success of an entire nation' (1990: 4).

The problem both with the obvious point and the logical extension to national success is that there is a marked dearth of evidence to support them. Indeed, at the most visible level, the national level, there is some evidence that on the most generalized assumptions taken here the evidence points in the opposite direction: countries with less evidence of HRM, those nations who allow least autonomy to their managements (with most legal regulations and trade union influence), tend to have been most successful in recent years. National differences in human resource management and in practices linked frequently with the American views of good HRM practice have no correlation with national differences in economic performance.

Part of the answer to this problem is undoubtedly methodological, based around the impossibility of finding nations (or organizations) which are equal in all substantial areas except HRM strategies. It seems unlikely, however, that better methodology would resolve the issue. This raises two possibilities: the first is that the link with economic success, despite its apparent logic, is a fallacy. The second, more promisingly, is that current conceptions of HRM are inadequate. This would go some way towards explaining the lack of correlation of a narrowly conceived view of organizational HRM strategies with economic success – by failing to include the external constraints the 'autonomous' HRM models ignore important factors.

It has been recognized from the earliest discussions of personnel administration and management that practice here has to be related to directly impinging environmental factors – such as labour markets and state legislation. Literature, perhaps, lagged rather behind practice. A paper at the end of the 1960s on the then dominant 'human relations' approach argued that the human relations literature of the immediate postwar years and the succeeding organization development and change literature ignored all external, economic variables (Strauss 1968). The same critique could well be applied to much of the more prescriptive HRM literature. This could be shown as in Figure 9.1. (The dotted line represents the situation where organizations can develop practices in HR without having any HRM policy).

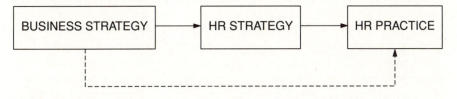

Figure 9.1 Popular prescriptive model of HRM

From the early 1980s this debate has been widened. Several authors in that period (see, for example, Nkomo 1980; Tichy *et al*. 1982; Fombrun 1982; Fombrun *et al*. 1984) argued that human resource management needed to follow the corporate strategy literature in acknowledging, and positioning itself in line with environmental influences. Indeed, Beaumont commented that, whatever the other failings of the latest writing on HRM, it 'no longer ignores external, economic variables' (Beaumont 1991a). This was, for example, included in the 'perspective' proposed by Lengnick-Hall and Lengnick-Hall where 'competitive strategy' and 'HR strategy' are still in separate boxes (but boxes which are connected or, in their terms, 'mesh') and which are both impacted on by external issues: for HR these issues are labour market, skills and values, culture and economic conditions. Only the last overlaps with issues for competitive strategy (Lengnick-Hall and Lengnick-Hall, 1988: 467). This and similar suggestions from other American authors are simplified into the position represented in Figure 9.2.

These approaches have been criticized in the USA. In the article just quoted on human relations, Strauss also attacked contemporary approaches as ignoring (or being anti) trade unions, and being based on a unitary view of organizations (Strauss 1968). The same criticisms have been made about theories of HRM. It is in response to this that Beer *et al*. supplemented the Figure 9.2 diagram with the notion of purality of interests by including (potentially conflicting) 'stakeholder interests' in their classic 'map of the HRM territory' (Beer *et al*. 1984: 16). Interestingly, however, much of their succeeding discussion reflects a unitarist concept of the organization, and in fact moves into a clearly normative and prescriptive path.

These models have been subject to significant criticism in Europe. Poole (1990) wishes to add to the Beer *et al*. map: 'globalization' (the practice of multinational corporations, including, centrally, the transfer of executives

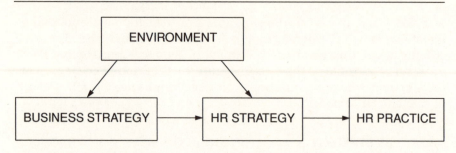

Figure 9.2 American environmental models of HRM

between countries (Brewster 1991); power; and strategic choice. Hendry and Pettigrew (1990) similarly start from the Beer *et al.* model and wish to amplify it to categorize the factors influencing strategic decision-making in HRM, under the headings of 'economic', 'technical', and 'socio-political'. Under 'economic' they include ownership and control, organizational size and structure, the growth path of an organization, industry structure and markets. Under 'technical' they refer to skill, work organization and labour force requirements of technologies. 'Socio-political' encompasses the institutional framework, particularly the national education and training system. The environmental factors have been central to discussions of this issue in other European countries too (see, for example, Bournois (1991b) in France; Remer (1986) and Pieper (1990) in Germany).

Whether these lists of environmental issues are external or are an intrinsic aspect of the HRM concept may be more than a matter of semantics. It is noteworthy that it is in general the American authors who have seen it as external and the European authors who have wanted to include these areas within the concept. Going down the route of seeing these issues as external has led to the often very detailed, case-study based and sophisticated attempts to create a 'contingency' approach to HRM. Thus Schuler (1989), a leading figure in this movement, has attempted to link HRM strategies to life-cycle models (as did Fombrun and Tichy 1983; and Kochan and Barocci 1985) and to Porter's models (1985) for achieving competitive advantage in different industry conditions (Schuler and Jackson 1987; Schuler, 1989). Other authors have argued that HRM should be contingent upon markets (Baird *et al.* 1983; Dertouzos *et al.* 1989) and upon groupings within organizational levels (Lorange and Murphy 1984). The examples could be multiplied (see also Macmillan and Schuler 1985, where the reciprocity of HR and strategy is clearly stated; Lengnick-Hall and Lengnick-Hall 1988; Schuler and Macmillan 1984; Schuler 1991).

This contingent determinism has been adopted by some authors in Europe (Staffelback 1986; Ackermann 1986; Besseyre des Horts 1987, 1988). However, contingency theory has come under attack in the corporate strategy literature (originated by Child 1976) and followed through by such authorities as Porter (1980, 1985) – see the recent debate on 'organizational economics' led by Donaldson in the *Academy of Management Review* (1990). A major critique is that it allows little role for managerial action other than that of identifying the current position and matching strategy to it. Many of the 'contingency' school of HRM writers fall into a form of strategy determinism in which management's task is essentially no more than to establish the 'fit' of HRM to a given – usually corporate strategy driven – scenario. Such attempts have been sharply criticized by Conrad and Pieper (1990); by Staehle (1988), who attacks the American literature accessible in Germany for its derivative approach to personnel management, which is seen as dependent upon corporate strategy, rather than contributory to it; and by Poole (1990: 5): 'strategic choices imply discretion over decision-making (i.e. no situational or environmental determinism)'.

THE EUROPEANIZATION OF THEORY

There is a general trend on theorizing on the eastern side of the North Atlantic towards arguing that an over-ready acceptance of American models has gone beyond its provable value and that the time is now ripe for distinguishing specifically European approaches. It is surely no co-incidence that this coincides with the revitalization of the European Community and Europe's economic success compared to the USA.

Thurley and Wirdenius (1991), for example, were concerned with the development of a functional model of management, particularly in the context of international business activities, rather than with HRM in particular or the comparative analysis of different national models of HRM. But they are relevant here because they try to distil what is particular to Europe rather than the USA or Japan. They focus on the cultural context of management, and, in the face of the predominance of American and Japanese conceptions of management, the need 'now to distinguish "European Management" as a possible alternative approach' (ibid.: 1228). They see this as necessary to reflect the different cultural values and legal institutional practices that are dominant in Europe. Such a European approach has the following characteristics:

> European Management
>> is emerging, and cannot be said to exist except in limited circumstances;
>> is broadly linked to the idea of European integration, which is continuously expanding further into different countries (i.e. the 12);
>> reflects key values such as pluralism, tolerance, etc., but is not consciously developed from these values;
>> is associated with a balanced stakeholder philosophy and the concept of Social Partners.
>
> (Thurley and Wirdenius 1991: 128)

There has been criticism of the importation of American theory else-where too (Cox and Cooper 1985). In the context of HRM specifically, European authors have argued that 'we are in culturally different contexts' and 'Rather than copy solutions which result from other cultural tradi-tions, we should consider the state of mind that presided in the search for responses adapted to the culture' (Albert 1989: 75; translations in Brewster and Bournois 1991).

A 'EUROPEAN MODEL'?

Our evidence here suggests two paradoxical trends run through HRM in Europe. First, there are clear country differences which can be understood and explained in the context of each national culture and its manifestations in history, law, institutions and trade union and employing organization structures; or in terms of regional clusters within Europe (Filella 1991). Second, there is an identifiable difference between the way in which HRM is conducted in Europe and the situation in the USA: a difference which allows us to speak of a European form of HRM and to question the appropriateness of the American concept of HRM in this other continent. (Of course, by implication, there may also be questions about the relevance of the US form of the concept in other continents.)

What is needed is a model of HRM that re-emphasizes the influence of such factors as culture, ownership structures, the role of the state and trade union organization. Clearly, the European evidence suggests that manage-ments can see the unions, for example, as social partners with a positive role to play in human resource management; and the manifest success of many European firms which adopt that approach shows the explicit or implicit anti-unionism of many American views to be culture bound.

Attempting to encompass these areas within a concept of HRM takes it back towards the industrial relations system approach first outlined by Dunlop (1958) in which the state and its agencies, employers and their associations and employees and their representative bodies formed the constituent elements.

Until recently a call to re-establish the primacy of the wider industrial relations concept may have been seen as a nostalgic attempt to deny the replacement of an older theory by a new one. However, the recent publication by Kochan *et al.* (1986) has breathed new life into the older theory. One weakness of a very important book is its lack of a comparative, international framework. The evidence presented here is that one element of the Kochan *et al.* argument – that governmental, market and labour management relations are interwoven – would have been all the stronger if they had drawn international comparisons.

It is contended here that HRM theory needs to adopt the wider perspective of the model proposed by Kochan *et al.*, and a more comprehensive view of the actors in the system, if it is to become a theory that stands the test of international application.

This article proposes a model of HRM (outlined in Figure 9.3) which places HR strategies firmly within, though not entirely absorbed by, the business strategy. The two-dimensional presentation does not show, but must be taken to include, an interaction between the two rather than one following from the other. The model also shows, in a simplistic form, that the business strategy, HR strategy and HR practice are located within an external environment of national culture, power systems, legislation, education, employee representation and all the other issues discussed above. The organization and its human resource strategies and practices in turn interact with and are part of that environment. The model places HR strategies in close interaction with the relevant organizational strategy and external environment in a way that is not unforeshadowed in much of the literature but is indicated simply and clearly here.

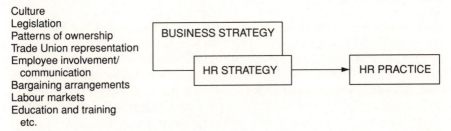

ENVIRONMENT

Culture
Legislation
Patterns of ownership
Trade Union representation
Employee involvement/
   communication
Bargaining arrangements
Labour markets
Education and training
   etc.

BUSINESS STRATEGY

HR STRATEGY

HR PRACTICE

Figure 9.3 International model of HRM

This different presentation of the HRM concept points towards a model which places HRM firmly within the national context, thus allowing fuller understanding of situations which differ from that existing in the USA. The advantages of this approach include a better fit of the model to the European scene and experience. This changes the debates in Europe from two angles. From the normative side, where commentators and consultants have criticized employing organizations for not adopting the 'American' model, this approach allows a change. Rather than searching for, and not finding, traditional HRM, and then criticizing employing organizations and their personnel specialists for not adopting these 'modern' approaches, the model enables the consultants to be more modest and employers to be less defensive. From the analytical side, where academics have found little evidence of HRM in practice and significant shortcomings in the concept as it has come across to us from the USA, the model enables analysts to move beyond discussions of whether HRM should be 'accepted' or 'rejected' to a more positive debate about the forms and styles of HRM.

By allowing for a greater input into HRM from the environment in which the organization is located this approach also enables the analysts to link HRM more clearly with some of the advantages in international competition which leading strategic theorists claim will accrue where organizations take greater account of personnel requirements, and so are more tolerant of ambiguity and challenge, in a position to take greater risks and more accepting of variability (Bartlett and Ghoshal 1989; Hedlund and Rolander 1990). Perhaps based partly on this reasoning the model provides a closer fit between HRM and national success. The fact that personnel aspects are brought into corporate strategy by culture, legislation, union involvement can be encompassed here, thus going a considerable way towards explaining why some countries, even including those with limited natural resources, that do not meet the traditional criteria of HRM are none the less among the most successful in the world. The link between positive HRM and economic success is restored.

COMPARING EUROPEAN AND US HRM

This article has focused upon outlining the challenge that the European perspective provides to at least many of the 'American' notions of HRM. Developing the concept to take account of the more limited autonomy (or greater support) of organizational managers which is evidenced in Europe, and including the external factors within a different presentation of the concept of HRM, has a value beyond the presentation of simple diagrams. Clearly, it needs refinement, but it does present a way forward. Without some adaptation to take account of the European (and perhaps other?) non-American situations, the HRM concept will continue to attract fundamental critiques, even in its most sophisticated form, for its failure to accept different degrees of managerial independence, different approaches to working with employee representatives and governmental involvement and, most damagingly, its inability to link HRM to economic performance. This paper, by attempting to clarify some of these fundamental bases of the concept, suggests one way forward.

The concepts, and their implications, can be summarized briefly in Figure 9.4 which abstracts (indeed perhaps caricatures) three approaches to the management of people. Column 1 indicates the traditional 'personnel management' approach still widespread within Europe – and possibly within the USA. Column 2 is an attempt to abstract the key features of the normative concept of HRM as it has reached Europe from the USA. Column 3 identifies what a 'European' view of HRM would look like. It can be seen that key features of this view are a combination of the practices of the two previous columns and a potential flexibility and tolerance of dual concerns.

The first row in each column identifies the preferred environment; the

	Personnel management	Prescribed human resource management	European human resource
Environment	Established legal framework	Deregulation	Established legal framework
Objectives	Social concern	Organizational objectives	Organizational objectives and social concern
	People as the organization	People as resource (internal or external)	People as key resource
Focus	Focus on systems formalization	Focus on cost/benefits autonomy	Focus on cost/benefits management and environment
Relationship with employees	Trade unions	Non-union	Union and non-union
Relationship with line managers	Specialist responsibility for systems	Specialists as support to line	Specialist/line liaison
Role of HR specialist	Intermediary/systems specialists	Labour costs/output specialists	Specialist managers: ambiguity tolerance flexibility

Figure 9.4 Three approaches to the management of people

second row, the objectives of people management; the third row, the focus of the personnel or human resource department activities. The first column indicates the established framework and the resultant drive towards formalization and systematization by personnel specialists, based on their view of the organization as consisting of the people within it – people who will be most effective if treated fairly. In contrast the second column indicates the normative view of HRM visible in much of the literature: governments should leave organizations and the labour market as free as possible and within that the HR department's job is to see people inside or outside the organization as resources which can be used to achieve corporate objectives. Echoes of the difference in approach in mainland Europe versus the UK throughout the 1980s may be detected here.

The fourth row addresses relationships with employees (union for personnel; 'non-union', or even anti-union, for HRM). Row five shows the different relationships with line managers, with personnel having responsibility for employee systems in the classic personnel model and HR serving the line in the prescribed HR model. The final row examines the role, or potential role, of the specialists.

Building on the arguments in this article, it is proposed that these simple approaches are, in practice, increasingly less adequate as explanations of what is happening. The HR challenge to personnel management has arisen partly as a way of expounding, or propounding, a new role for the personnel/HR department as the previous one is seen to be inappropriate to changing times. However, the evidence from this paper and from other data collected across Europe by the Price Waterhouse Cranfield project (Brewster and Holt Larsen 1992; Hegewisch and Brewster 1993; Brewster and Hegewisch 1994) is that HR is not developing as a straightforward opposite, or negative, of personnel management. What is happening in Europe at least is that, as the third column of Figure 9.4 indicates, there is a move towards the HRM concept but one which, within a clearly established external environment, accepts the duality of people management. Thus, objectives include both organizational requirements and a concern for people; the focus on both costs and benefits means fitting organizational policies to external cultures and constraints; union and non-union channels are utilized; the relationship with line managers at all levels is interactive rather than driven by either specialists or the line.

In this context the specialist department requires the ability to manage ambiguity and flexibility – issues which the management strategy gurus tell us are going to become ever more important, and perhaps issues where Europe has a lead.

This article has argued from European data and hence has restricted the analysis to Europe. It is believed that the 'European' approach projected here accords much better with the reality of current and developing practice than many of the more straightforward personnel management or HRM approaches elsewhere. And it may be that it is closer to reality in other continents and countries too.

Little directly comparable evidence is available from the USA and other parts of the world about practice in HRM elsewhere, and there is clearly a need for a considerable extension of research in the topic. It is arguable, however, that the 'European' model may well be more applicable to other countries than the 'Human Resource Management' model.

The conceptual limitations of this article will be apparent. One in particular is the conflating of Europe into a single entity. There is some rationale for this – the European Community provides a unifying political theme even for countries which at present only aspire to join it; and in many areas the similarities between countries in Europe in distinction to those in other continents are more obvious than differences within Europe. Nevertheless, differences within Europe are important and are touched on in this paper – and addressed in more detail in Brewster and Bournois (1991), Filella (1991) and Brewster and Holt Larsen (1992).

A second oversimplification in the model, and one where it clearly needs development, is in its relation to MNCs. Clearly it shows the need for international organizations, and particularly international managers (Brewster 1991), to be aware of, and to adapt to, local environments – as in practice they do. However, a more complicated, perhaps three-dimensional, model would be required to provide a full picture of the world environment within which many international organizations operate.

The methodological limitations are in one sense at least less important as the article has drawn on a range of data and other research. Nevertheless, a continual frustration is the lack of directly comparable data from the USA. In at least some respects the focus on case-study evidence in the United States has led to a theoretical debate which, it has been argued, is 'data-poor' (Kochan 1991). There is a real need for a substantial survey of organizations in the USA to establish hard data on the extent of particular practices in human resource management.

NOTES

1 For more detail on European HRM practices, see Brewster *et al.* (1992).
2 The closest German equivalent to the linguistic distinction between personnel management and human resource management is between *Personalwesen* or *Personalverwaltung* (administration) and *Personalmanagement*: this differentiation is much weaker and concentrates more on the shift from administration to management, rather than emphasizing a different valuation of employees.

REFERENCES

Ackermann, K.F. (1986) 'A Contingency Model of HRM Strategy – Empirical Research Findings Reconsidered', *Management Forum*, 6: 65–83.

Adler, N.J. and Jelinek, M. (1986) 'Is "Organisation Culture" Culture-Bound?', *Human Resource Management*, 25, 1: 72–90.

Albert, F.J. (1989) 'Les ressources humaines, atout stratégique', *Editions L'harmattan*, p. 75.

Baird, L., Meshoulam, I. and DeGive, G. (1983) 'Meshing Human Resources Planning with Strategic Business Planning, A Model Approach', *Personnel*, 60, 5: 14–25.

Bartlett, C.A. and Ghoshal, S. (1989) *Managing Across Borders: The Transnational Solution*, Cambridge, Mass.: Harvard Business School Press.

Beaumont, P.B. (1991a) 'The US Human Resource Management Literature: A Review'. In Salaman, G. (ed.) *Human Resource Strategies*, Milton Keynes: The Open University.

Beaumont, P.B. (1991b) 'Trade Unions and HRM' *Industrial Relations Journal*, 22, 4: 300–8.

Beer, M., Spector, B., Lawrence, P.R., Mills, Q.N. and Walton, R.E. (1984) *Managing Human Assets*, New York: The Free Press.

Beer, M., Lawrence, P.R., Mills, Q.N. and Walton, R.E. (1985) *Human Resource Management*, New York: The Free Press.

Besseyre des Horts, C.H. (1987) 'Typologies des pratiques de gestion des ressources humaines', *Revue française de Gestion*, 149–55.

Besseyre des Horts, C.H. (1988) 'Vers une gesion stratégique des ressources humaines', *Editions d'Organisation*, 69–84.

Beyer, H.T. (1991) *Personalarbeit als integrierter Bestandteil der Unternehmensstrategie*, paper to the 1991 DGFP Annual Congress, Wiesbaden.

Blanchflower, D. and Freeman, R. (1990) 'Going Different Ways: Unionism in the US and Other Advanced OECD Countries', *Centre for Economic Performance Discussion Paper 5*, London: LSE.

Bournois, F. (1991a) 'Gestion des RH en Europe: Données comparés', *Revue française de Gestion* mars-avril-mai: 68–83.

Bournois, F. (1991b) 'Gestion stratégique des ressources humaines: comparisons internationales', *Actes du collogue d l'Association Française de gestion des ressources humaines*, CERGY.

Brewster, C. (1991) *The Management of Expatriates*, London: Kogan Page.

Brewster, C. (1993) 'Human Resource Management in Europe: Reflection of, or Challenge to, the American Concept?' In Kirkbride, P. (ed.) *Human Resource Management in the New Europe of the 1990s*, London: Routledge.

Brewster, C. and Bournois, F. (1991) 'A European Perspective on Human Resource Management', *Personnel Review*, 20, 6: 4–13.

Brewster, C. and Hegewisch, A. (eds) *Policy and Practice in European Human Resource Management: Evidence and Analysis*, London: Routledge.

Brewster, C. and Holt Larsen, H., (1992) 'Human Resource Management in Europe: Evidence from Ten Countries', *International Journal of Human Resource Management*, 3, 3: 409–34.

Brewster, C. and Lockhart, T. (1992) 'Human Resource Management in the European Community'. In Brewster, C. *et al.* (eds) *The European Human Resource Management Guide*, London: Academic Press.

Brewster, C. and Teague, P. (1989) *European Community Social Policy: The Impact on the UK*, London: Institute of Personnel Management.

Brewster, C. Hegewisch, A., Holden, L. and Lockhart, T. (eds) *The European Human Resource Management Guide*, London: Academic Press.

Child, J. (1976) 'Organisational Structure, Environment and Performance: the Role of Strategic Choice', *Sociology*, 6: 1–22.

Conrad, P. and Pieper, R. (1990) 'HRM in the Federal Republic of Germany'. In Pieper, R. (ed.) *Human Resource Management: An International Comparison*, Berlin: Walter de Gruyter.

Cox, C. and Cooper, G. (1985) 'The Irrelevance of American Organisational Sciences to the UK and Europe', *Journal of General Management*, 11, 2: 27–34.

Dertouzos, M.L., Lester, R.K. and Solow, R.M. (1989) *Made in America: Regaining the Productive Edge*, Cambridge, Mass.: MIT Press.

Dunlop, J.T. (1958) *Industrial Relations Systems*, New York: Henry Holt.

Filella, J. (1991) 'Is there a Latin Model in the Management of Human Resources?' *Personnel Review*, 20, 6: 15–24.

Fombrun, C. (1982) 'Environmental Trends Create New Pressures on Human Resources', *Journal of Business Strategy*, 3, 1: 61–9.

Fombrun, C. and Tichy, N.M. (1983) 'Strategic Planning and Human Resources Management: at Rainbow's End'. In Lamb, R. (ed.) *Recent Advances in Strategic Planning*, New York: McGraw-Hill.

Fombrun, C., Tichy, N. and Devanna, M. (eds) (1984) *Strategic Human Resource Management*, New York: Wiley.

Gaugler, E. (1988) 'HR Management: An International Comparison', *Personnel*, 24–30.

Guest, D. (1990) 'Human Resource Management and the American Dream', *Journal of Management Studies*, 27, 4: 377–97.

Gunnigle, P., Brewster, C. and Morley, M. (1993) 'Evaluating Change in Industrial Relations: Evidence from the Price Waterhouse Cranfield Project', *P+: Journal of the European Foundation for the Improvement of Working and Living Conditions*.

Hedlund, G. and Rolander, D. (1990) 'Action in Heterarchies – New Approaches to Managing the MNC'. In Bartlett, C.A., Doz, Y. and Hedlund, G. (eds) *Managing the Global Firm*, London: Routledge, pp. 15–46.

Hegewisch, A. (1991) 'The Decentralisation of Pay Bargaining: European Comparisons', *Personnel Review*, 20, 6: 28–35.

Hegewisch, A. and Brewster, C. (eds) (1993) *European Developments in Human Resource Management*, Cranfield Research series, London: Kogan Page.

Hendry, C. and Pettigrew, A. (1990) 'HRM: An Agenda for the 1990s', *International Journal of Human Resource Management*, 1, 1: 17–25.

Hoftede, G. (1980) *Culture's Consequences: International Differences in Work-Related Values*, Beverly Hills, CA: Sage.

Kochan, T.A. (1991) 'Industrial Relations Research and HRM', paper to OECD Workshop, Paris.

Kochan, T.A. and Barocci, T.A. (1985) *Human Resource Management and Industrial Relations*, Boston, Mass.: Little Brown.

Kochan, T.A., Katz, H.C. and McKersie, R.B. (1986) *The Transformation of American Industrial Relations*, New York: Basic Books.

Kochan, T.A., McKersie, R.B. and Capelli, P. (1984) 'Strategic Choice and Industrial Relations Theory', *Industrial Relations*, 23: 16–39.

Legge, K. (1989) 'Human Resource Management: A Critical Analysis'. In Storey, J. (ed.) *New Perspectives on Human Resource Management*, London: Routledge.

Lengnick-Hall, C.A. and Lengnick-Hall, M.L. (1988) 'Strategic Human Resources Management: A Review of the Literature and a Proposed Typology', *Academy of Management Review*, 13, 3: 454–70.

Lorange, P. and Murphy, D. (1984) 'Bringing Human Resources into Strategic Planning: Systems Design Considerations'. In Fombrun, C.J. *et al.* (eds) *Strategic Human Resource Management*, New York: Wiley.

Macmillan, I.C. and Schuler, R.S. (1985) 'Gaining a Competitive Edge through Human Resources', *Personnel*, 62, 4: 24–9.

Nkomo, S.M. (1980) 'Stage Three in Personnel Administration: Strategic Human Resource Management', *Personnel*, 57: 189–202.

OECD (1991) *Employment Outlook*, Paris: Organization for Economic Co-operation and Development.

Pieper, R. (ed.) (1990) *Human Resource Management: An International Comparison*, Berlin: Walter de Gruyter.

Poole, M. (1990) 'Human Resource Management in an International Perspective', *International Journal of Human Resource Management*, 1, 1: 1–15.

Porter, M. (1980) *Competitive Strategies*, New York: The Free Press.

Porter, M. (1985) *Competitive Advantage*, New York: The Free Press.

Randelsome, C. (1993) *Business Cultures in Europe*, Oxford: Heinemann.

Remer, A. (1986) 'Personnel Management in Western Europe – Development, Situation and Concepts'. In Macharzine, K. and Staehle, W.H. (eds) *European Approaches to International Management*, Berlin: Walter de Gruyter.

Salaman, G. (ed.) (1991) *Human Resource Management Strategies*, Milton Keynes: The Open University.

Schuler, R. and Macmillan, S. (1984) 'Gaining Competitive Advantage through Human Resource Management Practices', *Human Resource Management*, 23, 3: 241–55.

Schuler, R.S. (1989) 'Human Resources Strategy: Focusing on Issues and Actions', *Organisational Dynamics*, 19, 1: 4–20.

Schuler, R.S. (1991) 'Strategic HRM: Linking People with the Strategic Needs of the Business', unpublished paper, New York University.

Schuler, R.S. and Jackson, S.E. (1987) 'Linking Competitive Strategies with Human Resource Management Practices', *Academy of Management Executive*, 1, 3: 209–13.

Staehle, W.H. (1988) 'Human Resource Management', *Zeitschrift für Betriebswirtschaft*, 5/6: 26–37.

Staffelbach, B. (1986) *Strategishes Personalmanagement*, Bern Stuttgart.

Strauss, G. (1968) 'Human Relations – 1968 Style', *Industrial Relations*, 7: 262–76.

Thurley, K. and Wirdenius, H. (1991) 'Will Management become "European"? Strategic Choices for Organisations', *European Management Journal*, 9, 2: 127–34.

Tichy, N.M., Fombrun, C.J. and Devanna, M.A. (1982) 'Strategic Human Resource Management', *Sloan Management Review*, 24: 47–61.

Trompenaars, A. (1985) 'Organisation of Meaning and the Meaning of Organisation: A Comparative Study on the Conception of Organisational Structure in Different Cultures', unpublished PhD thesis, University of Pennsylvania (DA 8515460).

Walsh, K. (1985) *Trade Union Membership, Methods and Measurement in the European Community*, Luxembourg: Eurostat.

Part II

International enterprise: communications, marketing, production and finance

Chapter 10

Tech talk

How managers are stimulating global R&D communication

Arnoud De Meyer

Today, no single industrial power can pretend, as the USA could in the 1950s and 1960s, to have a quasi-monopoly on high-tech development. Massachusetts and California are not the only places where technology is created. Certain universities and companies in Europe, Japan, and Korea have also become drivers of technological development. Transnational companies are thus thinking about how to manage technology globally.[1]

Companies have developed several strategies: acquiring technology, either by buying laboratories or negotiating licenses; forming strategic alliances or other collaborative efforts with companies, research institutes, or governments; and creating in-house international research and development capabilities. In this article I focus exclusively on the last strategy – developing an international network of laboratories.

Traditionally, one of the most important productivity problems in R&D is stimulating communication among researchers. How can one improve the flow of technology?[2] This problem becomes more difficult when laboratories are located far from each other. Steele observed that in many corporations coordination and communication become rather weak outside a one-day return traveling distance, and that in cases where communication and coordination do work, the corporations have long-standing multinational experience.[3]

This article reports on the practices of fourteen large multinational companies in order to get some insight into how they manage this communication problem. It also proposes some hypotheses for how the transnational or multinational company can improve the management of its international R&D operations.[4]

THE ROLE OF COMMUNICATION IN R&D

An essential element of an R&D engineer's work is the gathering, diffusion, and creative processing of information. Many studies about R&D have shown that the productivity of an R&D engineer depends to a large extent on his or her ability to tap into an appropriate network of information flows.[5]

Allen's seminal work has repeatedly supported the notion that individual, face-to-face contact is the backbone of an efficiently operating information network.[6] To exchange information, engineers and technologists have to talk to each other – in each other's presence. Engineers do read. But they limit their reading mainly to textbooks, to refresh their memories, or trade journals, to figure out what the competition is doing or to see what novel components and approaches suppliers are offering. Several studies, with different technologies and in different countries, have verified this core finding.

This conclusion is quite easy to accept. To be able to understand and digest information about new technologies, specific market conditions, or competitive developments, the engineer needs more than raw information or data. He or she also needs the context of the information. Knowing about the existence of a new micro-electronic component is often insufficient. The engineer also needs to know the primary application for which the component was developed. By acting upon the new information or rephrasing it, the engineer can better understand what the raw data means. Understanding is also facilitated when the receiver can control the speed with which information is offered.

We have all experienced this: learning something new, we want to repeat to the information source what we have understood in order to verify that we understood it properly. An audience that has listened to the delivery of a written speech has lower comprehension than an audience that has been involved in building up the argument with the speaker. By controlling the speed of delivery, or by providing feedback so the observant speaker can adapt the speed of delivery, the audience receives the information more efficiently.

Why is individual, face-to-face communication so important? One of the interesting findings of studies in the 1960s and 1970s was that telephone communication patterns, which are individual but not face-to-face, are strongly related to the pattern of face-to-face communication. Other than calls for simple exchanges of data, one only calls the people one knows well and sees fairly often. Thus, the telephone complements but does not substitute for face-to-face communication.

Individual, face-to-face communication seems to be essential to improve and maintain the productivity of an R&D organization. But geographically decentralized R&D operations make efficient communication patterns difficult. The tendency is to form efficient communication clusters in each country, with loose couplings between clusters. This may be sufficient for development laboratories that merely adapt products, developed elsewhere, to local market conditions. As Ghoshal and Bartlett have demonstrated in their empirical study of nine large transnational companies, innovation in local subsidiaries is positively associated with intrasubsidiary communication, though neutral with respect to inter-subsidiary communication.[7] But both adoption and adaptation by the subsidiary of innovations developed elsewhere, and diffusion of innovations created by the subsidiary to other parts of the company, are positively associated with both intra- and intersubsidiary communication. In other words, when the communication flows have to go in two or more directions, or when truly international developments are started, companies must develop mechanisms to replace or support individual, face-to-face communication.[8]

THE STUDY

My associates and I gathered data through interviews with fourteen large multinationally operating companies on their organization of international R&D operations. The number of interviews per company depended on the extent of its R&D network. In some cases we only interviewed the R&D manager. In other cases we interviewed several laboratory managers and eventual users of the research or development results (such as product or production managers). The interviews ranged from several hours to several days. Though we used a checklist of items to be discussed, in most interviews we kept the questions very open and adapted the interview format to the specific technology and market presence of the company.[9]

The fourteen companies do not form a representative sample of a particular industry or geographical region. Table 10.1 provides a description of the companies. Nine have a European headquarters, three are North American, but with a long presence in Europe, and two are Japanese. Ten of the companies have many years of experience carrying out R&D on an international scale. The number of laboratories per company ranges from two to nineteen, and each company has several hundred if not thousands of professionals working in R&D. Judging from financial performance over the last five years and evaluations in the international business press, each company was at the time of the interviews considered successful or very successful. This does not guarantee, however, the quality and success of their R&D performance. In fact, in more than one company we were allowed to do research because managers were concerned about the performance of their international R&D and hoped to get a benchmark evaluation out of the interviews.

The activities of the laboratories ranged widely, from basic research to applied development (we discarded from the analysis simple process engineering outlets). We found enormous variety in the definition of R&D. What one company classified as research, another company (even in the same industry) would have labeled applied development. Consequently, it does not seem useful to provide a table with laboratories by technical activity.

Table 10.1 The sample

Company activity	Number of laboratories	Total employees	Lab sizes (by number of employees)
Automotive	2 (+ 1 Test ground)	3,500	2,100 and 1,400
Automotive	3	7,800	70–7,500
Electronics	6	3,100	3–2,500
Electronics	8 (2 more planned)	300	15–70
Food	1 central research lab	450	450
	18 local development centers	Not disclosed	20–250
Petrochemicals	3 (1 closed after study)	400	200
Petrochemicals	2 central research labs	3,000	2,300 and 700
	60 business labs	2,000	10–several hundred
Petrochemicals	8 group central labs	4,560	150–1,600
	7 operating labs	2,280	60–1,680
Pharmaceuticals	3	750	30–500
Pharmaceutical	9	Not available	Not available
Speciality chemicals	1 primary research lab	660	660
	13 development labs	550	40–100
Speciality chemicals	3	1,200	Europe: 130 Japan: 70 US: 1,000
Telecommunication	13	1,300	40–250

SOLVING THE COMMUNICATION PROBLEM

We identified several elements that we expected to figure prominently in the companies' communication efforts: organizational structure, 'boundary-spanning' individuals, and communications technology. The literature on R&D communication has often stressed that communication patterns are highly influenced by project structure, organizational structure, and by change over time in the project structure.[10] Since open, person-to-person communication is often a result of people having worked together,[11] reallocating personnel to different project teams can create links between teams. But altering organizational structure, the technical assignment, or project groups can also destroy communication. In addition, the style of project management can have an important influence on the creation of links between project teams. Consequently, one could expect multinational companies to take organizational measures and use career planning to manage communication patterns.

Second, a constant element in the research on communication patterns is the important role played by 'boundary-spanning' individuals or 'gatekeepers'.[12] Information often comes from outside into a group by a two-step process. Particular individuals seem to have the capability of monitoring what is going on in the outside environment and translating that external information into messages comprehensible to the group to which they belong. They are different from the integrators or liaisons described in the literature on integration and differentiation. Indeed, gatekeepers do not integrate tasks and actions but only improve the flow of information. A boundary-spanning person, an international gatekeeper, might be able to manage the flow of information between international laboratories.

Third, recent technological innovations such as fax machines, tele-conferencing, and videoconferencing have considerably improved the tool kit for complementing individual, face-to-face communication. As with telephone calls, one wonders to what extent these technological means can support or even replace face-to-face communication. The images in videoconferencing and the pictures, graphs, and tables available with fax machines, electronic mail, and computer conferencing provide a quantum improvement over the simple telephone call.

In our study we saw a bit of everything. The companies were all strongly aware of the need to improve communications and often admitted that breakdown of the communication lines was the biggest recurring problem in their organization. We sorted the solutions they were pursuing into six broad categories:

- efforts to increase socialization in order to enhance communication and information exchange;
- implementation of rules and procedures in order to increase formal communication;
- creation of boundary-spanning roles – assigning individuals to facilitate communication flows;
- creation of a centralized office responsible for managing communication;
- development of a network organization;
- replacement of face-to-face communication by electronic systems.

None of the companies applied the methods with equal emphasis, and none limited itself to only one method. Below I describe each method in more detail.

Socialization efforts

Though every company recognized that organizational culture can improve R&D productivity, some companies strongly emphasized social-ization procedures to stimulate a positive culture. We heard the following comments:

> We need a cultural change so that people do not consider information a source of power. The amount of information you share with others should enhance your position in the company.

We are like a family; we share what we have. And it should stay that way.

We share our information in informal meetings. It is important that in such a meeting everybody is equal. Status or hierarchy should not play a role in evaluating the value of a piece of information. Only the factual content is important.

Companies attempted to create a 'family' atmosphere in four ways. One of the most important tools was the use of temporary assignments to other laboratories.[13] How long should an assignment last to have a meaningful impact? No strict rule emerged from our research, except that the companies that used transfers as a major policy element expected the engineer or scientist to move into the new country. One manager said, 'It has to be more than a visit where the engineer operates from a hotel. He has to get over the difficulties of settling in and increase his loyalty to the company family, which has helped him to overcome these difficulties.'

Reading between the lines, we can see an effort to turn the company into a protective environment that nurtures the engineer in a quasi-hostile foreign country. Such an approach can only work, of course, if the company is organized to support the employee looking for help.

A second element of socialization was constant traveling. In one particular company in 1988, the R&D department alone registered more than eight thousand business trips. Travel costs ranged from 3 per cent to 7 per cent of the total R&D budget. In some cases there was a conscious attempt to turn visits by representatives of central headquarters into more than a work related event. One manager said, 'I try to make sure that each time I or one of my people visit one of the decentralized research companies, they have an informal get-together organized.' Social events help create informal contacts, which are often the start of a healthy exchange on the task to be executed.

Some companies used rules and procedures to reinforce company culture. In one case, a company had two equally strong laboratories in the UK and West Germany. Training of German and British engineers is sufficiently different to create a tremendous potential for cultural clashes. But the company developed strong quality standards and procedures for execution and documentation of work: the engineers' pride in these standards helped them to identify with the company instead of with their previous training. Such a sense of pride and belonging was, in more than one company, linked to the feeling that the company had achieved technological leadership in a particular field.

A fourth method of improving company culture was the use of training programs. Language training was often strongly recommended. The difficulty here was to find a training program that increased identification with the company and did not negatively affect loyalty. If programs are too general, employees may use them to increase their value in the labor market.

None of the companies that emphasized organizational culture created a standard type of laboratory. On the contrary, they actively pursued diversity in research management. National characteristics and the historical background of the center and its strategic mission combined to create strong differences in the way the research laboratories operated. One manager summarized what companies hoped to achieve by improving socialization: 'We want to be a multicultural [family] with common goals and values.'

Rule and procedures

Many companies used rules and procedures to enhance formal communication. These efforts usually took one of two forms: emphasizing careful reporting and documentation, or developing a planning process that stimulated communication between laboratories.

During the study it became clear to us that, in comparison with single-laboratory companies we had studied in the past, these multilaboratory companies paid much more attention to the process of writing and distributing reports.[14] Originally, we thought this emphasis was a consequence of company size or government requirements, as in the case of pharmaceutical companies, which must meet certain government requirements during the approval stage. However, if this were the case, researchers would experience the reporting structure as an administrative burden. In several companies the reporting structure was really designed to minimize the burden and maximize the diffusion of acquired know-how throughout R&D laboratories. Some companies had strict rules about report designs aimed at increasing readability and accessibility. In other companies, information sheets were organized in treelike structures that allowed the individual laboratory manager or engineer quickly to scan the new results and problems. Some companies required a quick turnaround of highlight reports. In some companies the job description of the laboratory manager included reading reports from other laboratories and distributing them to the appropriate engineers. All these were efforts to use the reporting structure to enhance communication.

In those cases where development was strongly routinized, or in industries that had particular routine test procedures, such as pharmaceuticals, food, agro-chemical products, and mechanical engineering, the reporting structure made extensive use of electronic databases. These companies had often thought carefully about the design of the databases to give everyone in the company access (eventually with different levels of security) and to improve accessibility for inexperienced users. In laboratories or companies where the activities were more research oriented, less standardized, or more complex, most reporting was still not standardized on a database. This is probably temporary. The available commercial databases are perhaps not yet powerful enough to present unstructured information in a standardized and efficient form.

Companies also used the planning process itself to stimulate communication. A number of rituals and aspects of the planning process had more to do with rejuvenating the communication network and opening up new channels than with arriving at a plan.[15] Typical examples were scientific conferences that started the planning process, presentations made to other laboratories, and broad discussion of intermediate planning reports throughout the company. In one company, planning can be summarized as follows: the planning cycle starts with a number of regional minimeetings in preparation for the biannual conference. Representatives bring the topics from these discussions to the main conference, which has plenary sessions as well as small group meetings. Next, the business units or operating groups hold three- to four-day meetings to discuss major thrusts of the programs. Projects are not yet identified in detail at this stage. The purpose of the meetings is to obtain a portfolio of broad scientific and technical areas in which the company wants to invest and to guarantee that a balance exists between long-term and short-term research objectives, product differentiation, and cost reduction programs. The central research group participates actively in these discussions to encourage a long term perspective, inject ideas, and identify implications for the business of emerging technologies. Several steps into the planning process, participants obtain a sort of research guide and discuss it in the laboratories. This research guide describes the technical and commercial objectives and targets of different research programs and projects. On the basis of these discussions, the researchers provide program sheets detailing time planning and costs and discuss them with the business managers and fund providers. Once a final program is defined, the central research staff, in many cases the top R&D manager, visits each of the laboratories to review the detailed research plans and resource allocation. This whole process takes about one-and a-half years.

Although simplified, this is basically a description of a traditional, if elaborate, planning process. However, its length and complexity indicate that something more than a simple plan with targets and resource allocations is at stake. Planning has become a mechanism to force hundreds of researchers to talk to each other about their results, their know-how, and their technological forecasts. Later, it forces researchers to discuss these issues with the business groups, to anchor them in a realistic view of the market. Throughout, the central R&D staff plays an active role in fostering communication and diffusing the results of the planning exercise.

Though some companies were very successful in using the reporting structure or the planning process to foster communication, it became clear that rules and procedures cannot substitute for or even trigger informal communication. They probably can be a powerful mechanism for maintaining communication flows, complementary to other mechanisms that we describe here, but not a substitute for them. One of the companies, which admitted that interlaboratory communication was below expectations, had tried to use its planning procedures to create some kind of an exchange, but had failed miserably to do so. It was in the process of completely revamping the planning procedures. However, the effectiveness of rules and procedures to stimulate communication probably depends on their being built upon an already existing informal communication network.

Boundary-spanning roles

Many researchers have discussed the pre-eminent role of gatekeepers in technology transfer. We were not able to test whether a role like an international R&D gatekeeper exists – a person who has good contacts with other laboratories and can translate work from other laboratories into the jargon of his or her own laboratory. However, some companies had defined central staff's job as facilitating information flow. Central staff members had different (and sometimes inappropriate) job titles such as sponsor, liaison, or technology coordinator.

In one company, for example, the role of the sponsor was described as follows: 'The goal of the system is that every sponsor would encourage and support worldwide communication of developments and results in his [or her] product group. This is mainly done through the organization of a number of technological conferences.' This sponsor was placed high in the company and was responsible for organizing the communication process. In other companies, the sponsors or technological coordinators were lower in the hierarchy and had to travel around constantly to follow up on the evolution of the technology. They had actively to trigger the contacts between different individuals and groups in the laboratories. Obviously, the success of such a person was dependent on personality. At the minimum, a sponsor would need a combination of technological credibility and social listening and integrating skills.

One of the companies described this type of person as an 'ambassador'. Although the company had not appointed ambassadors officially, the research director commented that the success of a remote laboratory in attracting the attention of the central (and much bigger) laboratory had a lot to do with its ability to find a representative at headquarters. He said, 'There is a great need for intense communication. . . . The solution is, at least partially, to include inthe remote groups people from the central site. People who know the important people in the central offices and laboratory, who know the flow of information in the different departments. These people should act as ambassadors.'

In every organization we visited, we observed the use of individuals to transfer technology. In particular, it seemed to be the preferred way to construct a communication network when there was a major structural change in an R&D network. In those cases where such roles received a greater emphasis, or where they seemed to be the cornerstone of the communication process, the companies experienced a breakdown in communication when key individuals left the company and when new laboratories were created.

Organizational mechanisms

We distinguished two types of organizational mechanisms in use: a central coordination staff, with explicit communication responsibilities, and a network organization. In our research they seemed to be somewhat mutually exclusive: companies tended to adhere to either one or the other. Theoretically, we see no reason why this should be so.

In seven of the fourteen companies there was a small but important central staff that was not affiliated with a particular laboratory and whose explicit task was to coordinate R&D activities and stimulate communication. Of course, all fourteen companies had a central R&D manager and office, coordinating all the laboratory activities. But in some cases this central staff was an explicit component of the oldest or biggest laboratory and in some cases it was a very small administrative staff responsible mainly for coordination of planning and budgeting activities. In the seven companies we refer to here, the central staff did more than light co-ordination. A group of people, perhaps small, with no explicit research task, got involved in coaching, guiding, and monitoring the laboratories. These people explicitly managed the communication process. In some cases there was a clear overlap with the previously mentioned boundary-spanning individuals. But there was a difference: the central staff had responsibility for communication as an organizational unit. These organizations looked a bit like spider webs: the central staff, sitting in the middle, monitored all movements of information between the different nodes. Weak internodal communication could exist because the main force of the communication network was in the middle. The mechanisms were fairly simple: having meetings, traveling, bringing together engineers who had problems with engineers who had answers, managing the technical reporting process, disseminating reports and results, and monitoring the company database.

In contrast, six companies had an almost negligible central staff and believed strongly in the creation of a network. The R&D directors wanted to develop networks between the different laboratories at all hierarchical levels. Each person was supposed to be a node in an extensive network of equals, relaying messages to each other and making contact with any source of information by going through two or three nodes.[16] In such a network there was no preferred route for the message, while in the centralized organization the central staff was the preferred information exchange. None of the six companies that explicitly pursued such a system had been able to get to such an ideal state.

These six companies fell into two categories: companies with a limited number of laboratories (two or three) and companies in the communication and electronics industry. It would be interesting to check whether network communications were favored by those managers who had actually been involved in electronic network design. But the fact that organizations with a limited number of laboratories favored such networks is not surprising. Organizational networks in R&D are not easy to create. Successful creation seems to require the fulfillment of three conditions, all of which are easier to implement in smaller, less complicated organizations.

First, the central staff has to accept, not only at a rational level, but also at an emotional level, that information will flow freely in the organization. Given the secrecy that is often needed in R&D, it is hard for the central office to accept that each engineer can decide what can be shared, or that there will be no secrets within the company. Not all companies are willing to shoulder the increased risk of information leaks that come with such a system.

Second, individual engineers have to be prepared to share their contacts with others. It takes time for the individual engineer to create and maintain a network, and this network is perceived to be a source of individual competitive advantage within the company. A successful network depends on the transformation of this protective attitude into one in which sharing is perceived as a source of competitive advantage.

Third, the company has to be prepared to support the network with the appropriate tools. At a minimum, these tools are a career planning and job rotation system, extensive meetings at different hierarchical levels, inter-laboratory travel, and an electronic communication system.

Only one company was attempting both to create a network and to stimulate the network with a central R&D staff. Since the firm had only started promoting the network two years before the interviews were conducted, it was too early to judge the potential for success.

Electronic communication

Each of the companies was experimenting in some way with electronic means of communication. Though not all had gone beyond the stage of pilot experiments, each had used computer networks, electronic mail, and computer conferencing in some way. Needless to say, fax machines were standard equipment six months after their introduction in the market. Nearly all the companies had electronic mail systems or worldwide engineering databases, if appropriate. In at least four companies, serious experiments with videoconferencing were underway. In only one company had videoconferencing become a normal way of communicating between R&D sites.

The evaluation of these electronic means was mixed. Nobody doubted that electronic communication systems could complement other channels for communication. But the mere fact that videoconferencing had not been introduced at the same sweeping pace as fax machines indicated that there was much reluctance about new forms of communication media.

Hauptmann has categorized information shared during development projects as either innovative or coordinative information.[17] Innovative information is helpful in solving technical problems. It is information on the experimental and analytical efforts researchers make to develop the product. Coordinative information includes tasks and time schedules, expected output, and the day-to-day coordination of activities. Most firms in our study used computerized communication systems to send coordinative information – schedules, results of experiments, lists of publications, and so on. They found this to be the most effective use of electronic media. However, we observed that the capacity to share innovative, problem-solving information was dependent on the nature of the R&D work, including its analyzability and complexity. Analyzability reflects the degree to which there exist standard procedures and methods to identify, describe, and solve the problems posed by the technology's development. The higher the analyzability and the lower the complexity of the technology, as in the case of electronic assembly or simple chemical experiments, the more effective the computer supported communication systems seemed to be. With increasing complexity and decreasing analyzability, the problem-solving content of the information exchange decreased, while the coordinative content of the information could still be communicated.

The companies that were experimenting with videoconferencing hoped that these real-time picture systems could replace some direct personal contacts. But firms did not seem confident that they could, even in their most sophisticated forms, be more than a temporary replacement for face-to-face contact.

The senior product development manager of the company with the most sophisticated electronic communication system in the sample said:

Videoconferencing, integrated CAD/CAM databases, electronic mail, and intensive jet travel all contribute to lowering the communication barriers. All things considered, however, the most effective communication, especially in the beginning of a project, is a handshake across a table to build mutual trust and confidence. Then and only then can the electronics be really effective.

We sensed the same feeling in all the managers who had some experience with electronic communication systems. These systems can make a valuable contribution once a certain level of confidence between the partners has been established. The 'handshake' is an important preceding condition for their effective use.

Weick has made a similar observation.[18] He argues that in the electronic world, information and representations can lose their meaning because the set of assumptions that give them life are lost. He sees a risk that representations of events cease forming an ordered cosmos and become chaotic. Electronic data excludes sensory information, feelings, intuition, and context. One engineer with considerable experience on videoconferencing systems summarized his own relation to the system:

> [Although it is a great system], I have two difficulties with it. I still cannot express emotions on a videoconferencing system. It seems so silly to become angry, to joke, to deviate from the subject and to talk about your family, to complain about your boss, all those things you need to do to get to know each other. And I am never sure that my colleagues at the other end will not tape me, to use my own words against me. I know it is silly, because I am not scared of being taped on the phone, but videoconferencing meetings still create many more formal commitments than a simple phone call.

Weick also argues that the people who manage the data cannot process it accurately. When people are forced to make judgments based on cryptic data, they cannot resolve their confusion by comparing different versions of the event registered in different media. When comparison is not possible, people try to clear up their confusion by asking for more data. More data of the same kind clarifies nothing. More and more human-processing capacity is then used to keep track of unconnected details.

We have arrived at two conclusions. First, electronically transmitted data cannot be the sole source of information. This seems obvious, but the relative convenience of electronic data communications as opposed to travel, direct contact, or even telephone calls between laboratories in different time zones gives people reason to fool themselves and to be satisfied with it.

Second, if electronic data is to be effective, there must be some level of confidence that the two parties are really communicating. This confidence comes from sensory information, feelings, and context – all of which require personal interaction. We observed that even with the best electronic communication systems, confidence between the team members of a worldwide development project seemed to decay over time. We have sometimes used the expression 'the half-life effect of electronic communications' to describe, like the decay of nuclear radiation, this decreasing confidence.[19] Thus, periodic face-to-face contact seems necessary to maintain confidence at a level high enough to promote effective team work (see Figure 10.1). When one starts a new cross-laboratory project or program, one should bring the team members together to establish that initial confidence. But once everybody returns to their respective laboratory benches and starts communicating through terminals, faxes, and videoconferences, confidence will decay. One must then organize another face-to-face meeting. The frequency of confidence maintaining meetings can be lower with intensive use of electronic media than without them, but it will not drop below a minimum level. However, we have not been able to determine how one knows that the confidence level has decayed enough to merit another face-to-face meeting.

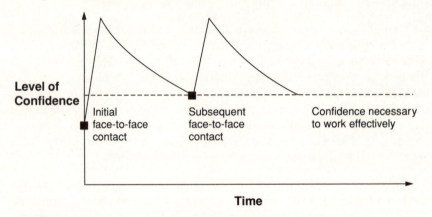

Figure 10.1 Strategy for maintaining confidence

A PORTFOLIO OF MECHANISMS

Our categorization of communication mechanisms is, of course, somewhat artificial. The companies did not think in these categories; they consciously or unconsciously made efforts in nearly all categories. But none of the companies made strong efforts in all the categories either. Table 10.2 gives an over-view of the utilization of the different categories. Socialization was the most intensively used mechanism; rules and procedures and electronic communication were used least. Electronic communication has probably not been fully deployed yet.

Table 10.3 shows that companies usually had a portfolio of mechanisms. An electronic company invested in the development of five of the six approaches. Only one company had focused its communication improvement efforts on one single activity (rules and procedures). Furthermore,

Table 10.2 Number of companies deploying mechanisms

	Chemicals and Pharma-ceuticals (7 companies)	Automotive (2 companies)	Electronics and Tele-communication (4 companies)	Food (1 company)	Total
Socialization	3	2	3	1	9
Rules and procedures	3	—	2	—	5
Boundary-spanning roles	3	1	2	1	7
Centralized coordination	3	1	2	1	7
Networks	3	1	2	—	6
Electronic communication	2	1	2	—	5

Table 10.3 Mechanisms deployed by companies

Number of mechanisms	*Number of companies*
5	1
4	1
3	8
2	3
1	1

there seemed to be a few patterns that we have formulated here as hypotheses:

- Building up a communication network is harder in an international environment that in a single laboratory, but just as important. Companies use portfolios of mechanisms to create and maintain communication networks.
- Integrating a new laboratory into an existing communication network, or drastically restructuring a network, requires identifying individuals to act as network builders.
- Procedural mechanisms such as cleverly designed reporting structures, or planning processes that stimulate communication, cannot create a network. However, they may help to maintain the network or adapt it slightly.
- Electronic communication cannot replace individual, face-to face contact, but it can help to postpone the decay of confidence. It has a longer half-life effect than either written or telephone communications.
- Organizational design may influence communication patterns. We found two approaches: a spider web pattern with a central staff coordinating the flow of communication, and a network with no dominant nodes. Networks are attractive, but the difficulties in creating

them should not be underestimated. They require a serious investment of effort by both the company and the individual engineers.

CONCLUSION

Though global technology development may remain of marginal interest for most companies, those that went to compete globally must recognize the necessity of tapping sources of technology around the world. International R&D is one way to do this. If a company chooses to create an international network of laboratories, it will have to pay considerable attention to the creation and maintenance of an effective communication network. This is not a new problem in R&D management, but the problem is more complex now because of the geographical distance between laboratories. Future research should test our hypotheses and track the results of the programs we studied.

NOTES AND REFERENCES

1   C.A. Bartlett and S. Ghoshal, *Manging Across Borders* (Boston: Harvard Business School Press, 1989).
2   T.J. Allen, *Managing the Flow of Technology* (Cambridge, Massachutsetts: MIT Press, 1977).
3   L.W. Steele, *Innovation in Big Business* (New York: Elsevier North Holland Publishing Company, 1975).
4   In this paper I do not discuss at length why companies internationalize their R&D operations. See: A. De Meyer, 'Technology Strategy and International R&D Operations' (Fontainebleau, France: INSEAD, Working Paper No. 89/62, 1989).
5   See Allen (1977); A. De Meyer 'The Flow of Technical Information in an R&D Department', *Research Policy* 14 (1985): 315–328.
6   Allen (1977).
7   S. Ghoshal and C.A. Bartlett, 'Creation, Adoption, and Diffusion of Innovations by Subsidiaries of Multinational Companies', *Journal of International Business Studies* 19 (1988): 365–388.
8   A. De Meyer and A. Mizushima, 'Global R&D Management', *R&D Management* 19 (1989): 135–146.
9   Two cases have been published after reworking into pedagogical cases. See: W.H. Davidson and J. de la Torre, *Managing the Global Corporation* (New York: McGraw Hill, 1989).
10 J.L. Utterback, 'Innovation in Industry and the Diffusion of Technology', *Science* 183 (1975): 620–626.
11 M. Kanno, 'Effects in Communication between Labs and Plants of the Transfer of R&D Personnel', (Cambridge, Massachusetts: MIT Sloan School of Management, Master's thesis, 1968).
12 Allen (1977); M.L. Tushman, 'Special Boundary Roles in the Innovation Process', *Administrative Science Quarterly* 22 (1977): 587–605.
13 See J. Van Maanen and E.H. Schein, 'Toward a Theory of Organizational Socialization', in *Research in Organizational Behavior*, ed. B. Shaw (Greenwich, Connecticut: JAI Press, 1979); A. Edstrom and J.R. Galbraith, 'Transfer of

Managers as a Coordination and Control Strategy in Multinational Organizations', *Administrative Science Quarterly* 22 (1977): 248–263.

14 See, for example, A. De Meyer, 'Management of Technology in Traditional Industries: A Pilot Study in Ten Belgian Companies', *R&D Management* 13 (1983): 15–22; R. Moenaert, J. Barbe, D. Deschoolmeester, and A. De Meyer, 'Turnaround Strategies for Strategic Business Units with Aging Technology', in *The Strategic Management of Technological Innovation*, eds. R. Loveridge and M. Pitt (Chichester, England: Wiley, 1990).

15 A.P. De Geus, 'Planning as Learning' *Harvard Business Review*, March–April 1988, pp. 70–74.

16 For networks in R&D see: H. Hakansson and J. Laage-Hellman, 'Developing a Network R&D Strategy', *Journal for Product Innovation Management* 4 (1984): 224–237; De Meyer (1989); and S. Ghoshal and N. Nohria, *Requisite Complexity: Organising Headquarters-Subsidiary Relations in MNCs* (Fontainebleau, France: INSEAD, Working Paper No. 90/74, 1990).

17 O. Hauptmann, 'Influence of Task Type on the Relationship between Communication and Performance: The Case of Software Development', *R&D Management* 16 (1986): 127–139.

18 K.E. Weick, 'Cosmos versus Chaos: Sense and Nonsense in Electronic Contexts', *Organisational Dynamics* 13 (1984): 51–64.

19 De Meyer and Mizushima (1989).

Chapter 11

Rattling SABRE

New ways to compete on information

Max D. Hopper

I have built my career, and American Airlines has built much of its business, around massive, centralized, proprietary computer systems. Developing these systems consumed millions of man-hours and billions of dollars, but their marketplace advantages were huge. As a result, our experience underscored the competitive and organizational potential of information technology. At the risk of sounding immodest, we helped to define an era.

That era is over. We are entering a new era, one in which the thinking that guided 'best practice' as recently as five years ago is actually counterproductive. In this new era, information technology will be at once more pervasive and less potent – table stakes for competition, but no trump card for competitive success. As astute managers maneuver against rivals, they will focus less on being the first to build proprietary electronic tools than on being the best at using and improving generally available tools to enhance what their organizations already do well. Within their companies, they will focus less on developing stand-alone applications than on building electronic platforms that can transform their organizational structures and support new ways of making decisions.

Who, by now, cannot recite the computer-based success stories of the 1970s and 1980s?

- SABRE, American Airlines's reservation system, which eventually became a computerized reservation system [CRS], and Apollo, the other leading CRS, transformed marketing and distribution in the airline industry.
- American Hospital Supply's ASAP order-entry and inventory control system generated huge sales increases for the company's medical products and turned it into an industry leader.
- United Service Automobile Association used its Automated Insurance Environment – a collection of telecommunication systems, databases, expert systems, and image-processing technologies – to outperform consistently its insurance industry rivals in service quality, premium growth, and profitability.

- Mrs. Fields Cookies relied on its Retail Operations Intelligence system, an automated store management network, to build and operate a nationwide chain of 400 retail outlets without a costly and stifling headquarters bureaucracy.

These and a handful of other well-known computer systems (the Information Technology Hall of Fame, if you will) represent an important chapter in the application of electronic technologies to build competitive advantage and enhance organizational effectiveness. But it is time to turn the page. In 1984 F. Warren McFarlan published an influential article in *HBR* on the competitive potential of information technology.[1] He asked managers to consider how information systems might benefit their companies. Could the technology build barriers to competitive entry? Could it increase switching costs for customers? Could it change the balance of power in supplier relationships? He went on to argue that for many companies the answer was yes. By being the first to develop proprietary systems, pioneers could revolutionize their industries.

Increasingly, however, the answer is no. While it is more dangerous than ever to ignore the power of information technology, it is more dangerous still to believe that on its own, an information system can provide an enduring business advantage. The old models no longer apply.

THE INFORMATION UTILITY

The new era is driven by the greatest upheaval in computer technology since the first wave of modern computer developments thirty years ago. We are finally (and just barely) beginning to tap the real potential of computer functionality. As we change what computers can do, we must change what we do with computers.

Think of it as the emergence of an 'information utility'. Using superfast RISC architectures, hardware suppliers are delivering enormous processing power at remarkably low costs. UNIX and other software and communications standards are bringing unprecedented portability among different classes of products. Software tools like relational databases, expert systems, and computer-aided software engineering are helping to create powerful applications that meet specialized needs at reasonable costs. The ultimate impact of these and other technical developments is to give end-users greater power to shape their computer systems and manage their information needs. Increasingly, technology is allowing groups and individuals within companies to perform many of the functions once reserved for data processing professionals.

It is hardly news to most managers that technology is changing faster than ever. Yet I wonder how many appreciate just how radical and rapid the changes are. Over the past two decades, price/performance ratios for computer technology improved at an annual compound rate of roughly 10 per cent. In recent years, those ratios improved at a compound rate closer to 40 per cent. This massive acceleration in performance will have profound implications for how computers are used and how useful computers are. Three features of the new environment will be particularly important.

Powerful workstations

Powerful workstations will be a ubiquitous presence in offices and factories, and organizations will use them far more intensively and creatively than they do today. One of the paradoxes of the information age is that computers become easier to use as they become more powerful and complex. This is what is so important about dramatic hardware advances like microprocessors with a million transistors on a chip. Personal workstations running at near supercomputer speeds will finally be powerful enough to be simple and thus truly useful. Meanwhile, new graphical user interfaces are creating screen environments (electronic desktops) that make it quicker for employees to become skilled with their workstations, to move between systems without extensive retraining, and to develop the confidence to push the functionality of their machines.

In the not-so-distant future, computers will be as familiar a part of the business environment as telephones are today. They will also be as simple to use as telephones, or at least nearly so. As a result, companies will find it harder to differentiate themselves simply by automating faster than the competition. It will be easier for every organization to automate and to capture the efficiency benefits of information technology. This leaves plenty of room for competitive differentiation, but differentiation of a new and more difficult sort.

Application of technology

Companies will be technology architects rather than systems builders, even for their most critical applications. The widespread adoption of standards and protocols in hardware, software, and telecommunications will dramatically recast the technology-management function. At American Airlines, for example, we have spent thirty years handcrafting computer systems. We like to think that we are better at this than most and that our skills in hardware evaluation, project management for software development, and systems integration have given us an important leg up on the competition. But we look forward to the day when we can buy more and more of our hardware and software from third-party vendors capable of tailoring their systems to our needs – and that day is rapidly approaching.

InterAAct, our major new initiative for organizational computing, is a good example. Unlike SABRE, which incorporates a vast amount of AMR-developed technology, InterAAct is built around hardware and software provided by third-party vendors: workstations from AT&T, IMB, and Tandy; minicomputers from Hewlett-Packard; HP's NewWave presentation software and Microsoft Windows; local area networks from Novell. We play a role in systems integration (in particular, merging the networks), but outside suppliers are capable of delivering more value than ever before.

Of course, if we can buy critical hardware and software from outside vendors, so can our competitors. Our skills as electronic-tool builders, honed over decades, will become less and less decisive to our information technology strategy. This may sound like bad news, but we welcome it. We're not in business to build computer systems; our job is to lead in applying technology to core business objectives. We do not much worry if the competition also has access to the technology; we think we can be smarter in how we use it.

Economies of scale

Economies of scale will be more important than ever. We have entered the age of distributed computing, an age in which a young company like MIPS Computer Systems delivers a $5,000 workstation with processing speeds comparable to those of a $3 million IBM 3090 mainframe. Yet the amount of information required to solve important business problems also keeps growing, as does the capacity of telecommunications systems to transmit data quickly and reliably between distant locations. More than ever, then, the benefits of distributed computing will rely on access to vast amounts of data whose collection and storage will be managed on a centralized basis. The proliferation of desktop workstations will not erode the importance of scale economies in information processing.

Consider the airline industry. American Airlines began working on a computerized reservation system in the late 1950s as the volume of reservations began to outrun our capacity to handle them with index cards and blackboards. In 1963, the year SABRE debuted, it processed data related to 85,000 phone calls, 40,000 confirmed reservations, and 20,000 ticket sales. Today there are 45 million fares in the database, with up to 40 million changes entered every month. During peak usage, SABRE handles nearly 2,000 messages per second and creates more than 500,000 passenger name records every day. As we enhance SABRE, we are aggressively replacing 'dumb terminals' in travel agents' offices, airline reservation offices, and airports with workstations capable of intensive local processing. But as a system, SABRE still works only in a centralized environment. The level of data collection and management it must perform dwarfs the demands of the 1960s just as thoroughly as the performance of today's computers dwarfs the performance of their ancestors.

The continued importance of scale economies has at least two major implications for information technology. First, truly useful computer systems are becoming too big and too expensive for any one company to build and own; joint ventures will become the rule rather than the exception. Second, organizations (like AMR) that have developed centralized systems will eagerly share access to, and sometimes control of, their systems. For companies to remain low-cost providers of information, they must tap the enormous capacities of their systems. Tapping that capacity requires opening the system to as many information suppliers as possible and offering it to as many information consumers as possible.

FROM SYSTEMS TO INFORMATION

I do not mean to diminish the pivotal role of information technology in the future or to suggest that technology leadership will be less relevant to competitive success. Precisely because changes in information technology are becoming so rapid and unforgiving and the consequences of falling behind so irreversible, companies will either master and remaster the technology or die. Think of it as a technology treadmill: companies will have to run harder and harder just to stay in place.

But that's the point. Organizations that stay on the treadmill will be competing against others that have done the same thing. In this sense, the information utility will have a leveling effect. Developing an innovative new computer system will offer less decisive business advantages than before, and these advantages will be more fleeting and more expensive to maintain.

The role of information technology has always been to help organizations solve critical business problems or deliver new services by collecting data, turning data into information, and turning information into knowledge quickly enough to reflect the time value of knowledge. For thirty years much of our money and energy has focused on the first stage of the process – building hardware, software, and networks powerful enough to generate useful data. That challenge is close to being solved; we have our arms around the data-gathering conundrum.

The next stage, and the next arena for competitive differentiation, revolves around the intensification of analysis. Astute managers will shift their attention from systems to information. Think of the new challenge this way: in a competitive world where companies have access to the same data, who will excel at turning data into information and then analyzing the information quickly and intelligently enough to generate superior knowledge?

On Wall Street, there are stock traders who wear special glasses that allow for three-dimensional representations of data on their screens. They need three dimensions to evaluate previously unimaginable quantities of information and elaborate computer models of stock patterns. Manufacturers Hanover has developed an expert system to help its foreign-currency traders navigate through volatile markets.

In our industry, powerful new tools are helping us to answer faster and more precisely questions we have struggled with for years. What is the best price to charge for each perishable commodity known as an airline seat? How do you reroute aircraft after a storm disrupts airport operations? How do you distribute your aircraft between airports? How do you meet the special needs of each passenger without pricing your basic service out of reach? As the process of analysis intensifies, decisions we once made monthly will be made weekly. Those we made weekly, we'll make daily. Those we made daily, we'll make hourly.

Consider yield management, the process of establishing different prices for seats on a flight and allocating seats to maximize revenues – that is, calculating the optimal revenue yield per seat, flight by flight. Yield management is certainly one of the most data-intensive aspects of the airline business. Computers review historical booking patterns to forecast demand for flights up to a year in advance of their departure, monitor bookings at regular intervals, compare our fares with competitors' fares, and otherwise assist dozens of pricing analysts and operations researchers. During routine periods, the system loads 200,000 new industry fares a day. In a 'fare war' environment, that figure is closer to 1.5 million fares per day.

The initial challenge in yield management was to build software powerful enough to handle such demanding analyses. We spent millions of dollars developing SABRE's yield-management software, and we consider it to be the best in the world. Indeed, we believe our pricing and seat-allocation decisions generate hundreds of millions of dollars of incremental annual revenue. For years we guarded that software jealously. Since 1986, however, we have sold SABRE's revenue-management expertise to any company that wanted to buy it. One of our subsidiaries – called AA Decision Technologies, many of whose members built our original yield-management applications – is knocking on the doors of airlines, railroads, and other potential customers. Why? Because we believe our analysts are better at using the software than anyone else in the world. Whatever 'market power' we might enjoy by keeping our software and expertise to ourselves is not as great as the revenue we can generate by selling it.

Similarly, Mrs. Fields has begun marketing to other retail chains the sophisticated networking and automation system with which it runs its cookie operations. Price Waterhouse is helping companies like Fox Photo evaluate and install the Retail Operations Intelligence system, the backbone of Mrs. Fields's nationwide expansion.

This is the competitive philosophy with which American Airlines is entering the new era: we want to compete on the use of electronic tools, not on their exlusive ownership.

COMPUTERS AND COMPETITION: SABRE RECONSIDERED

Perhaps no case study better illustrates the changing competitive role of computer technology than the evolution of the system that helped define the old era – SABRE. According to conventional wisdom on SABRE, the fact that American Airlines developed the world's leading computerized reservation system generated substantial increases in traffic for us by creating market-power advantages over the competition. This has always been a difficult proposition to document. Analysts once pointed to so-called 'screen bias' as a source of marketing advantage, even though the government-mandated elimination of such biases in 1984 produced no appreciable decline in bookings for American Airlines. Others argued that American's access to CRS data regarding the booking patterns of travel agents gave us an incalculable information and marketing edge over our rivals – an argument that has proven groundless. Now the experts speak of a halo effect that by its very nature is impossible to identify or document.[2]

We are proud of what SABRE has achieved, and we recognize that it represents a billion-dollar asset to the corporation. But I have always felt the folklore surrounding SABRE far exceeded its actual business impact. SABRE's real importance to American Airlines was that it prevented an erosion of market share. American began marketing SABRE to travel agents only after United pulled out of an industry consortium established to explore developing a shared reservation system to be financed and used by carriers and travel retailers. The way American was positioned as an airline – we had no hubs, our routes were regulated, and we were essentially a long-haul carrier – meant that we would have lost market share in a biased reservation system controlled by a competitor. SABRE was less important to us as a biased distribution channel than as a vehicle to force neutral and comprehensive displays into the travel agency market.

My concerns about the conventional wisdom surrounding SABRE, however, go beyond the issue of market power. SABRE has evolved through four distinct stages over the past thirty years. In each stage, it has played different roles within American Airlines, and each role has had a different impact on the industry as a whole. Unfortunately, most analysts mistake the CRS distribution stage for the entire story. To do so is to invariably draw the wrong lessons.

SABRE took shape in response to American's inability to monitor our inventory of available seats manually and to attach passenger names to booked seats. So SABRE began as a relatively simple inventory-management tool, although by the standards of the early 1960s it was a major technical achievement.

Over the years the system's reach and functionality expanded greatly. By the mid-1970s SABRE was much more than an inventory control system. Its technology provided the base for generating flight plans for our aircraft, tracking spare parts, scheduling crews, and developing a range of decision-support systems for management. SABRE and its associated systems became the control center through which American Airlines functioned.

American installed its first SABRE terminal in a travel agency in 1976, inaugurating its now familiar role as a travel-industry distribution mechanism. Over the decade that followed we added new services to the database (hotels, rail, rental cars), built powerful new features to help travel agents offer better service, increased the installed base of SABRE terminals, and created a training and support infrastructure. SABRE now operates in more than 14,500 subscriber locations in 45 countries. Largely as a result of the proliferation of such systems, travel agents now account for more than 80 per cent of all passenger tickets as compared with less than 40 per cent in 1976. SABRE and its CRS rivals truly did transform the marketing and distribution of airline services.

Today, however, SABRE is neither a proprietary competitive weapon for American Airlines nor a general distribution system for the airline industry. It is an electronic travel supermarket, a computerized middleman linking suppliers of travel and related services (including Broadway shows, packaged tours, currency rates) to retailers like travel agents and directly to customers like corporate travel departments. Speak with any of the 1,800 employees of the SABRE Travel Information Network, the system's marketing arm, and you will hear that their division doesn't treat American Airlines materially differently from the other 650 airlines whose schedules and fares are in the system. American pays SABRE the same booking fees as other airlines do. SABRE's capacity to write tickets and issue boarding passes works similarly on other large carriers as it does on American flights. Although limited performance differences remain (largely as a result of SABRE's technical heritage as an in-house reservation system), SABRE programmers are working to overcome these limitations and put all carriers on an equal footing in the long term.

I do not deny that there is some halo effect from SABRE that benefits American Airlines in the marketplace, although we have never been able to determine the magnitude or causation. But the core identifiable benefit American Airlines now receives from SABRE is the revenue it generates. This is not an inconsequential advantage, to be sure, but it is difficult to argue that the SABRE system tilts the competitive playing field in ways that uniquely benefit American Airlines. This is not necessarily how we would prefer it, but it is what the technology, the market, and the US government demand. There is no compelling reason for a travel agency to accept a CRS that does not provide the most comprehensive and unbiased system for sorting through thousands of potential schedules and fares. If SABRE does not do the job, another system will. SABRE's industry-leading US market share of 40 per cent means that rival systems account for three out of every five airline bookings.

I receive weekly reports on our 'conversion wars' with Covia, whose Apollo reservation system remains our chief competitor, and the other US-based CRS systems. Subject to contract-term limitations that are established by the US government, it takes only thirty days for a travel agent who is unhappy with SABRE to pull the system out and install a competing system. If a CRS can be replaced within a month by a rival system, can it really be considered a source of enduring competitive advantage? The old interpretations of SABRE simply no longer apply.

As a group of HBR authors argued, 'Early developers of single source or biased sales channels should plan for the transition to unbiased electronic markets. That way, they can continue to derive revenues from the market-making activity.'[3] The alternative, they might have added, is for the biased channel to disappear altogether in favor of unbiased markets offered by other suppliers.

This is the future of electronic distribution. It is increasingly difficult, if not downright impossible, for computerized distribution systems to bind customers to products. Smart customers simply refuse to fall into commodity traps. (Indeed, American Hospital Supply has opened ASAP to products from rival companies.) It is increasingly difficult to design information systems that locked-out competitors can't eventually imitate or surpass. It is increasingly difficult for one company to marshal the financial resources to build new information systems on the necessary scale.

We are applying these new rules outside the airline realm. AMRIS, a subsidiary of AMR, is developing a computerized reservation and yield-management system for the hotel and rental car industries. Its power and sophistication will exceed anything currently available. We expect that the introduction of the Confirm system, scheduled for 1991, will affect pricing strategies and marketing techniques in the hotel and rental car industries in much the way Apollo and SABRE transformed the airline business. But we are not approaching the system itself in the same way we approached SABRE – at least three major differences stand out.

For one, we are not going it alone. AMRIS has formed a joint venture with Marriott, Hilton, and Budget Rent-A-Car to develop and market the Confirm system. Moreover, there will be nothing biased about Confirm's reservation functions – no tilted screen displays, no special features for the sponsors. Finally, the management aspects of the system, such as the yield-management software, will be generally available to any hotel or rental car company that wants to buy them. Confirm's sponsors are participating in the creation of the most sophisticated software in the world for their industries; but the moment the system is operational, they will offer its tools to their competitors around the world.

Not all companies will benefit equally from this new system. As is true with marketing or finance or employee development, some organizations will excel in manipulating, analyzing, and responding to the data Confirm generates. But no company will be locked out of access to the data or the opportunity to use it to compete. As in airlines and so many other industries, competition shifts from building tools that collect data to using generally available tools to turning data into information and information into knowledge.

BUILDING THE ORGANIZATIONAL PLATFORM

As with competition between companies, technological change will have profound consequences for the role of computers within companies. Until recently I was not a champion of office automation. Workstations were simply not powerful enough, nor affordable enough, nor easy to use, nor capable enough of being integrated into networks, to justify large investments in organizational computing. Indeed, a visitor to my office would be hard-pressed to find more than a handful of personal computers on the desks of the information technology professionals.

In the last few years, though, as a result of the technology changes I have outlined here, my caution has given way to genuine enthusiasm. But in this area too, it is time for new thinking. Understandably, given the earlier limitations of the technology, most companies approached office automation with an 'applications' mind-set. They developed discrete systems to make administration more efficient, to improve planning and control, or to deliver particular services more effectively.

We are taking a different approach. AMR has embarked on a multiyear, $150 million initiative to build an information technology platform modeled directly on the utility concept. This platform, called InterAAct, provides for the convergence of four critical technologies: data processing, office automation, personal computing, and networking. InterAAct will provide an intelligent workstation for every knowledge worker at AMR and will guarantee that every employee, no matter the rank or function, has easy access to a workstation. These workstations will be part of local area networks connecting work groups and a corporatewide network linking every location in the company, from departure gates in Boston to the underground SABRE facility in Tulsa, Oklahoma to the CEO's office in Dallas/Fort Worth.

The goal of InterAAct is not to develop stand-alone applications but to create a technology platform – an electronic nervous system – capable of supporting a vast array of applications, most of which we have not foreseen. InterAAct is an organizational resource that individuals and groups can use to build new systems and procedures to do their jobs smarter, better, and more creatively. It should eliminate bureaucratic obstacles and let people spend more time on real work – devising new ways to outmarket the competition, serve the customer better, and allocate resources more intelligently.

InterAAct began to take shape in 1987, and rollout started last June. It will take at least three years to extend the platform throughout the AMR organization. We are approaching the project with four guiding principles.

1 The platform must give each employee access to the entire system through a single workstation that is exceptionally easy to use and that operates with a standard user interface throughout the company.
2 The platform must be comprehensive, connecting all managerial levels and computing centers within the company, and be connectable to other companies' platforms.
3 The project must generate hard-dollar savings through productivity gains that are quantifiable in advance, and it should be rolled out in stages to ensure that it is delivering those hard-dollar savings.
4 The project must be managed as much as an *organizational* initiative as a technology initiative. Installing a powerful electronic platform without redesigning how work is performed and how decisions are made will not tap its true potential.

Installing InterAAct is partly a matter of faith. But $150 million projects cannot be justified on faith alone. After extensive study (including in-depth analyses of how 300 AMR employees from different parts of the company actually spend their time), we estimated that extensive automation could produce enough hard-dollar savings to generate a 10 per cent return on the InterAAct investment. AMR's standard hurdle rate is 15 per cent, so corporate directors with a pure financial mind-set would not have approved this project. That's where faith comes in. We are confident that the 'soft-dollar' benefits – better decisions, faster procedures, more effective customer service – will boost returns on InterAAct well above the hurdle rate. Still we are rolling out the project in stages and testing its impact along the way to be sure the hard-dollar savings materialize first.

I do not know how InterAAct will change our company's organizational structure and work practices over the next five years. But I guarantee there will be major changes. Most large companies are organized to reflect how information flows inside them. As electronic technologies create new possibilities for extending and sharing access to information, they make possible new kinds of organizations. Big companies will enjoy the benefits of scale without the burdens of bureaucracy. Information technology will drive the transition from corporate hierarchies to networks. Companies will become collections of experts who form teams to solve specific business problems and then disband. Information technology will blur distinctions between centralization and decentralization; senior managers will be able to contribute expertise without exercising authority.[4]

We are currently at work on a series of InterAAct applications to reduce common sources of frustration and delay within AMR. Why should employees remain in the dark about the status of resource requests? On-line forms and electronic signature control, to be introduced later this year, will help speed such approval processes. Why should an employee's personnel file remain locked away and inaccessible? A pilot project at the Dallas/Fort Worth airport allows baggage handlers to use a workstation to check how much overtime they have accrued. Eventually, employees should be able to file their own insurance claims or check on their reimbursement status. With respect to bureaucratic procedures, the potential of an electronic platform is obvious: eliminate paper, slash layers, speed decisions, simplify the information flows.

Other organizational possibilities are even more far-reaching. InterAAct standardizes spreadsheets and databases, provides direct access to the corporate mainframes, and will eventually support automatic report generation. The new ease and speed with which analysts will be able to accumulate and dis-aggregate data, conduct 'what if' scenarios, and share information should accelerate the planning and budgeting process. It's not our job to design a new planning process. InterAAct gives our analysts the potential to redesign systems to best suit their needs.

Finally, and perhaps of greatest importance, InterAAct will allow senior executives to make their presence felt more deeply without requiring more day-to-day control. Eventually, executives should be able to practice selective intervention. The information system, by virtue of its comprehensiveness, will alert senior managers to pockets of excellence or trouble and allow them to take appropriate action more quickly. Over time, the role of management will change from overseeing and control to resolving important problems and transferring best practices throughout the organization.

WHO NEEDS THE CIO?

The ultimate impact of the hardware, software, and organizational developments I have described is to proliferate and decentralize technology throughout the organization. Piece by piece and brick by brick, we and others are building a corporate information infrastructure that will touch every job and change relationships between jobs. Much work remains to be done. We need better tools, more connectivity, and richer data that reflect the real business needs of our companies. But in all these areas, momentum is moving in the right direction.

As technology reshapes the nature of work and redefines organizational structures, technology itself will recede into the strategic background. Eventually – and we are far from this time – information systems will be thought of more like electricity or the telephone network than as a decisive source of organizational advantage. In this world, a company trumpeting the appointment of a new chief information officer will seem as anachronistic as a company today naming a new vice-president for water and gas. People like me will have succeeded when we have worked ourselves out of our jobs. Only then will our organizations be capable of embracing the true promise of information technology.

NOTES AND REFERENCES

1 F. Warren McFarlan, 'Information Technology Changes the Way You Compete', *HBR* May–June 1984, p. 98.
2 For a comprehensive review of CRS technology in the airline industry, see Duncan G. Copeland and James L. McKenney, 'Airline Reservation Systems: Lessons from History', *MIS Quarterly,* June 1988.
3 Thomas W. Malone, Jo Anne Yates, and Robert I. Benjamin, 'The Logic of Electronic Markets', *HBR* May-June 1989, p. 168.
4 For a good overview of the organizational possibilities, see Lynda M. Applegate, James I. Cash, Jr., and D. Quinn Mills, 'Information Technology and Tomorrow's Manager', *HBR* November–December 1988, p. 128.

Chapter 12

Technik

Managers and management in Germany

Peter Lawrence

A dimension to the consciousness of German managers is the pervasive influence of *Technik*. This is a word and concept which has equivalents in other languages, for instance, *Teknik* in Swedish and *Techniek* in Dutch, but not in the English language. The starting point is that there are differences in the ways in which societies perceive and evaluate skill and knowledge; differences in the way they group and label branches of knowledge.

In English-speaking countries we distinguish between Arts and Sciences. The distinction is there in common speech and assumptions, is reflected in school timetables and college prospectuses and is actually thought to connote something. The distinction was formalized, publicized and given a further thrust by C.P. Snow's famous 'Two Cultures' lecture at Cambridge over twenty years ago. The key question here is: what is the role of engineering in the two cultures scheme, or the Arts versus Sciences distinction? C.P. Snow solved the problem by fitting in engineering as 'applied science', and this is a common, if not invariable convention, in the English-speaking world.

This 'applied science' label is, however, rather damaging to engineering. It tends to accord engineering a junior, dependent and subordinate status under the aegis of science. This is unfortunate for the status of engineering in Britain. It is also misleading since it tends to suggest that any advance in engineering is dependent on a prior advance in science, and this is simply not true. Sometimes this relationship and dependency exists. Sometimes it does not. The 'applied science' label also implies some misconception of engineering work. That is, it suggests that engineering work consists of the application of knowledge and principles derived from science, and again this is only partly and sometimes true. The 'applied science' formula also suggests a similarity between science and engineering, albeit with engineering as the junior partner. This is totally false. The output of science is knowledge; the output of engineering is three-dimensional artefacts. Much scientific work takes place in laboratory conditions where the influence of undesirable variables has been controlled: most engineering work is conducted 'on site' and is subject to environmental influences. Scientists who study things seek ideal solutions and universally valid laws. Engineers who make things seek workable solutions which do not cost too much. In short the 'applied science' label is damaging and misleading. And it does not exist in Germany.

It is indeed linguistically and culturally difficult to represent the two cultures thesis in German. This is not because the Germans do not make distinctions, but because they make different distinctions. Engagingly, they use the same word for Arts and Sciences. The German term *Wissenschaft* covers all formal knowledge subjects whether arts, natural sciences, or social science in the British scheme of things. And particular subjects are often designated by compound nouns based on *Wissenschaft*; economics, for instance, is *Wirtschaftwissenschaft*, literature, as a university subject, is *Literaturwissenschaft*. The Germans employ a second term *Kunst* to refer to art. Not to 'the Arts' in the British sense of the humanities, but to the end products of art – the paintings and statues and symphonies. And third, the Germans use the term *Technik* to refer to manufacture and the knowledge and skills relevant to it. That is, of course, to engineering knowledge and engineering and craft skills. It was noted that more German managers are qualified in engineering than in anything else, that engineers enjoy higher status in Germany than in Britain, and many reasons for this status differences were advanced. The existence in German culture of the concept of *Technik* not only avoids the demotion and misconception of engineering implicit in 'applied science', it also tends to dignify and even glamorize engineering under its distinctive rubric.

It is important to grasp that *Technik* really does not have any equivalent in English. The English word 'technique' is not a contender. It simply means a way of doing something, and the something is not necessarily technical or related to manufacture. Neither is the English word 'technology' an equivalent of the German concept of *Technik*. there are various objections to 'technology' in this context. First, it is a newfangled and imposed word, not a culturally rooted concept like *Technik*. Second, it again over-stresses the engineering/science link; when examples of 'technology' are offered they are typically from the 'science based' industries such as aerospace and electronics. Third, even if technology connotes some of the relevant knowledge, it does not connote relevant skills – *Technik* does. Fourth, technology is a rather vague word; there are no agreed definitions of technology, and the word is most often used by politicians wishing to strike a modern pose, politicians who would be hard put to define it. The corresponding word *Technologie* exists in German with the same vague connotations: it tends to be used by journalists, politicians and social scientists; managers and engineers talk about *Technik*.

It is also fair to add that the word *Technik* is actually used in German, and used in quite homely ways. It is not a term for the exclusive use of those who write books on the philosophy of science. In recent conversations with German managers the present writer has come across such gems as *'die Technik ist sauber'* (*'Technik* is wholesome – a manager denouncing the American practice of using pretty girls in machinery advertisements) and *'Ich bin eigentlich Technik Liebhaber'* ('Actually I'm a *Technik* lover' – production manager expounding on his job satisfaction). A standard German phrase is *'technisch gesteuert'*, meaning technically guided or directed in terms of *Technik*. One hears of advertising departments which are *'technisch gesteuert'*, or sales departments, or whole companies.

In short *Technik* exerts a pervasive influence in German firms and on German managerial thinking. The idea of *Technik*, however, affects the ethos of the typical German company as a whole, as well as the pronouncements of individual managers. The influence of *Technik* tends to account for the uncomplicated view taken by top managers of company goals and the means to achieve them. The goals are in the German view 'technicized', to the German manager they are self-evident and there is no need to have a seminar on it. *Technik* similarly accounts for the relative lack of interest in techniques of planning, control and decision-taking. The German is more likely to feel that *Technik* is in the foreground and managerial technique and corporate strategy take second place. The standing of *Technik* again supplies the clue to German apathy on foreign investments, mergers and takeovers. These measures are outside *Technik*; they are not the way in which German firms have traditionally expected to make money.

Technik is also, all things being equal, a force for integration. The German company is *Technik* in organizational form. The skilled worker, the foreman, the superintendent, the technical director are all participants in *Technik*. Of course there are many things which they do not have in common, but *Technik* is something which transcends hierarchy. It may also transcend particular functions in the company. This is most obviously true for various technical functions – Research and Development, Design, Production, Production Control, Maintenance and Quality Control. The fact of qualificational homogeneity in these functions (nearly everyone has one of two different qualifications and they are all engineers) tends to integrate these functions and *Technik* provides them with a cultural umbrella. It is also conceivable, though we would not press this point, that *Technik* is sufficiently pervasive to have some integrating effect as between technical and commercial functions. The first occasion on which the present writer heard the word *Technik* used by a German manager was in the observation of a public relations manager in a commercial vehicle company that *'Die Firma lebt schliesslich von der Technik'* ('After all, the firm lives from *Technik*').

Chapter 13

Finance and global competition

Exploiting financial scope and coping with volatile exchange rates

Donald R. Lessard

Two major shifts over the last decade have radically changed the battle for competitive advantage among corporations and, with it, the potential contribution of the finance function to that advantage. The first is the shift toward global competition. Multinational corporations (MNCs) not only participate in most major national markets, but they are also increasingly integrating and coordinating their activities across these markets in order to gain advantages of scale, scope, and learning on a global basis.[1] The second major change is the globalization of financial markets, which has been accompanied by the increased volatility of exchange rates and other key international financial variables.

The emergence of global competition represents a major threat, as well as an opportunity, to those European and American companies that gained competitive advantage under an older mode of multinational competition. Labeled 'multi-domestic' competition by Michael Porter, this now passing phase in the development of international business was characterized by large MNCs with overseas operations which operated for the most part independently of one another.[2] What centralization existed in this stage of the evolution of the MNC was typically restricted to areas such as R&D and finance. With global competition, a much larger proportion of value added is coordinated globally, including aspects of manufacturing, important aspects of marketing, and virtually all of R&D.

The emergence of global competition reflects the merging of previously segmented national markets caused by a variety of forces, including reductions in trade barriers, a convergence of tastes, and the introduction of new corporate strategies and structures. These new strategies and structures spearheaded primarily by the Japanese, have been successful in exploiting new competitive opportunities provided by placing both domestic and foreign markets in a global context. This adoption of a global perspective is reflected in large part in the increasing proportion of value added in many industries in the form of 'up front' intangibles, such as product and process design and software. The multidomestic era, in contrast, was characterized by transfers of fixed capital outlays and by recurring unit manufacturing costs. New global strategies also take advantage of changes in information technology and increased organizational sophistication to improve coordination among geographically dispersed operations.

This new competitive and financial environment places important demands on the corporate finance function. Broadly conceived, the role of the finance function under global competition is to:

1 provide the appropriate yardstick for evaluating both current operations and strategic alternatives;
2 raise the funds required for these operations and, in so doing, minimize the firm's cost of capital;
3 minimize taxes;
4 manage the risks inherent in the firm's activities.

The larger stakes associated with world-scale operations require greater financial resources and flexibility. Further, global competition in product and factor markets reduces the ability of companies to pass through to their customers any financing or tax costs in excess of those facing the lowest-cost producers. And this means that global competition affects not only MNCs with international operations, but also those largely domestic firms which face global competitors in their home goods and factor markets.

Especially critical and difficult, however, is the task of coping with volatile exchange rates in the new competitive environment. Volatile exchange rates create much greater challenges for a firm facing global competition than one operating in a largely multidomestic mode. Under global competition, exchange rate fluctuations not only change the dollar value of the firm's foreign profits and foreign currency denominated contractual assets and liabilities (such as accounts receivable and debt), they also alter the firm's competitive position and often call for changes in operating variables such as pricing, output, and sourcing. These decisions are complicated by the fact that volatile exchange rates distort traditional measures of current and long-term profitability, creating illusions that depend on the currency in which strategic alternatives are weighed and operating managers' performances evaluated.

A firm wearing 'dollar-colored' eyeglasses or, for that matter, 'yen-colored' eyeglasses will have a distorted view of its competitive position and is likely to make costly mistakes. A firm that sees through these effects will be in a much better position to judge its evolving competitive strengths. As a result, it will be more likely to make appropriate pricing, output, and sourcing choices in response to exchange rate shifts. It will also be in a better position to measure management's contribution to current performance by taking account of the effects of macroeconomic events beyond management's control.

These views are borne out by the experiences of 1978 and 1979, when the weak dollar favored global competitors with US production facilities, and of the period from 1981 through the end of 1985, when the strong dollar had the opposite effect. In the first period, many American firms were lulled into a false sense of security; their margins were 'holding up' in the face of increasing foreign competition when in fact they should have been doing much better than the norm. As a result, they were poorly prepared for the shift in competitive position *vis-à-vis* their foreign competitors caused by the 'dollar shock' of late 1980.

While it is impossible to forecast exchange rate movements, it is likely that extreme shifts such as these will reoccur, again altering international competitive positions and requiring major adjustments by firms. To make the proper adjustments to such changes, however, will require major changes in conventional corporate financial perspectives as well as considerably more and better dialogue between operating and financial management.

In this paper, I begin by describing changes in financial markets that have accompanied the shift to global competition. Second, I describe the changing role of finance in the context of global competition, and contrast it with the finance function under multidomestic competition. Third, I explore in greater depth the implications for the finance function of volatile exchange rates coupled with global competition. In so doing I argue that adoption of a global financial perspective critically affects a company's ability to maintain or strengthen its competitive position. Such a perspective must be incorporated into the firm's performance measurement scheme, its method of evaluating strategic alternatives, and its incentive compensation plan for local operating managers.

THE CHANGING FINANCIAL ENVIRONMENT

The emergence of global competition has coincided with and, to some extent, has given rise to major changes in the international financial environment. National financial markets have been linked into a single global market. At the same time, governments have continued or increased their use of financial instruments in pursuit of various policy goals, with the result that the world economy has become more volatile as reflected in the behavior of exchange and interest rates.

Increased international linkage of financial markets

The increased linkage of national money and capital markets has been caused by a variety of factors.[3] These include the dismantling of many restrictions on financial flows across national borders,[4] the deregulation of financial institutions both at home and abroad,[5] financial innovations that allow a separation of the choice of currency and other attributes of contracts from the jurisdiction in which they take place,[6] and increased corporate awareness of the intricacies of international finance.[7]

This increased integration of financial markets implies, of course, an evening of the cost of funds in various countries and a consequent reduction in the benefits accruing to a firm from spanning national financial markets.[8] At the same time, however, global competition puts more pressure on MNCs to take advantage of the remaining gains from global financial scope.

Increased financial intervention in domestic economies

Counteracting this trend toward a level international financial playing field is the increased use by governments of financial intervention to favor home firms or home production. Credit allocation, with its implicit subsidies to firms with access to credit, continues in several industrialized countries and is the rule in most developing countries. Many governments also offer concessional loans and explicit or implicit guarantees, to the point that these have become a major source of contention in international trade. Finally, most governments modify their basic tax structures by providing tax holidays, special deductions or credits, or the ability to issue securities exempt from personal tax to favor particular activities.[9] (While much of this intervention has been scaled back by the recent tax reforms in the USA and the UK, it is too early to tell whether these changes will last.)

Such intervention has led to intense 'shopping' for tax and financing benefits by MNCs and increasing competition among governments for projects.[10] In many cases, access to these financial benefits is linked to performance requirements such as the location of the plant or the level of employment or exports.[11] However, the value of such incentives to an MNC often depends on how it arranges its internal and external finances. For example, a firm with no need for borrowing in a country with cheap credit can shift its interaffiliate accounts so as to increase its apparent local borrowing requirements, while a firm investing in a start-up venture that will not break even for several years in a country offering a tax holiday can use transfer prices to shift profits from related operations to the tax-sheltered unit. Similarly, a firm engaged in overseas oil exploration may obtain a tax benefit from having operations in the USA because it can deduct these expenses from taxable profits in the USA, but not from profits in most other countries.[12] Later I will show that the ability of an MNC to exploit these conditions will depend on how many options it has for shifting funds or profits among subsidiaries across national boundaries, which in turn will depend on the number of places it operates and on the volume and complexity of the ongoing real and financial interactions among its component corporations. For this reason alone, a firm's international financial scope is likely to be an important factor in its competitiveness.

Exchange and interest rate instability

A major characteristic of the current world economy involving both the financial and real spheres is the extreme volatility of exchange and interest rates. This volatility is inextricably linked to differing degrees of integration internationally of finance, industry, and politics. Because of the high degree of integration among financial markets in major industrialized countries, factors influencing interest rates are readily transmitted across national boundaries. Given the lesser degree of integration in markets for goods and real factors of production, and the almost total lack of co-ordination in macroeconomic policies among nations, the result has been a high degree of volatility in nominal and real exchange rates.[13] This volatility, in turn, has led to sharp swings in the competitiveness of production facilities based in different countries.

In the short run, the volatility of exchange rates obscures longer-term trends in the international competitive position of particular industries. Over time, though, given that changes in exchange rates tend to offset cumulative differences in rates of inflation among countries,[14] the competitive effects of exchange rate changes are likely to be swamped by microeconomic factors such as the firm's productivity growth compared to that of its host economy.[15]

This long-run tendency for exchange rates and inflation differentials to offset each other is illustrated in Figure 13.1. Cumulative changes in the nominal exchange rate – the dollar price of the foreign currency – are depicted on the vertical axis, while changes in the real exchange rate – defined as changes in the nominal exchange rate relative to cumulative inflation differences – are shown on the horizontal axis.[16] Over relatively long periods, from 1973 until 1980 (points represented by open rectangles) or 1985 (triangles), for example, the spread of cumulative movements in real rates is much less than that of nominal rates.

In the short term of from six months to as long as two or three years, though, when inflation differentials are small, both real and nominal exchange rates move together. Between December 1980 and June 1982, for example, the dollar strengthened against most currencies in real terms and reduced the competitiveness of US producers. From June 1982 to December 1983, there was a further strengthening of the dollar relative to major currencies. By September 1986, however, this appreciation had been partially reversed in most cases, and more than completely reversed in the case of the yen.

This volatility of real exchange rates, as I shall later show, gives rise to

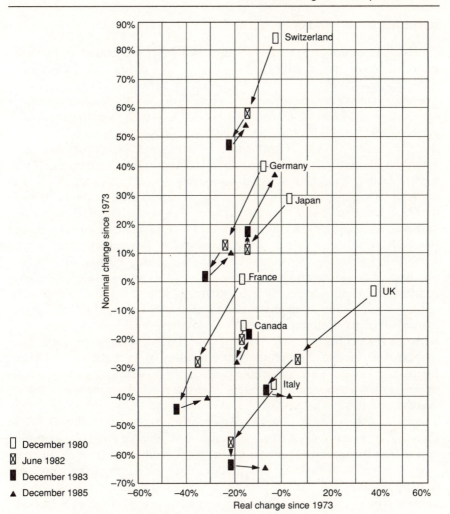

Figure 13.1 Nominal and real changes in exchange rates relative to US dollar

an exaggerated variability in corporate operating margins. This variability in turn creates two problems:

1 a potentially significant currency operating exposure;
2 great difficulty in evaluating the real profitability of overseas operations, both for purposes of strategic planning and compensating operating management.

Resulting threats and opportunities

Global competition, together with an increasingly integrated and volatile financial environment, gives rise to both opportunities for firms whose activities span real and financial markets in various countries. A major threat is the exposure to exchange rate volatility and its impact on the firm's competitive position. A closely related threat, which is more subtle and therefore more difficult to address, is the potential for management error due to illusions associated with short-run movements in exchange rates.

On the positive side, exchange rate volatility provides an opportunity to exploit relative price shifts, but this requires production flexibility that is costly and organizational flexibility that is difficult to sustain.[17] For example, in order to be able to switch sources to exploit changes in wage rates, a firm or its suppliers would have to invest in excess capacity; managers would have to devise (and, perhaps, rehearse) alternative sourcing and marketing responses that would be undertaken only in the case of major exchange rate shifts; and those geographic units within the firm whose competitive position is undercut by exchange rate shifts would have to be willing to concede market share to units that were favored by the change.

In addition to its effects on operations, exchange rate volatility combined with less than complete integration of financial markets and the significant degree of government intervention also results in new challenges for firms' financial activities. The treasurers of MNCs are now daily confronted with opportunities to speculate or engage in arbitrage across financial markets and tax regimes via internal financial transactions. At the same time, they also face greater risks if they do not carefully hedge their positions. While there is a reason to believe that profitable cross-border and cross-currency speculative and arbitrage opportunities are becoming scarcer as financial markets become more integrated, global competition creates more pressure to exploit those that remain because it shifts the incidence of differential taxes and financing costs to the firm. Thus, finance not only comes into play in addressing issues that arise because of global competition in product markets, but also becomes a direct factor in that competition.

Each of these threats and opportunities has significant implications for the finance function and its interaction with other aspects of the firm. In order to trace these implications we review the role of finance in the corporation and then consider how this role is or should be changed in the context of global competition.

THE ROLE OF FINANCE IN THE CONTEXT OF GLOBAL COMPETITION

Notwithstanding the periodic attempts of conglomerateurs or asset strippers to create value by repackaging financial claims, finance derives most of its value from the real business operations it makes possible. In an idealized world characterized by complete information, perfect enforceability of all contracts, and neutral-taxation, the principal roles of the finance function would be to provide a yardstick for judging business options to ensure that they meet the 'market test' for the use of resources, to raise sufficient funds to enable the firm to undertake all projects with positive present values, and to return funds to shareholders when they cannot be reinvested profitably.

Of course, the world does not match this idealization. Managers often possess information that they cannot or will not disclose to investors, and investors often disagree among themselves as well as with managers regarding future prospects. As a result, defining and monitoring contractual relationships between managers and various classes of claimants is extremely complex and imperfect.[18] Further, taxes are not neutral and access to particular capital markets is often restricted in a discriminatory fashion. As a result, financial contracts at times are not fairly priced.

In such an environment, finance can contribute to the firm's value in several ways in addition to its basic role of evaluating and funding investment opportunities.[19] Finance can add value by allowing the firm to:

1 exploit pricing distortions in financial markets;
2 reduce taxes:
3 mitigate risks and allocate them among different parties in order to maximize diversification benefits, create appropriate managerial incentives, and reduce costs of financial distress.

The nature and potential contribution to value of each of these functions will differ according to the type of international strategy pursued by the firm. For the sake of simplicity, I will view all multinationals as falling into three stylized categories:

1 international opportunists – firms that focus primarily on their domestic markets but engage in some international sales and/or sourcing from time to time;
2 multidomestic competitors – firms committed to a number of national markets with substantial value added in each country, but with little cross-border integration or coordination of primary value activities;
3 global competitors – firms that focus on a series of national and supra-national markets with substantial cross-border integration and co-ordination of primary value activities.

To what extent, then, does the finance function differ in these three different contexts?

The nature and potential contribution of some aspects of finance would appear to depend on the firm's multinationality – that is, the extent to which it spans different currency areas or tax jurisdictions – rather than on the degree of integration or coordination of the firm's primary activities such as manufacturing or marketing. Other aspects, however, especially those related to exchange rate risk, will differ dramatically depending on the pattern of competition. For this reason, a multinational firm may have a global orientation in finance but not in other activities. On the other hand, merely the fact of having multinational operations does not guarantee that it will realize the benefits of global scope in finance. Nevertheless, there are many reasons why the nature and potential contribution of the multinational financial function will differ in the context of global competition.

Table 13.1 provides an overview of the changing nature of the finance function and its linkages to the firm's overall competitive position under international, multidomestic, and global competition. It classifies firms into these three categories according to their method of dealing with a number of tasks assigned to the corporate treasury and planning staffs: evaluation of new investment, funding, performance measurement, and exchange risk management. I also include tactical pricing and output changes to exchange rate changes – not typically thought of as finance functions – because they are closely linked to exchange risk management and strongly influenced by a firm's currency perspective.

In the remainder of this section I review the implications of increased global competition together with the increased integration of financial markets for each of the major finance functions identified in Table 13.1.

Evaluating investment opportunities

A clear implication of the current competitive and financial environment is an increase in the complexity of investment opportunities and the corresponding increase in the potential for management error. The estimation of incremental benefits from resource outlays must take into account increased international interdependence among the various activities of the firm in terms of the benefits of scale, scope, learning and, hence, future opportunities.

In analyzing alternative plant locations, for example, the firm must evaluate not only differences in the direct costs of operating in each location, but also the impact of different choices on other strategic factors such as access to particular markets and the scale and experience 'platforms' that each alternative provides for future operations. Consider the case of the Korean consumer electronics companies whose US operations appear to break even at best.[20] This poor financial performance is often offered as evidence of uneconomic behavior on the part of Korean firms or, alternatively, of extensive Korean government subsidies of its firms' operations abroad. Another explanation, however, is that the financial performance of their US operations is only one component of their contribution to Korean firms' value. Others include the effect of unit cost

Table 13.1 Implications of global competition for finance function

| | Nature of competition | | |
	International opportunist	Multidomestic	Global
Function			
Investment Evaluation	Domestic perspective, few 'foreign' considerations	Yes/no decision to enter market or change mode to serve local market	Mutually exclusive global choices, currency and tax issues central
Funding operations*	Meet domestic norms	Meet local norms	Match global competitors' cost of capital
Exchange risk management	Focus on exposure of foreign currency contracts	Focus on exposure of converting foreign profits into dollars	Focus on exposure of home and foreign profits to competitive effects of exchange rate shifts
Output/pricing responses to exchange rate movements	No change in home currency price	No change in local currency price	Change in home and local price to reflect global competitive position
Performance measurement	Measure all operations in dollars at actual rates	Measure foreign operations in local currency	Measure all operations relative to standard that reflects competitive effects of exchange rate

*The entries in this row reflect typical behaviors of firms. Clearly, firms can and some do pursue global cost-minimizing financing strategies regardless of degree of global linkage of operations.

reduction due to the scale made possible by entering the US market on the profits of these firms in Korea (where they are oligopolists with substantial market power), and the benefits of learning from present US operations on future investment opportunities both in the USA and elsewhere. Choices among alternative product and marketing programs are even more complex because gains in some product market segments will result in erosion in others; in still other cases there may be positive carryover from success in one segment to others.

Given the varying patterns of government intervention, management must make choices among strategic alternatives that are further complicated by the need to trade off such direct and indirect benefits against alternative packages of investment incentives and performance requirements. Such decisions must be made on the basis of calculations of the present value of each package, which in turn will depend on the corporation's anticipated (worldwide) cash flow and its tax position in various jurisdictions. While similar complications existed under multidomestic competition, in general there were fewer interdependencies to contend with; each decision influenced only whether a firm should enter a particular national market rather than which of a number of (mutually exclusive) alternatives should be chosen as the best way of serving a world market.

A further complication is the problem of the 'bent measuring stick'.[21] Unless the firm conducts all interaffiliate transactions at arms' length, the profits (incremental cash flows) of any activity to any corporate unit will not equal the incremental flows to the corporation as a whole. There are many reasons, such as the desirability of reducing taxes, why a firm will not choose to adopt arms-length transfer pricing (even provided it is able to produce accurate estimates of such prices). Under global competition, this problem is exacerbated not only by the increased interdependencies among companies' operations, but by the overwhelming impact of exchange rate fluctuations on revenues, costs, and profits. In projecting future profits and cash flows, firms must see through the short-term effects on profits of currency movements to focus on their evolving competitive position assuming 'normal' exchange rates. I return to this point in the next section.

These complexities have contributed to a general view that discounted cash flow (DCF) techniques are no longer valid and that their use by US management has contributed to the decline of America's competitive position.[22] Nothing could be farther from the truth. It is probably true that US managers' overreliance on short-term return on investment (ROI) goals, coupled with a simplistic use of DCF techniques, does result in a bias against projects with indirect future benefits.[23] When properly employed, however, DCF measures provide a powerful framework for combining the effects of scale, scope, and learning on present and future activities.[24] What is needed is a closer linkage of competitive analysis and DCF techniques, not a surrender of quantitative techniques to more subjective approaches.

Funding business requirements

The increased scope of the competitive arena implies larger stakes for most major business gambles.[25] But the increased integration of financial markets in different countries has enhanced MNCs' external financing capacity as well, especially for those based in smaller countries with isolated capital markets.[26] Firms that consider themselves global competitors are broadening their funding bases to ensure that they will not find themselves at a competitive disadvantage in this regard.[27] Even a multidomestic competitor is not safe; the emergence of a firm with a global financing advantage will alter the terms of competition in much the same way as the emergence of a firm with globally-integrated production in an industry hitherto characterized by production only on a national scale.

Exploiting financing bargains

To the extent that financial markets are not fully integrated or that financing concessions differ among countries, MNCs' ability to span these markets will increase not only their ability to fund global operations, but also the likelihood that they can identify and exploit financing bargains. If a firm can identify financial investment or borrowing opportunities that are mispriced, it can add value by engaging in arbitrage or speculation. In general, opportunities for such gains are rarer than for gains arising from real market advantages; whereas real advantages are typically protected by barriers to entry, there are likely to be fewer and far less formidable barriers to financial transactions. Nevertheless, such opportunities do exist from time to time, especially in capital markets that are distorted and isolated by controls on credit and exchange market transactions. Exxon, for example, was able to issue zero-coupon bonds at a rate lower than the US Treasury yield on the comparable maturity, defuse the issue by buying an offsetting portfolio of Treasuries, and pocket a profit of nearly $20 million – largely because of differences in the Japanese tax code and restrictions on Japanese foreign investment.[28]

Because they are at once domestic and foreign, multinationals are more likely to encounter such exploitable distortions in financial markets than firms operating in single countries. They often can circumvent the credit market and exchange market controls that create these profit opportunities.[29] The internal financial networks of MNCs provide them with considerable latitude in the timing of interaffiliate transfers as well as in the choice of channels through which they transfer cash or taxable profits among their various national corporate components.[30] For example, a firm can advance funds to a subsidiary through an injection of funds in the form of equity or a loan, through a transfer of goods (or intangibles such as technology) at less than an arm's-length price, or by providing it with a guarantee that enables it to borrow locally. Depending on how the subsidiary is funded, the firm then has a similar array of channels through which it can withdraw funds. It can accelerate or delay transfers by leading or lagging interaffiliate settlements relative to their scheduled dates or, if such behavior is prohibited, by shifting the timing of the shipment of goods within the corporation.

This discretion over the channels and timing of remittances among related corporations is of little value within a single tax and monetary jurisdiction because transfers among units typically involve little cost and have no tax consequences. But when the firm operates across jurisdictions, certain channels may be restricted by virtue of exchange controls, and the use of others will trigger additional tax liabilities. Under these circumstances, the firm benefits from 'internalizing' these transactions.[31]

The increase in global competition is likely to increase the pressure on firms to pursue such gains because they are less able to pass through to their customers financing costs in excess of those facing the industry cost leaders. In a multidomestic context, in contrast, the competitive impact of these costs depends only on the relative position of firms in each country.

Reducing taxes

By appropriately 'packaging' the cash flows generated by business operations, firms often can substantially reduce the present value of government's tax take.[32] The simplest example in a single country setting is the use of debt as a way to reduce corporate income taxes. Firms operating internationally may be in a position to shift income into jurisdictions with relatively low rates or relatively favorable definitions of income. While some of these profit shifts occur through transfer prices of real inputs and outputs, the pricing of interaffiliate financial transactions often provides the greatest flexibility.[33]

In the current global competitive environment, though, a new factor is coming into play. As governments seek actively to manipulate their fiscal systems for nationalistic or distributional gains, MNCs 'shop' fiscal regimes and bargain over the distribution of rents resulting from a given activity. This is especially true of facilities on a world scale such as, for example, a plant to produce automobile engines located in a country with a relatively small local market. Such investments, by definition, are not premised on access to any single market. In these cases, tax system arbitrage becomes an area of active bargaining as well as gaming of passive fiscal systems.[34]

A final way that an international firm can reduce (the present value of expected) taxes is to structure interaffiliate commercial and financial dealings – as well as hedging the risks of individual units through external transactions – so as to minimize the chance that any of its corporate components will experience losses on its tax accounts and, as a result, have to carry forward some of its tax shields. Virtually all corporate income tax regimes are asymmetric in that they collect a share of profits but rebate shares of losses only up to taxes paid in the prior, say, three years. Otherwise, the losses must be carried forward with an implied reduction in the present value of the tax shields.[35]

As with financing costs, global competitors will be under much greater pressure than multidomestic competitors to match the lowest tax burden obtainable by any firm in the industry while, at the same time, increasing their flexibility in where to locate and how to coordinate value-adding activities. Thus, tax and financial management aimed at minimizing the firm's cost of capital, once an optional activity pursued by a handful of sophisticated firms, has become an integral element of global competitive strategy.

Managing risks

A final, often critical, role of finance is to offset particular risks inherent in the firm's undertakings and/or shift them to other firms or investors. Global competition, for example, increases firms' exposure to exchange rate volatility, but the firm can to a large extent lay off this risk through hedging transactions such as currency futures, swaps, options, or foreign currency borrowing. Some aspects of exchange risk can also be shifted to suppliers or customers through the choice of invoicing currencies. Alternatively, the firm can retain this risk and, in effect, pass it on to its shareholders.

An important insight of modern financial theory is that in an idealized capital market, the allocation of risk among firms, as well as the form in which it is passed on to investors, does not affect the value of the firm's securities. The reasoning is that sophisticated investors, simply by holding diversified portfolios, can manage most risks just as efficiently as corporate management. Under these circumstances, hedging by the corporation does not add to the value of a company's shares; and, as long as hedging prices are 'fair', contractual risk-sharing with suppliers or customers is of no consequence.

In practice, however, firms devote a great deal of effort to risk allocation in the form of hedging and risk-sharing. While much of this behavior can be traced to attempts by managers to 'look good' within imperfect control systems, several recent analyses provide a rigorous basis, consistent with shareholder value maximization, for hedging under some circumstances. In particular, as we have seen above, it can reduce the (present value) of taxes. It can also increase diversification benefits, improve managerial incentives, and reduce the probability (and thus the expected costs) of financial distress.[36]

Volatile earnings and cash flows may reduce a firm's ability to compete by distorting management information and incentives, hindering access to capital markets, and threatening the continuity of supplier and customer relationships. In the case of risks which, although outside the control of individual firms, affect many companies, such as the effects of variable exchange rates or relative prices of key commodities, firms with large specific exposures will benefit by laying off these risks to other firms or investors that have smaller or perhaps even opposite exposures. To the extent that the risks affecting particular business undertakings are at least partially controllable by one or more potential participants, risk allocation to create appropriate strategic stakeholdings is likely to reduce risk.

Although capital markets are becoming more integrated, there are barriers to cross-border investment in the form of taxes, controls on foreign investment, and political risks that have different effects on domestic and foreign investors, particularly transfer risks. Because of these barriers, investors in various countries will differ in their scope for diversifying particular risks and, hence, will place different values on particular securities.[37] They also may differ in their ability to mitigate those risks that are at least in part the result of choices by governments or other firms.[38] A firm may exploit this comparative advantage in risk-bearing by issuing securities either directly or indirectly (that is, by contracting with a firm with a different set of investors) to the investor group which will value them most highly. A global firm will not limit itself to any particular capital market base and, hence, will exploit this potential to the fullest.

Organizational implications

Global competition results in a blurring of the boundaries between finance and operations. Investment choices involve tax and financing considerations that depend on the firm's overall cash and profit position. Exchange rate impacts, typically the realm of the treasury function, are critical factors in the shifting competitiveness of the firm's operations. Operating profitability cannot be separated from financing considerations and must be judged relative to the macroeconomic environment.

Further, just as global competition blurs national product market boundaries, it also blurs national boundaries in finance. The use of finance to offset exchange exposures and to exploit distortions in financial markets requires a high degree of global coordination and centralization of decision-making. It may interfere with the management of operations sensitive to local conditions, especially in cases where global optimization reduces the profits of a local affiliate. Already bent, measuring sticks used in evaluating the performance of operations in a multidomestic context will be further distorted.

A further consequence of global management of the finance function is that it may require affiliates to act in conflict with local national interests, especially given MNCs' ability to bypass financial controls by using their internal networks.[39] In recent years, governments of major industrialized countries appear to have conceded the battle over the control of international capital flows and, as a result, have found themselves severely constrained in terms of policies to stabilize currency values. The battle is still being fought on fiscal terrain, but the advent of global competition and the resultant aggressive tax shopping by firms and fiscal promotion by particular countries is transforming the conflict from one between firms and nation-states to one among states.

The bottom line

Many of the differences between the finance function under global and under multidomestic competition are differences of degree rather than kind. Because of the ability it provides to span national financial markets, multinationality confers financial benefits on firms whether they compete globally or multidomestically. However, the ability of the firm to pass on differential financing costs and taxes is reduced by global competition. Thus, to compete effectively, MNCs will have to match their competitors' 'cost of capital'. As a result, the value of an effective finance function to a global firm will be overwhelming.

Furthermore, the greater currency volatility of the current period and its greater proportionate effect on firms' cash flows and profits, given global competition, increase the importance of effective foreign exchange management, both in terms of limiting risks and providing management information for tactical and strategic choices. The biggest differences appear to lie in this latter area, the role of finance in evaluating business options. The boundaries between finance and competitive behavior are blurred, and appear to becoming even more so.

COPING WITH EXCHANGE RATE VOLATILITY

Given the vital importance of exchange rate volatility in the new global environment, it is necessary to examine in greater depth how exchange rate volatility affects firms engaged in global competition and how these firms cope with this volatility. We focus on three specific issues arising from the coincidence of volatile currencies and global competition. These are:

1 the impact of exchange rate fluctuations on competitive position;
2 corporate management of exchange risk;
3 the effect of firms' currency perspectives on their strategic and tactical choices.

THE IMPACT OF EXCHANGE RATE SHIFTS ON COMPETITIVENESS

A major difference between multidomestic and global competition is the impact of exchange rates on the competitiveness and underlying profitability of an MNC. Under multidomestic competition, markets are national in scope and, typically, a substantial proportion of value added is local. In this case, exchange rate shifts do not significantly change the relative costs of operating in a particular market. As a result, revenues and costs move together in response to shifts in exchange rates and profits from foreign operations, when converted into dollars, move roughly proportionally with exchange rates.[40]

In contrast, under global competition prices in various national markets are more closely linked and larger proportions of firms' value added are likely to be concentrated in particular countries as they seek to exploit scale economies.[41] Therefore, unless all firms in a given industry have the same geographic patterns of value added, shifts in exchange rates will change their relative costs and profit margins. With the increased importance of Japanese and European firms in many industries, such exchange rate effects on operating profits are becoming the rule rather than the exception.[42]

The responsiveness of operating profits to shifts in exchange rates is comprised of two effects: a conversion effect and a competitive effect. The conversion effect is the proportional adjustment of foreign currency operating profits into dollars. By definition, it applies only to foreign operations. The competitive effect, in contrast, is the response of local currency operating profits to exchange rate shifts resulting from the interaction of the various competitors' supply and price responses. It applies to domestic as well as overseas activities.

Whereas financial exposure is caused by the sensitivity of the parent currency value of its money-fixed assets and liabilities to exchange rate movements, competitive or operating exposure is measured by the sensitivity of a firm's operating profits (margins) measured in the parent currency. Unlike financial exposures, which are sensitive to changes in nominal exchange rates, operating profit margins are exposed only to changes in real exchange rates (that is, exchange rate changes adjusted for offsetting inflation differentials). In further contrast to financial exposure, the extent of operating exposure depends on the structure of the markets in which the firm operates and not necessarily on the country or currency in which the firm purchases or sells its product.

Consider the case of Economy Motors, a hypothetical US manufacturer of small cars.[43] Economy produces components and assembles its products in the Midwest and sells them throughout the USA. Its products sell in direct competition with Japanese imports, which dominate the market and are the price leaders. The shifting competitive position of Economy under different real exchange rate scenarios is illustrated in Figure 13.2.

In the base year, when the yen and dollar are 'at parity', the Japanese set US prices so that they (and Economy) earn normal margins. In some later year, if the yen strengthens in line with the difference in inflation between the two countries, Economy remains on par with the Japanese. But, if the yen weakens while Japan's inflation remains below that of the USA (that is, the yen depreciates in real terms), the Japanese firms will have lower dollar costs, they will cut prices to gain share, and Economy will face lower profit margins.

The reason Economy faces an operating exposure, even though it operates entirely in its domestic market, is that the market in which it sells its output is much more integrated globally than the markets in which it purchases its inputs.

The sensitivity of a firm's profits to shifts in exchange rates under global competition may be greater than one for one. Extending the Economy

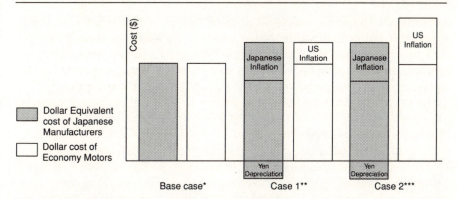

Figure 13.2 The effects of Japanese yen depreciation on the competitive position of Economy Motors

* Dollar equivalent costs of Economy Motors and its Japanese competitors are equal with exchange rates at parity.
** A change in the nominal exchange rate with no change in the real exchange rate does not change competitive position.
*** A change in the real exchange rate changes competitive position.

Motors example, assume that the operating margin under normal (parity) conditions is 15 per cent, that all costs are in US dollars, but that a 1 per cent change in the real yen/dollar rate results in a 0.5 per cent change in dollar prices of small cars in the USA. In this case, assuming that the optimal response to exchange rate involves matching price and holding volume constant, the sensitivity of profits would be 3.33 to 1.[44] In other words, a 10 per cent change in the real exchange rate would result in a 33 per cent change in operating profits!

A useful way to think of the price effects of exchange rate changes is to determine the currency habitat of each product or input. This currency habitat is defined as the currency in which the price of the good tends to be most stable.[45] The determinants of the currency habitat can be summarized along the two dimensions illustrated in Figure 13.3:

1 the geographical scope of the product market (that is, whether national or global);
2 the relative influence on price of both producer costs and consumer demand in a given market (that is, are prices determined largely by costs or demand?).

The geographic scope of the market will depend on the ability of the firm – or, in the case of inputs, its suppliers – to segment national markets, either by limiting transshipment or by differentiating the products it sells in various markets. As product markets become more globally integrated, prices in various national markets tend toward a world price.

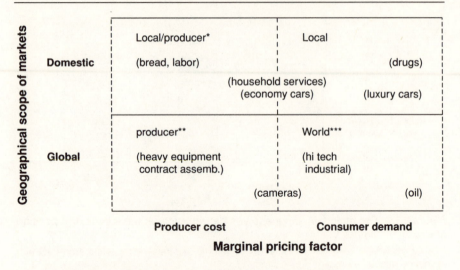

Marginal pricing factor

Figure 13.3 Determinants of currency habitat of cost/price

* Local if recurring costs of production are local.
** Currency of marginal firm/price leader depending on industrial structure.
*** Basket weighed by relative importance (income and elasticity) of consumers. As a first
approximation, this is the basket comprising special rights (SDRs).

The second dimension, the marginal pricing factor, captures the relative importance of supply and demand considerations which reflect, among other things, the competitive structure of the industry, the price elasticity of demand, the existence of complements and substitutes, and the structure of costs – in particular the level of nonrecurring costs.[46]

The two dimensions are not entirely independent because firms with signficant market power will be able to discriminate among national market segments by 'bundling' local services (e.g. warranties) with products or otherwise precluding transshipment by distributors or customers. For example, the recent collaboration of Mercedes Benz and other luxury auto manufacturers with the US government in requiring the stamping of various component parts, although ostensibly intended to reduce theft, was squarely aimed at stamping out the gray market. The same effect was also intended by MBZ's ads stressing that, while they stood behind all their cars, they could only promise exceptional service to owners who had purchased their cars from authorized US dealers. Quotas have performed the same role for Japanese manufacturers, preventing American importers from arbitraging the difference in the price of Toyotas in Japan and in the US.

In the case of local markets (as shown in the upper half of Figure 13.3), the currency habitat will clearly be the local currency if costs are locally determined as well; in such cases international supply and demand will play little or no role. The more interesting cases, however, are those in which a significant proportion of value added is global in nature – that is, cases where the degree of global configuration and coordination is high, but producers have sufficient market power to engage in some price discrimination across borders. Because such firms can effectively segment national markets through their own market power and with the collaboration of regulatory authorities, they face local currency-denominated marginal revenue curves. If recurring costs are low, therefore, they will tend to maintain constant local prices in the face of exchange adjustments. If these costs are high, in contrast, they will adjust both local price and volume.

Manufacturers of patented drugs with local currency habitats, for example, represent one extreme in this regard; they are able to segment national markets, and thus maintain market power and high margins, with the help of national regulations of the drug industry. In contrast, the price habitat of mid-range autos such as Toyota and Nissan, in the absence of quotas, would involve a combination of local and producer currencies. The currency habitat for luxury cars, which face less elastic demand because of greater product differentiation, and with higher margines of sales prices over recurring costs, will also involve a mix of local and producer currencies, but with a much greater weight on the local currency.

In those cases where transshipment cannot be barred – whether because of the portability of the product, the inability of manufacturers to control distribution channels, or the power of key customers – prices will tend to a single world level (lower half of Figure 13.3). The camera industry is a case in point, with gray marketeers denying manufacturers the ability to fully segment national markets. The same is true of industrial equipment and components that are sold to sophisticated buyers which themselves are multinational. The currency habitat of these world prices will depend on the weighted importance of demand from various countries and the currency habitat of the costs incurred.

FOREIGN EXCHANGE RISK MANAGEMENT UNDER GLOBAL COMPETITION[47]

Exposure to exchange rate movements is a serious problem for firms in the current environment, especially those that are global competitors.[48] Unfortunately, current corporate methods of managing exchange risk are unlikely to help firms compete effectively and, indeed, are likely to provide misleading signals. In fact, as currently practiced, corporate exchange risk management differs little from staking the assistant treasurer with a sum of money to be used to speculate on stock options, pork bellies, or gold.

There are two reasons for this. First, foreign exchange risk management is concerned primarily with deciding whether to hedge or retain particular exposures arising from operations. Instead of this residual or reactive approach, management should take a more anticipatory or 'proactive' stance, seeing to it that operating exposures and their expected effect on profits are factored into operating decisions. The second shortcoming of conventional corporate practice is that it tends to focus on exposures that lead to identifiable foreign exchange gains or losses – that is, on effects on contractual items instead of operating profits.

Foreign exchange exposure can be defined as the sensitivity to shifts in exchange rates of a number of variables but, for hedging purposes, the choice comes down to two alternatives: reported profits or operating cash flows. While the cash flow perspective makes more economic sense, the reporting perspective also matters to the extent that it affects managerial decisions or financial market reactions.[49]

Figure 13.4 shows the major categories of foreign exchange exposures on these two dimensions: earnings and cash flow. Accounting impacts are classified in terms of their recognition in accounting reports. Under FAS 52, transaction gains or losses are separately identified in earnings,

Accounting exposures		Contractural	Noncontractural	Fictitious
	Transaction	Contracts including accts payable, receivable, and debt 'closed out' during period	not applicable	not applicable
	Translation	Contracts on books at end of period	not applicable	fixed assets
	Operating	Gains/losses on 'unbooked' contractural items incl. backlogs, purchase contracts	gains/losses on items not contracted for (e.g. future revenues, expenses)	not applicable

Cash flow exposures

Figure 13.4 Types of foreign exchange exposures

translation adjustments bypass earnings and go directly to net worth, while operating impacts are mixed in with all other sources of variation in profits. Cash flow effects are classified in terms of the nature of the cash flows in question, whether they are contractually fixed in some currency or depend on competitive interactions. The fictitious category refers to those accounting adjustments that have no cash flow counterpart.

The category that differs most under global, as opposed to multidomestic, competition is the operating/noncontractual cell; it reflects the effect of exchange rate fluctuations on operating profits via adjustments in revenues and costs that have not been contracted for. This is what we refer to as operating exposure; and it consists of both a conversion effect and a competitive effect. The conversion component is readily identifiable. The competitive component, however, is much more difficult to isolate because it is mixed in with a host of other variables, both macroeconomic and microeconomic, that affect local operating profits. As a result, few firms have fully incorporated it into their foreign exchange management function. Furthermore, they often do not take into account the effects of these exposures on current and projected operating profits in making strategic and tactical choices. I review each of these points in turn below.

Measuring operating exposures

While most firms are aware of their operating exposures, it appears that few have defined or estimated them very carefully or developed explicit procedures for dealing with them. In reviewing the 1982 and 1983 annual reports of thirty firms, Mark Trusheim found that while twenty-two mentioned the impact of the strong dollar, sixteen of them focused on the reduced dollar value of foreign revenues and only six discussed the impacts of the strong dollar on their margins or overall competitive position.[50]

While these external reports do not provide a full picture of internal procedures, they do show that the treatment of operating exposure by US firms is less than complete. This is corroborated by more detailed reviews of the practices of a few firms. In in depth interviews with three firms, Alberto Boiardi found that all three had a rough notion of their operating exposures, but none had acted on this estimate.[51] In discussions with six firms, we have found the same thing – a growing awareness of the general concept, but little or no progress in addressing it.[52] One reason for this is the relative difficulty of assessing operating exposures. The second is the difficulty of managing them appropriately in the typical firm.

Managing operating exposures

Firms have both business and financial options for reducing exchange rate exposures. Three kinds of business options are available for managing operating exposure:

1 configure individual businesses to have the flexibility to increase production and sourcing in countries that become low cost producers due to swings in exchange rates;
2 configure individual businesses to reduce operating exposure by matching costs and revenues;
3 select a portfolio of businesses with offsetting exposures.

The first option, configuring operations to increase flexibility, can actually increase a firm's expected operating profits while reducing their variability. The other two can at best reduce variability with no reduction in expected operating profits, but they are more likely to result in some reduction in expected operating profits. In the case of configuring individual businesses to match revenues and costs (or the currency habitats), such matching typically will require some departure from the optimal configuration in terms of scale and locational advantages. In the case of selecting a portfolio of businesses with offsetting exposures, reduced profits are likely to result from the increased administrative costs and reduced efficiency associated with managing diverse businesses without other synergistic linkages.

After having considered and exhausted its business options, the firm can then hedge its remaining exposure using the available financial options. These include long-dated forwards, swaps, or borrowing in foreign currencies as well as long-dated currency options. None of these provides an exact hedge because they are keyed to nominal rather than real exchange rates. But they do have the advantage that, when competitively priced, they reduce the variability of operating profits with little or no reduction in the anticipated level of such profits.[53]

Given the magnitude of operating exposures and the fact that they do not necessarily have even the same sign as contractual exposures, firms that hedge only their contractual exposures may actually increase their total exposures.[54] If a firm doesn't understand its operating exposure, its best policy is not to hedge at all.

STRATEGIC AND TACTICAL RESPONSES TO EXCHANGE RATE VOLATILITY

Volatile exchange rates create havoc for operations in a globally competitive industry. Shifts in rates require decisions regarding pricing, output, and sourcing. Such decisions will typically involve a balancing act between vaguely understood limits to sustainable price differentials across countries and the impact of local currency price shifts on demand and hence profits. Further, given the emergence of global oligopolies in many industries, pricing decisions must reflect anticipations of competitor actions or reactions. Estimating these reactions is likely to be complicated by the fact that competitors differ significantly in the currency composition of their costs and, perhaps more importantly, in the currency 'eyeglasses' they wear.

Currency fluctuations also introduce noise into measures of current performance, reducing the firm's ability to monitor its evolving competitive position and distorting its results-based managerial incentives. If these distortions are significant, and if many key decisions are made on a decentralized basis, the firm's choices are likely to be distorted as well. Finally, the impact of currency fluctuations on the accounting-based performance of current operations is likely to distort management's perception of the long-term profitability of strategic choices.

The finance function plays a key role in terms of the perspective it can provide on these choices (though, again, this does not involve finance in the classic sense of raising funds). This financial perspective on operating choices, and the rules of thumb that follow from it, are part of a firm's culture. The perspective is the result of corporate experience and is unlikely to change rapidly. Thus, given the drastic change in the competitive and financial environment over the last ten years, we expect that this perspective is only now catching up with the new reality. This is clearly borne out in the relatively slow evolution of corporate management of exchange risk; and we expect it to have major operational implications as well.

Currency illusions and pricing/output choices

A perennial pricing error that results from a currency illusion is the practice of setting foreign currency prices by multiplying the domestic price by the spot rate and, perhaps, adding an 'uplift' for the extra costs of doing business overseas. The illusion is that the foreign currency proceeds can be converted into dollars at the spot rate. In fact, the prices quoted are for future payment and, hence, can be converted only at the forward rate (or expected future spot rate) corresponding to the time of cash payment.[55] Foreign currency receivables are often 'booked' at spot rather than forward rates with the result that operating profits are initially over(under)stated in the case of depreciating (appreciating) currencies, and subsequently exposed to potentially large transaction gains or losses that on average will offset the initial error. Depending on when and at what rate these receivables are 'handed off' to treasury, the true profitability of one or both functions will be misstated and, as a result, management decisions based on such measures are likely to be misguided.[56] If operating managers are held responsible for the ultimate exchange gains or losses, their contribution is likely to be buried in the noise created by exchange rate movements; if they are not, their contribution will be systematically misstated.

This illusion can be readily overcome by valuing all contracts at forward rates, but this requires an explicit recognition that generally accepted accounting rules are misleading and requires a shift in procedures.[57] While many firms have changed procedures to do this, it is surprising how many have not. A survey of corporate practices found, for example, that 55 per cent of all firms included transaction gains and losses in measures of managers' performance.[58] This illusion affects all international transactions and is not unique to global competition. It does illustrate, however, how traditional perspectives can interfere with appropriate choices in a changing environment.

With global competition, the problem is compounded by the fact that pricing must take into account not only the relative value of future claims in various currencies, but also the possibly asymmetric impact of exchange rate shifts on the firm's costs and prices relative to competitors'. If prices in local currencies are left unchanged subsequent to an exchange rate shift, prices will differ across countries inviting transshipment and entry by competitors in 'high-priced' markets. On the other hand, if prices in the parent currency are maintained by 'passing through' the exchange rate variations to local customers, sales volumes may react abruptly (as Volkswagen discovered when the DM strengthened in the early 1970s, and as Caterpillar later discovered in 1980).

Therefore, even with full information and a 'rational' economic perspective, pricing adjustments to exchange rates will be extremely complex. In practice, though, we expect that choices will be strongly influenced by the firm's view of the world. The easiest response to a change with complex implications is to do nothing. Doing nothing, however, can be defined in many different ways. In the case of pricing responses to exchange rate changes, it could mean either maintaining parent currency (dollar) prices or maintaining local prices. Active responses, in turn, could involve either maintaining market share or adjusting both price and volume to maximize long-term profit.

Under multidomestic competition, with its largely autonomous business operating units, the likely choice is for the firm to 'do nothing' by maintaining local prices (although the parent currency, as I argue below in discussing control systems, may play a role as well). But with global competition, firms' activities are more integrated or coordinated across national boundaries; and, therefore, such companies are more likely to 'do nothing' in terms of maintaining parent currency prices. This may be a reasonable approximation to the correct response for a firm that dominates world markets, but it will not be for a member of a global oligopoly with players based in several different countries and with different currency perspectives and exposures.

The heavy construction equipment industry, once dominated by a handful of US firms but now including major Japanese and European players in global markets, is an excellent case in point. A study by David Sharp found that distributor prices of construction equipment sold in the UK by US firms tended to remain stable in dollars through 1980, when they shifted abruptly in response to Japanese inroads and subsequently appeared to be sensitive to the dollar-yen relationship as well.[59] Sharp's finding of different pricing responses to exchange rate changes for virtually identical products produced and sold in the UK by a US- and a UK-based firm supports the view that at least some of this effect can be traced to organizational factors rather than to technical demand or cost considerations.

An ironic example of this type of pricing is the reported satisfaction of many US firms with their ability to hold their own and maintain dollar prices during the 1978–9 period. In fact, given the general weakness of the dollar in that period, they should have been able to raise dollar prices. And US firms are not alone in their susceptibility to this kind of illusion. The Swedish auto firms, especially Volvo, nearly priced themselves out of US markets in this same period. They apparently attempted to pass through to US customers most of the appreciation of the kroner, while they should have maintained relatively stable dollar prices.[60]

The picture is not all bleak, of course. Sharp's findings do suggest an awakening of US firms to the realities of global pricing; and Boiardi found that pricing decisions were consistent with market structures, although two of the three firms he studied faced multidomestic product market competition.

Interaffiliate pricing

A large proportion of the production of firms engaged in global competition moves through interaffiliate sales on its way to the final customer. Apart from their effect on taxes and tariffs, the transfer prices on these sales have no economic impact except through their effect on the behavior of managers. These behavioral impacts, though, are often substantial and represent a key determinant of the firm's pricing of final sales. Firms with strong, centralized (or coordinated) production units often apply tranfer pricing rules based on standard costs measured in the parent currency, imposing the full impact of currency swings on the downstream stages of the value-added chain. The shift to global competition strengthens this effect because the pursuit of global scale and scope economies requires greater integration and coordination of production.

There are several different ways to address this problem. The first is to create a mechanism whereby transfer prices are negotiated to approximate arms-length prices, in essence forcing production and marketing to share the exchange rate impact. This clearly is most feasible where there are alternative sources of supply. The second is to leave the transfer prices as they are, but adjust the performance standards (margin or ROI) of the marketing units to reflect the baseline effect of the exchange rate shifts. This requires substantial prior analysis of exchange rate impacts and appropriate operating responses at the corporate and business unit levels. A third is to substitute narrower performance standards (e.g. market share or some measure of production efficiency) for profits at one or more stages in the value-added chain. This approach, however, presupposes that the firm can specify such standards appropriately, which may be as complex as solving the cross-unit profit conflicts. This clearly is one the most challenging issues arising in global competition and is likely to push key operating responsibilities up to higher levels within the firm.

Measurement of current performance

Currency fluctuations clearly have an impact on measured performance, and these measures presumably feed back to a host of operating choices. While there are many technical issues in measuring performance in the face of fluctuating exchange rates, the debate among practitioners appears to be centered on whether performance should be measured in local currency or parent currency terms. Under conditions of global competition, neither is appropriate.

An ideal performance measurement system should hold managers responsible for those aspects of performance over which they have substantial control, but should limit responsibility for performance shifts due to factors largely beyond their control. Of course, this ideal is seldom met because, for example, fluctuations in aggregate demand are inextricably linked with managerial success in producing and selling a product. The emphasis of many firms on market share, however, is an attempt to separate these two effects. In the case of currency fluctuations, some aspects of the problem are easily separable while others are not. Gains or losses on accounts receivable due to currency surprises, for example, are outside the control of operating managers and can be split by transferring these claims to treasury at forward rates. If this is done, treasury's contribution through 'selective hedging' (that is, speculation in the form of market timing) is measured fairly as well.

In contrast, with the competitive component of operating exposures, such a clear separation is not possible because managers can and should react to exchange rate shifts by altering prices, output, and sourcing. However, so long as there is some degree of global competition it should be recognized that profits in either local or parent currency should fluctuate in line with real exchange rates. A failure to incorporate this in the control system is likely to lead managers to 'leave money on the table' when they are favored by exchange rates, and to sacrifice too much market share by attempting to hold constant dollar margins when exchange rates work against them. What is required is a budgetary standard that adjusts for exchange rate impacts. The process of developing such a budget should involve a joint exploration by corporate and business unit managers of the impacts of and appropriate responses to exchange rate movements, thus providing a dress rehearsal of future tactics as well as a standard against which future performance can be judged.[61]

The controller of a US firm's UK plant, in an interview with Sharp, stated that he would have no trouble in meeting his firm's goal of 'cutting real dollar costs by x percent' because in the period since the program was announced the pound had already fallen by a large fraction of that amount relative to the dollar. His response would have been quite different if the corporation had demanded an x per cent cut relative to costs normalized for exchange rate circumstances.

Assessment of strategic options

Just as currency fluctuations affect current performance, they alter the attractiveness of the firm's strategic options. The long-run profitability of a given business unit will depend on its evolving competitive advantage, but in the short-run this advantage can be swamped by exchange rate impacts. In some cases, the firm will be able to enhance its average profitability over time by building a degree of flexibility that allows it to shift sourcing and value-added activities as exchange rates move.[62] In general, though, it will have to look past the current circumstances to assess its long run competitiveness. This requires a multi-stage procedure:

1 Assess future expected cash flows conditional on purchasing power parity, concentrating on micro-competitive factors such as the firm's likely experience gains relative to anticipated wage increases.[63]
2 Assess how these (conditional expected) cash flows would differ under alternative exchange rate scenarios.
3 Estimate expected cash flows across scenarios given their relative probability.

In general, management should choose the alternative with the highest (net present value of) expected cash flows, without regard for exposure to exchange rate movements, because as noted above these exposures can be offset by financial hedges that have little or no cost in present value terms.

While there have been several recent surveys of capital budgeting practice,[64] none have focused on this issue; so I do not know whether academic observers are lagging behind practice or whether practice is lagging behind changes in the competitive environment. I suspect some of both.

SUMMARY AND CONCLUSIONS

The emergence of global competition, coupled with both an increased integration of financial markets and continued exchange rate volatility, represents a major threat and challenge to corporations that have been accustomed to world market leadership under conditions of multidomestic competition.

In this article I have argued that the finance function plays a critical role in such firms' ability to respond to this challenge, both because of the demands it places on the finance function *per se* and its requirement for a much more sophisticated financial perspective on strategic and tactical choices. Because a company's financial eyeglasses are part of its culture, these changes in outlook inevitably lag changes in the competitive environment. Nonetheless, it does appear that many firms are rapidly moving down the 'financial learning curve' and changing their standard operating procedures to accommodate the economic realities of global competition. Within the traditional realm of finance – which includes primarily the treasury functions of raising funds externally and maneuvering them efficiently within the corporation – companies will find that, in order to compete globally, they must fully exploit the benefits of multinational financial scope to match their competitors' costs of capital and effective rates of taxation. The structure of external financing will have to become more global; the corporate convention of home currency borrowing at the parent level and local currency borrowing on the part of foreign subsidiaries must give way to a more complex pattern which recognizes the interaction between three distinct objectives: minimizing taxes, exploiting financial incentives and distortions in financial markets, and offsetting exchange rate exposures.

Even greater changes will be required in areas where finance interacts more closely with operations, most notably in the area of management of foreign exchange exposures. Financial managers, with their knowledge of the dynamics of foreign exchange, must assist operating managers in configuring operations to cope with exchange rate volatility and in responding to shifts as they occur. The corporate treasury should also provide internal hedging facilities (or contingent performance standards) to insulate operating managers from the inevitable exposures resulting from strategic bets to the fullest extent consistent with maintaining incentives for proper operating responses. At the same time, they must expand the scope of exchange risk management to deal with operating exposures – a task which multinationals are only beginning to address.

Another important area where there is great room for improvement is performance measurement for overseas operating units. Each unit's performance should be measured relative to a standard that takes into account key changes in the macroeconomic environment, especially the exchange rate. Further, the measures employed must capture trade-offs that improve corporate profits at the expense of the one unit in question. To do this, firms will have to redefine business units along the dimensions where greatest coordination is required. But because no structure can simultaneously capture geographic, product, and stage of value added leverage points, they will also have to create more effective processes for mediating conflicts among units. This will involve, among other things, the substitution of relatively narrow measures of business performance such as market shares and unit costs for the 'bottom line' measures of financial profitability now favored by most US firms.

NOTES

1 By scale economies I refer to reductions in unit costs and/or product enhancements resulting from increases in production volume in a single location. Scope economies, in contrast, are reductions in unit costs and/or product enhancements associated with current production volume in related facilities and include the benefits of coordination of multiple facilities. Learning, or experienced-based, gains are unit cost reductions or quality improvements resulting from cumulative volume in one location or in related facilities.

2 See Porter (1986) for a number of perspectives on global competition. Full citations for all references are provided at the end of this chapter.

3 For an overview of recent evidence on financial market integration see Kohlhagen (1983).

4 For recent studies of border controls and their effects on financial markets see Dooley and Isard (1980) and Otani and Tiwari (1981).

5 The deregulation of financial institutions first took the form of an escape from national regulations by banks operating 'offshore' as described by Dufey and Giddy (1981), Grubel (1977), Kindleberger (1974), Tschoegl (1981) and others. Subsequently, partly in response to this offshore competition and partly to shifts in domestic considerations, it has taken the form of reduced regulation of financial intermediation within individual national markets.

6 For a review of recent financial innovations see Dufey and Giddy (1981) and Antl (1984).

7 This integration of financial markets, however, is as yet far from complete. Many less-developed countries, in response to foreign exchange crises brought about by their own external borrowing coupled with the world recession, have imposed new or tighter exchange controls and other measures that isolate the domestic financial markets from world markets. As a result, private firms based in these countries have seen their access to international financial markets cut back to pre-1970 levels. Nevertheless, financial markets are considerably more integrated on balance than they were in 1970. For a review of exchange restrictions see International Monetary Fund (1985). Rosenberg (1983) discusses the (in)effectiveness of these controls given the mechanisms firms can use to circumvent them.

8 For overviews of the benefits of spanning national financial markets see Robbins and Stobaugh (1973) and Lessard (1979).

9 These include the ability to make use of tax-exempt bond issues, '80/20' offshore financing in the US and similar measures in most other industrialized countries.

10 These two points are discussed in Baldwin (1986) and Encarnation and Wells (1986), respectively.

11 See Guisinger and Associates (1985).

12 This has been given as one explanation of BHP's (Australia) recent acquisition of a US exploration company.

13 For recent views of the determinants of exchange rates see Dornbusch (1983), Frenkel and Mussa (1980), and Stockman (1980).

14 This tendency, known as purchasing power parity, was first outlined by Cassel (1923). For a recent review of its various meanings see Shapiro (1983). For evidence on how well it holds see Roll (1979), Frenkel (1981), and Adler and Lehman (1983).

15 For a discussion of the strategic implications of purchasing power parity in the long run, see Keichel (1981).

16   The real exchange rate, therefore, is a statistical construct that measures the relative price of a composite of goods in the US relative to a similar composite in the foreign country. In this particular case, wholesale price indices are used as measures of the prices of composite goods in the two countries.

17   See Baldwin (1986) and Kogut (1983).

18   Myers (1984) and Barnea, Haugen, and Senbet (1981) discuss the impact of these agency effects on financing choices.

19   Here we refer to the warranted (present discounted) value of the firm's shares, the most complete financial measure of a firm's performance.

20   This discussion draws on Jun (1985).

21   This term was coined by Robbins and Stobaugh (1973) in their pathbreaking study of the multinational finance function.

22   This theme is developed by Hayes and Abernathy (1980) and echoed by Hout, Porter, and Rudden (1982). Donaldson (1972) provides an earlier indictment of DCF techniques, but also indicates where the problems lie and suggests ways to overcome them.

23   Surveys by Schall, Sundem, and Geijsbeek (1978), Wicks (1980) and Oblak and Helm (1980) show that managers continue to favor DCF rate of return calculations in spite of the clear superiority of additive present value calculations when a projects gives the firm access to significant future growth options. Hodder and Riggs (1985) discuss how methodological biases distort decisions. Hodder (1984) finds substantial differences between the capital budgeting practices of US and Japanese firms. US firms appear to be more 'number driven', but devote much less attention to alternative scenarios and strategic options.

24   One line of development of DCF techniques that is capable of taking many of these effects into account is the valuation by components method. Under this approach, cash flows are segregated into equity equivalents, debt equivalents and option equivalents and each component is valued using techniques most appropriate to its characteristics. Developed by Myers (1974), it has been extended to the international context by Lessard (1979, 1981). Recent work on valuing option equivalents in investment decisions by Brennan and Schwartz (1985) and Myers and Majd (1983) is particularly promising in the treatment of future options to invest, abandon, or receive various forms of government support. Booth (1982) and Lessard and Paddock (1980) discuss the advantages of valuation by components relative to more traditional single discount rate approaches.

25   Vernon (1979) argues that, in contrast to the 1960s, a much larger proportion of new product launches will be on a global scale with correspondingly larger outlays.

26   An interesting case in point is the Danish firm Novo whose entry into US equity markets is chronicled by Stonehill and Dullum (1982). Firms such as Schlumberger and Ciments LaFarge also have shifted their funding from small home markets to integrated world markets; and, most recently, Jardine-Mathieson is shifting its 'window' on world capital markets from Hong Kong to Bermuda. (NYT, March 29, 1984). Adler (1974) and Agmon and Lessard (1977) discuss the basis for such capital market-seeking behavior of firms.

27   Hitachi, for example, recently announced the creation of five offshore financing centers for its worldwide business.

28   See the discussion of this transaction by John Finnerty (1985).

29   For a discussion of the relationship between credit market and exchange controls and pricing distortions in financial markets, see Dooley and Isard (1980) and Otani and Tiwari (1981).

30 The source of profit shifting in this case comes from manipulating the transfer prices among affiliates. See Brean (1985) for an in-depth discussion of financial transfer prices.

31 The concept of internalization has been extended to many other aspects of multinational firms' activities. See in particular, Buckley and Casson (1976), Hennart (1982), and Rugman (1981). Robbins and Stobaugh (1973), studying a set of multidomestic multinationals, showed that the potential gains from exploiting internal financial systems were often significant. They also found, however, that larger firms tended not to fully exploit this potential because of external constraints (or self-policing to avoid sanctions) and organizational limitations.

32 Packaging can involve setting up tax-minimizing ownership chains as discussed by Rutenberg (1970) or choosing the nature of the parent's financial claim – equity, debt, or a claim on royalties – as discussed by Horst (1977) and Adler (1979).

33 Examples of the impact of interaffiliate financial transactions of a firm's taxes are presented by Horst (1977) and Brean (1985).

34 The industry studies in Guisinger and Associates (1985) confirm that fiscal incentives are most important when several alternative sites provide access to the same (common or world) market.

35 As explained by Smith and Stulz (1985), the tax authorities effectively hold a call option on profits. As a result, the expected tax rate is an increasing function of the variability of the taxable profits of each entity that comprise the firm.

36 See for example, Barnea, Haugen and Senbet (1985), Shapiro and Titman (1985), and Smith and Stulz (1985).

37 For an introduction to the impact of cross-border barriers on the valuation of securities see Stulz (1985).

38 See Blitzer *et al.* (1984).

39 See Robbins and Stobaugh (1973) for an early discussion of this point.

40 In more technical terms, given a change in the real exchange rate, the demand and supply curves facing the firm will remain unchanged in the local currency (adjusted for inflation). Hence the optimal output and local currency price will remain unchanged, as will local currency profit. From a dollar perspective, of course, both curves will shift by the same amount, and the dollar profit will change in proportion to the change in the exchange rate.

41 An exception may be IBM, which, because of its very large scale and its responsiveness to national goals, is able to balance global scale production of specific products with a matching of value added and sales in most major markets.

42 Under these circumstances, a change in the real exchange rate will result in a relative shift of demand and supply curves, regardless of the reference currency of the firm. This implies that the optimal price and volume will change as well.

43 This example is drawn from Lessard and Lightstone (1986).

44 If volume does not change, the sensitivity of operating profits can be defined as:

$$\text{sensitivity (profits)} = \text{sensitivity} \cdot \frac{\text{revenues}}{\text{profits}} - \text{sensitivity (costs)} \cdot \frac{\text{costs}}{\text{profits}}$$

See Levi (1982) and Flood and Lessard (1986) for a fuller explanation.

45 The term currency habitat is introduced by Flood and Lessard (1986). It also has been defined as the 'currency of price (cost) determination'. It may differ from the currency in which prices are quoted, invoices issued, or transactions settled. For example, the prices of various products are quoted in currencies (e.g. crude oil in dollars, certain chemicals in DM, etc.) and as shown by

Grassman (1973), and Magee (1974), certain currencies are favored in invoicing, but the prices of the products in these currencies are not necessarily independent of the exchange rate.

46 If nonrecurring costs (e.g., 'up front' capital investment including R&D and capital equipment) are a large proportion of total costs, then the marginal unit costs of production will be small and pricing will be dictated primarily by demand considerations.

47 This section draws substantially on Lessard and Lightstone (1986).

48 For a discussion of why a firm should concern itself with managing foreign exchange risk see Logue and Oldfield (1977), Wihlborg (1980), Dufey *et al.* (1984), and the references cited in note 36 above.

49 There is no clearcut evidence on the financial market reactions to alternative approaches for reporting exchange rate impacts. For one attempt, and reasons why one should not expect definitive findings, see Dukes (1980) and the accompanying discussion by Lessard.

50 See Trusheim (1984).

51 See Boiardi (1984).

52 The same point is made by Waters (1979) and several corporate finance officers interviewed in 'Coping with Volative Currencies Multinationals Go For Safety First', *Business Week*, January 30, 1984.

53 Lessard and Lightstone (1986) describe an alternative hedge that is keyed to real exchange rates and, hence, is more appropriate for operating exposures.

54 This is especially likely for firms facing global competition that hedge their transactions as well as transaction exposures because under FASB 52 foreign plant often is classified as a foreign asset, without regard to whether the prices of its inputs and outputs are determined locally, the prices of its inputs are determined locally but its outputs are priced internationally, or vice versa. While this contradiction can be resolved to some extent by clever choices of functional currencies, it is unlikely that any translation scheme will capture the exposure of a firm's future operating profits that is so important in the context of global competition.

55 For a recent example, See Hintz-Kessel-Kohl, a Harvard Business School case prepared by Professor Thomas Piper.

56 See Lessard and Lorange (1977) and Lessard and Sharp (1984) for further discussion of this point.

57 Strictly speaking, valuing contracts at forward rates only makes them comparable to contracts for future payment in the home currency. Both should still be discounted to reflect the time value of money measured in that currency.

58 See Chesowitz, Choi, and Bavishi (1982). The question asked does not quite address the issue we raised, since transaction gains/losses include anticiapted gains/losses and surprises. We would contend, however, that neither component should be included in a manager's evaluation. See Lessard and Sharp (1984) for further discussion.

59 See Sharp (1984).

60 The reason why the dollar/kroner relationship should have had little or no impact on dollar prices of Saabs and Volvos was that transshipment was limited and demand, presumably, relatively price elastic. Further, the effect of the exchange rate on short run variable costs measured in dollars was quite small given that under Sweden's labor policies, wages are a fixed cost in the short run, and most inputs are internationally sourced.

61 Lessard and Sharp (1984) discuss alternative ways that this recognition of exchange rate effects can be incorporated in the control system.

62 This point is discussed by Kogut (1983, 1984) and Baldwin (1986).

63 As might be expected, there is no unambiguous measure of purchasing power parity. An instructive attempt to estimate parity rates, though, is provided by Williamson (1983). A further issue that has not been resolved in the literature is whether real exchange rates tend to return to parity or to move randomly. The results of Adler and Lehman (1983) and Roll (1979) support the latter view, but the macroeconomic models of Dornbusch (1983) and others suggest that there must be some type of adjustment over time.

64 See Note 23.

REFERENCES

Adler, Michael (1974) 'The Cost of Capital and Valuation of a Two-Country Firm,' *Journal of Finance* 29, 119–37.

Adler, Michael (1979) 'U.S. Taxation of U.S. Multinational Corporations'. In M. Sarnat and G. Szego (eds) *International Trade and Finance*, Vol. 2., Cambridge, MA., Ballinger.

Adler, Michael and Bernard Dumas (1983) 'International Portfolio Choice and Corporate Finance: A Survey', *Journal of Finance* 38, 1471–87.

Adler, Michael and Bruce Lehman (1983) 'Deviations from Purchasing Power Parity in the Long Run', *Journal of Finance* 38, 1471–87.

Agmon, Tamir and Donald Lessard (1977) 'Financial Factors and the International Expansion of Small Country Firms', in Agmon and Kindleberger (eds), *Multinationals from Small Countries*, Cambridge, MA.: MIT Press.

Antl, Boris (1984). *Swap Financing Techniques*, London: Euromoney Publications.

Baldwin, Carliss (1986) 'The Capital Factor: The Impact of Home and Host Countries on the Global Corporation's Cost of Capital', in Michael Porter (ed.) *Competition in Global Industries*. Cambridge, Mass.: Harvard Business School Press.

Barnea, Amir, Robert A. Haugen and Lemma W. Senbet (1981) 'Market Imperfections, Agency Problems, and Capital Structure: A Review', *Financial Management* 10 No. 2 (Summer), 7–22.

Barnea, Amir, Robert A. Haugen and Lemma W. Senbet (1985) 'Management of Corporate Risk', *Advances in Financial Planning and Forecasting*, JAI Press, Vol. 1, 1–2345.

Blitzer, Charles, Donald Lessard and James Paddock (1984) 'Risk Bearing and the Choice of Contract Forms for Oil Exploration and Development', *The Energy Journal 5*, 1–28.

Boiardi, Alberto (1984) 'Managing Foreign Subsidiaries in the Face of Fluctuating Exchange Rates', unpublished master's thesis, MIT Sloane School of Management.

Booth, Lawrence D. (1982) 'Capital Budgeting Frameworks for the Multinational Corporations', *Journal of International Business Studies 8*, No. 2, 113–23.

Brean, Donald J.S. (1985) 'Financial Dimensions of Transfer Pricing', in Rugman and Eden (eds) *Multinationals and Transfer Pricing*, London and Sydney: Croom Helm.

Brennan, Michael J. and Eduardo S. Schwartz (1985) 'Evaluating Natural Resource Investments', *Journal of Business 58*, No. 2, 135–58.

Buckley, Peter and Mark Casson (1976) *The Future of Multinational Enterprise*, London: Macmillan.

Carsberg, Bryan (1983) 'FAS # 52–Measuring the Performance of Foreign Operations', *Midland Corporate Finance Journal 1* No. 2, 47–55.

Cassell, Gustav (1923) *Money and Foreign Exchange after 1914*, London: Macmillan.

Caves, Richard (1986) 'Entry of Foreign Multinationals into U.S. Manufacturing Industries', in Michael Porter (ed.) *Competition in Global Industries*, Cambridge, Mass.: Harvard Business School Press.

Chesowitz, James, Frederick Choi and Vinod Bavishi (1982) *Assessing Foreign Subsidiary Performance: Systems and Practices of Leading Multinational Companies*, New York: Business International.

Cornell, Bradford and Alan C. Shapiro (1983) 'Managing Foreign Exchange Risk', *Midland Corporate Finance Journal 1* No. 3 (Fall).

Donaldson, Gordon (1972) 'Strategic Hurdle Rates for Capital Investment', *Harvard Business Review 50*, (March–April) 50–55.

Dooley, Michael and Peter Isard (1980) 'Capital Controls, Political Risks and Deviations from Interest Rate Parity', *Journal of Political Economy 88* 370–84.

Dornbusch, Rudiger (1980) 'Exchange Rate Economics: Where Do We Stand?' *Brookings Papers on Economic Activity 1*, 143–85.

Dornbusch, Rudiger (1983) 'Equilibrium and Disequilibrium Exchange Rates', *Zeitschrift fur Wirtschafts–und Sozial Wissenschaften 102*, New York: Prentice-Hall.

Dufey, Gunter and Ian Giddy (1978) *The International Money Market*, New York: Prentice-Hall.

Dufey, Gunter and Ian Giddy (1981) 'Innovation in the International Financial Markets', *Journal of International Business Studies 7*, No. 2, 33–52.

Dufey, Gunter, Ian Giddy and S. L. Srinivasulu (1984) 'The Case for Corporate Management of Foreign Exchange Risk', *Financial Management 12*, No. 4.

Dukes, Roland (1980) 'Forecasting Exchange Gains (Losses) and Security Market Response to FASB 8', in Levich and Wihlborg (eds.) *Exchange Risk and Exposure*. Lexington, MA.: Heath Lexington.

Encarnation, Dennis and Louis T. Wells (1986) 'Negotiating Global Investments: A View From the Host Country', in Michael Porter (ed.) *Competition in Global Industries*. Cambridge, Mass.: Harvard Business School Press.

Finnerty, John (1985) 'Zero Coupon Bond Arbitrage: An Illustration of the Regulatory Dialectic at Work', *Financial Management* (Winter).

Flood, Eugene (1985) 'Global Competition and Exchange Rate Exposure', Research Paper # 837, Graduate School of Business, Stanford University (September).

Flood, Eugene and Donald Lessard (1986) 'On the Measurement of Operating Exposure to Exchange Rates: A Conceptual Approach', *Financial Management*, Vol. 16, No. 1 (Spring).

Frenkel, Jacob A. (1981) 'The Collapse of Purchasing Power Parities During the 1970's'. *European Economic Review 16*, 145–65.

Frenkel, Jacob A. (1983) 'Flexible Exchange Rates, Prices and the Role of 'News': Lessons from the 1970s'. *Journal of Political Economy.*

Frenkel, Jacob A. and Michael Mussa (1980) 'The Efficiency of Foreign Exchange Markets and Measures of Turbulence', *American Economic Review 70* 374–81.

Grassman, Sven (1973) 'A Fundamental Symmetry in International Payment Patterns', *Journal of International Economics* (May).

Grubel, Herbert (1977) 'A Theory of International Banking', *Banca Nazionale del Lavoro Quarterly Review.*

Guisinger, Steven E. and Associates (1985) *Investment Incentives and Performance Requirements: Patterns of International Trade, Production, and Investment*, New York: Praeger.

Hayes, Robert and William Abernathy (1980) 'Managing Our Way to Economic Decline', *Harvard Business Review 58* No. 4, 67–77.

Hennart, Jean-Francois (1982) *A Theory of Multinational Enterprise*, Ann Arbor: University of Michigan Press.

Hodder, James E. (1984) 'Evaluation of Manufacturing Investments: A Comparison of U.S. and Japanese Practices', Technical Report 84–8, Department of Industrial Engineering and Engineering Management, Stanford University (November).

Hodder, James E. and Henry E. Riggs (1985) *Pitfalls in Evaluating Risky Projects'*, *Harvard Business Review 85*, No. 1 (January – February), 128–35.

Horst, Thomas (1977) 'American Taxation of Multinational Firms', *American Economic Review 67* 376–89.

Hout, Thomas, Michael Porter and Eileen Rudden (1982) 'How Global Companies Win Out', *Harvard Business Review 60*, No. 5, 98–108.

Ijiri, Yuji (1983) 'Foreign Exchange Accounting and Translation', in R.J. Herring (ed.) *Managing Foreign Exchange Risk*. New York: Cambridge University Press.

International Monetary Fund (1985) *Annual Report on Exchange Arrangements and Exchange Restrictions*.

Jun, Yong Wook (1985) 'The Internationalization of the Firm: The Case of the Korean Consumer Electronics Industry', unpublished Ph.D. Thesis.

Keichel, Walter, 3rd (1981) 'Playing the Global Game', *Fortune 104*, (November 16), 111–26.

Kindleberger, Charles P. (1969) *American Business Abroad*, New York: Yale University Press.

Kindleberger, Charles P. (1974) *The Formation of Financial Centers: A Study in Comparative Economic History*, Princeton Studies in International Finance, No. 36.

Kindleberger, Charles P. (1985) 'Plus Ça Change – A Look at the New Literature', in Kindleberger (ed.) *Multinational Excursions*. Cambridge, MA.: M.I.T. Press.

Kogut, Bruce (1983) 'Foreign Direct Investment as a Sequential Process', in Kindleberger and Audretsch (eds), *The Multinational Corporation in the 1980s*. Cambridge, MA.: M.I.T. Press.

Kogut, Bruce (1985) 'Designing Global Strategies: Profiting from Operating Flexibility', *Sloan Management Review* (Fall) 27–38.

Kohlhagen, Steven (1983) 'Overlapping National Investment Portfolios: Evidence and Implications of International Integration of Secondary Markets for Financial Assets', in R. Hawkins, R. Levich, and C. Wihlborg (eds), *Research in International Business and Finance*, Greenwich, CT.: JAI Press.

Lessard, Donald (1979a) 'Transfer Prices, Taxes and Financial Markets: Implications of Internal Financial Transfers within the Multinational Firms', in R. B. Hawkins (ed.), *Economic Issues of Multinational Firms*. Greenwich, CT: JAI Press.

Lessard, Donald (1979b) 'Evaluating Foreign Projects: An Adjusted Present Value Approach', in D. R. Lessard (ed.), *International Financial Management*. New York: Warren, Gorham, and Lamont.

Lessard, Donald (1981) 'Evaluating International Projects: An Adjusted Present Value Approach', in R. Krum and F. Derkindiren (eds), *Capital Budgeting under Conditions of Uncertainty*. Hingham, MA: Martinus Nijhoff.

Lessard, Donald and John Lightstone (1986) 'Coping with Exchange Rate Volatility: Operating Financial Responses', *Harvard Business Review* (July / August).

Lessard, Donald and Peter Lorange (1977) 'Currency Changes and Management Control: Resolving the Centralization/Decentralization Dilemma', *Accounting Review 52*, No. 3, 628–37.

Lessard, Donald and James Paddock (1980) 'Evaluating International Projects: Weighted-Coverage Cost of Capital versus Valuation by Components', unpublished manuscript.

Lessard, Donald and Alan Shapiro (1984) 'Guidelines for Global Financing Choices', *Midland Corporate Finance Journal 1*, No. 4, 68–80.

Lessard, Donald and David Sharp (1984) 'Measuring the Performance of Operations

Subject to Fluctuating Exchange Rate." *Midland Corporate Finance Journal 2*, No. 3, 18–30.

Levi, Maurice (1982) *International Finance*, New York: McGraw Hill.

Logue, Dennis and George Oldfield (1977) 'Managing Foreign Assets when Foreign Exchange Markets are Efficient', *Financial Management 7*, No. 2, 16–22.

Magee, Stephen (1974) 'U.S. Import Prices in the Currency Contract Period', *Brookings Papers on Economic Activity*, No. 1, 303–23.

Magee, Stephen and Ramesh Rao (1980) 'Vehicle and Nonvehicle Currencies in Foreign Trade', *American Economic Review 70*, 368–73.

Mason, Scott and Robert C. Merton (1985) 'The Role of Contingent Claims Analysis in Corporate Finance', in Altman and Subrahmanyan (eds) *Advances in Corporate Finance*. New York: Dow Jones Irwin.

Myers, Stewart (1974) 'Interactions of Corporate Finance and Investment Decisions', *Journal of Finance 29*, 1–25.

Myers, Stewart (1984) 'The Capital Structure Puzzle', *Journal of Finance 39*, 575–92.

Myers, Stewart and Saman Majd (1983) 'Calculating Abandonment Value Using Option Pricing Theory', M.I.T. Sloan School of Management, Working Paper # 1462–83 (August).

Oblak, David J. and Roy J. Helm, Jr. (1980) 'Survey and Analysis of Capital Budgeting Methods Used by Multinationals', *Financial Management 9*, No. 2, 37–40 (Winter).

Otani, Ichiro, and Siddarth Tiwari (1981) 'Capital Controls and Interest Rate Parity: The Japanese Experience 1978–1980', *Staff Papers 28*, 798–815.

Porter, Michael (1986) 'Competition in Global Industries: A Conceptual Framework', in Michael Porter (ed.) *Competition in Global Industrie*, Cambridge, MA.: Harvard Business School Press.

Robbins, Sidney and Robert Stobaugh (1973) *Money in the Multinational Enterprise*, New York: Basic Books.

Roll, Richard (1979) 'Violations of Purchasing Power Parity and Their Implications for Efficient International Commodity Markets', in Sarnat and P. Szego (eds.) *International Finance and Trade*, Vol 2, Cambridge, MA: Ballinger.

Rosenberg, Michael (1983) 'Foreign Exchange Controls: An International Comparison', in A. George and I. Giddy (eds.), *International Finance Handbook*. Vol. 1. New York: John Wiley.

Rugman, Alan (1981) *Inside the Multinationals: The Economics of Internal Markets*, New York: Columbia University Press.

Rugenberg, David (1970) 'Maneuvering Liquid Assets in a Multinational Company: Formulation and Deterministic Solution Procedures', *Management Science 16*, No. 10, B671–84.

Schall, Lawrence D., Gary L. Sundem, and W. R. Geijsbeek, Jr. (1978) 'Survey and Analysis of Capital Budgeting Methods', *Journal of Finance 33*, No. 1, 281–7.

Schydlowsky, Daniel (1973) 'Simulation Model of a Multinational Enterprise', in S. Robbins and R. Stobaugh, *Money in the Multinational Enterprise*.

Shapiro, Alan (1983) 'What Does Purchasing Power Parity Mean?' *Journal of International Money & Finance 2*, 295–318.

Shapiro, Alan and Sheridan Titman (1985) 'An Integrated Approach to Corporate Risk Management', *Midland Corporate Finance Journal 3*, No. 2, 41–56.

Sharp, David (1984) 'Organization and Decision Making in the U.S. Multinational Firm: Price Management Under Floating Exchange Rates', Dissertation, M.I.T. Sloan School of Management.

Smith, Clifford W. Jr., and Rene Stulz (1985) 'The Determinants of Firms' Hedging Policies', *Journal of Financial and Quantitative Analyses 20*, No. 4 (December).

Sophonpanich, Chartsiri (1984) 'Exchange Rates and Corporate Performance', unpublished master's thesis. M.I.T. Sloan School of Management.

Stockman, Alan (1980) 'A Theory of Exchange Rate Determination', *Journal of Political Economy 88*, 673–98.

Stonehill, Arthur and Kare Dullum (1982) *Internationalizing the Cost of Capital*, New York: John Wiley.

Stulz, Rene (1985) 'Pricing Capital Assets in an International Setting: An Introduction', *Journal of International Business Studies*, 15, No. 3, 55–73.

Tobin, James (1978) 'A Proposal for International Monetary Reform', Cowles Foundation Discussion Paper 506, Yale University.

Trusheim, Mark (1984) 'An Exploration of Foreign Exchange Operating Expense', unpublished master's thesis. M.I.T. Sloan School of Management.

Tschoegl, Adrian (1981) *The Regulation of Foreign Banks: Policy Formation in Countries Outside the United States*, NYU Monograph series in Finance and Economics (1981–2).

Vernon, Raymond (1979) 'The Product Cycle Hypothesis in a New International Environment', *Oxford Bulletin of Economics & Statistics 41*, 4.

Waters, Somerset (1979) 'Exposure Management is a Job for all Departments', *Euromoney* (December) 79–82.

Wicks, Marilyn E. (1980) *A Comparative Analysis of Foreign Investment Evaluations Practices of U.S. based Multinational Companies*, New York: McKinsey and Co.

Wihlborg, Clas (1980) 'Economics of Exposure Management of Foreign Subsidiaries of MNCs', *Journal of International Business Studies 6*, No. 3, 9–18.

Williamson, John (1983) *The Exchange Rate System*, Washington, D.C.: Institute for International Economics.

Chapter 14

Trade, location of economic activity and the multinational enterprise

A search for an eclectic approach

John H. Dunning

The main task of this article is to discuss ways in which production financed by foreign direct investment, that is, undertaken by MNEs, has affected our thinking about the international allocation of resources and the exchange of goods and services between countries. The analysis takes as its starting point the growing convergence between the theories of international trade and production, and argues the case for an integrated approach to international economic involvement, based both on the location-specific advantages of countries and the ownership-specific advantages of enterprises. In purusing this approach, the article sets out a systemic explanation of the foreign activities of enterprises in terms of their ability to internalize markets to their advantage. It concludes with a brief examination of some of the effects which the MNE is allegedly having on the spatial allocation of resources, and on the patterns of trade between countries.

We begin by looking at the received doctrine on international economic involvement. Until around 1950 this mainly consisted of a well-developed formal theory of international trade and a complementary but less well-developed theory of capital movements. With the notable exceptions of John Williams (1929)[1] and Bertil Ohlin (1933), international economists of the interwar years were less concerned with explanations of the composition of goods and factors actually traded across boundaries (and implicitly, at least, of the spatial distribution of economic activity) as with theorizing on what would occur if, in the real world, certain conditions were present. The Heckscher–Ohlin model, for example, asserted that, provided certain conditions were met, countries would specialize in the production of goods which required relatively large inputs of resources with which they were comparatively well endowed, and would export these in exchange for others which required relatively large inputs of factors with which they were comparatively poorly endowed. The conditions included that countries had two homogeneous inputs, labour and capital, both of which were: locationally immobile (i.e. they were to be used where they were located); inputs were converted into outputs by the most efficient (and internationally identical) production functions; all entrprises were price-takers, operating under conditions of atomistic competition; there were no barriers to trade and no transaction costs; and international tastes were similar.

The Heckscher–Ohlin model has been criticized in the literature on various grounds, including the unreality or inapplicability of its assumptions. Here, I would underline some of the implications of three of these assumptions: factory immobility, the identity of production functions and atomistic competition. These are, first, that all markets operate efficiently; second, there are no external economies of production or marketing; and third, information is costless and there are no barriers to trade or competition. In such a situation international trade is the only possible form of international involvement; production by one country's enterprises for a foreign market must be undertaken within the exporting country; and all enterprises have equal access to location-specific endowments.

One of the deductions of the Heckscher–Ohlin theory is that trade will equalize factor prices. Replacing the assumption of factor immobility with that of the immobility of goods, it may be shown that movements of factors also respond to differential resource endowments. This was the conclusion of the early writings of Nurkse (1933), Ohlin (1933) and Iversen (1935) which explained international (portfolio) capital movements in terms of relative factor prices, or differential interest rates. For many years trade and capital theory paralleled each other, it being accepted that, in practice, trade in goods was at least a partial substitute for trade in factors. Eventually, the two were formally integrated into the factor price equalization theorem by Samuelson (1948) and Mundell (1957).

In the late 1950s there was a striking shift of direction in the interests of international economists brought on, *inter alia*, by the tremendous postwar changes in the form and pattern of trade and capital exports. Building on the empirical work of MacDougall (1951) and Leontief (1953 and 1956), and taking advantage of much improved statistical data, the 1960s saw the first real attempts to explain trade patterns as they were, rather than as they might be. Contemporaneously, the emergence of international production as a major form of non-trade involvement was demanding an explanation.

Over the past twenty years the positive theory of international economic involvement has 'taken off'. For most of the period it comprised two quite separate strands. The first concerned explanations of trade flows. Here, contributions were mainly centred on introducing more realism into the Heckscher–Samuelson–Ohlin doctrine. Basically, there were two main approaches. The first was that of the neofactor theories, which extended the two-factor Heckscher–Samuelson–Ohlin model to embrace other location-specific endowments (notably natural resources) and differences in the quality of inputs, especially labour. The second group of theories was more path-breaking, as it cut at the heart of the Heckscher–Samuelson–model by allowing the the possibility of differences in the production function of enterprises and of imperfect markets. These theories, which included the neotechnology and scale economy models, were different in kind to the neofactor theories because they introduced new explanatory variables which focused not on the specific resource endowments of countries but on the exclusive possession of certain assets by enterprises. Sometimes, in addition to, but more often as a substitute for, orthodox theories, these new hypotheses of trade flows have been exposed to various degrees of testing. Yet as Hufbauer (1970) has shown, the predictive power of the neofactor and the neotechnology theories is scarcely better than that of the crude factor proportions theory. In his own words, 'No one theory monopolises the explanation of manufacturing trade'.

The second strand of research in the 1960s centred on explaining the growth and composition of foreign direct investment, or of production financed by such investment. At first causes were sought either from orthodox location theory (witness the plethora of microeconomic field studies and more macro-oriented econometric studies) or from neo-classical investment doctrine; but for various reasons, discussed elsewhere (Dunning, 1973a), neither approach proved very helpful. More rewarding were the attempts to identify the distinctive features of foreign direct investment in terms of ownership advantages of foreign firms. Though the gist of this idea was contained in the writings of Southard (1931) and Dunning (1958), it was left to Stephen Hymer in his seminal PhD thesis (Hymer 1960) to explore it in depth. Out of this approach, later refined and extended by Caves (1971, 1974a, 1974b) several hypotheses, focusing on particular kinds of ownership advantages of MNEs, were put forward: for example, access to superior technology (Johnson 1970), better capabilities for product differentiation (Caves 1971), underutilization of entrepren-eurial and managerial capacity (McManus 1972; Wolf 1977), while a more behavioural perspective was taken by Vernon and his colleagues, notably Knickerbocker (1973), who chose to emphasize the role played by defens-ive oligopolistic strategy. These theories, too, have been subject to some testing,[2] but again it seems clear that no single hypothesis offers a satisfactory explanation of non-trade involvement.

Though these new theories of trade and production originated quite independently of each other, by the early 1970s it was clear that they were converging on, and even overlapping, each other. Though expressed differently, the same variables were being increasingly used to explain both trade and non-trade involvement. Comparable to the technological gap theory of trade was the knowledge theory of direct investment; analogous to monopolistic competitive theories of trade were theories of direct investment focused on product differentiation and multi-plant economies. Yet, with the exception of Vernon's early integration of trade and investment as different stages of the product cycle (Vernon 1966), which took as its starting point the innovative advantages of enterprises in a particular country, and the later discovery of Horst (1972) that the same variable – size of firm – which best explained foreign investment also explained investment plus trade, no attempt was made to integrate the two forms of involvement into a single theory, although the need for this had been discerned by Baldwin (1970) and others. Nor, indeed, was there any explicit recognition that, because the decisions to trade or engage in foreign production are often alternative options to the same firm, any explanation of one must, of necessity, take account of the other.

The last decade has seen the first, albeit faltering, attempts to do just this. In a paper published in 1973, this author suggested that only by considering trade and foreign production as alternative forms of international involvement in terms of ownership and location endowments could the economic implications of the UK joining the EEC be properly evaluated (Dunning 1973b). Seev Hirsch (1976) formalized these concepts into a model that specifies, very clearly, the conditions under which foreign markets will be serviced by alternative routes. Tom Parry (1975) applied these concepts to a study of the pharmaceutical industry; his contribution is especially noteworthy as he included licensing as a third form of economic involvement. Buckley and Dunning (1976) examined comparative US and UK trade and non-trade in these terms. Birgitta Swedenborg (1979) uses a similar approach in her analysis of the international operations of Swedish firms. In the belief that this is a helpful route towards an eclectic theory of international economic involvement, I now explore it in more detail.

INTERNATIONAL ECONOMIC INVOLVEMENT

Exactly what is to be explained? Here an important point of taxonomy arises. A country's economic involvement outside its national boundaries may be perceived in two ways. First, it may mean the extent to which its own resources, that is, those located within its boundaries, are used by economic agents (irrespective of their nationality) to produce goods or services for sale outside its boundaries; or the extent to which it imports either resources or the products of resources located in other countries. This is the interpretation of orthodox international economics; *inter alia* it implies arm's length trade in inputs and outputs. But second, a country's involvement may mean the extent to which its own economic agents[3] service foreign markets with goods and services, irrespective of where the resources needed to do this are located or used, and the extent to which its own economic agents are supplied goods by foreign owned firms, irrespective of where the production is undertaken. Here, a country's economic space is perceived more in terms of the markets exploited by its institutions than of its geographical boundaries.

Like the distinction between gross national product and gross domestic product[4] which of the two interpretations is the more appropriate depends on the purpose for which it is being used. But for an evaluation of the contribution of a country's international economic involvement to the economic welfare of its citizens, the second has much to commend it, particularly where inward or outward investment account for a substantial proportion of its net capital formation.

Economic involvement by one country's enterprises in another may be for purposes of supplying both foreign and home markets. Production for a particular foreign market may be wholly or partly located in the home country, in the foreign market, in a third country or in a combination of the three. Similarly, production for the home market may be serviced from a domestic or a foreign location.

The capability of a home country's enterprises to supply either a foreign or domestic market from a foreign production base depends on their possessing certain resource endowments not available to, or not utilized by, another country's enterprises. We use resource endowments in the Fisherian sense (Johnson 1968) to mean assets capable of generating a future income stream. They include not only tangible assets, such as natural resources, manpower and capital, but intangible assets, such as knowledge, organizational and entrepreneurial skills, and access to markets. Such endowments could be purely location specific to the home country, in other words they have to be used where they are located[5] but are available to all firms, or they could be ownership specific, that is, internal to the enterprise of the home country, but capable of being used with other resources in the home country or elsewhere.[6] In most cases, both location and ownership endowments affect competitiveness.

For some kinds of trade it is sufficient for the exporting country to have a location-endowment advantage over the importing country, that is, it is not necessary for the exporting firms to have ownership-endowment advantage over indigenous enterprises in the importing country. Much of the trade between industrialized and non-industrialized countries (which is of the Ricardian or H/O type) is of this kind. Other trade, such as that which mainly takes place between developed industrialized countries, is of high skill intensive or sophisticated consumer goods products, and is based more on the ownership advantages of the exporting firms;[7] but, observe, this presupposes that it is better to use these advantages in combination with location-specific endowments in the exporting rather than in the importing (or in a third) country. Where, however, these latter endowments favour the importing (or a third) country, foreign production will replace trade. Foreign production then implies that location-specific endowments favour a foreign country, but ownership endowments favour the home country's firms, these latter being sufficient to overcome the costs of producing in a foreign environment (Hirsch 1976). (Again we assume that transfer costs can be considered as a negative endowment of countries other than the country of marketing.)

From this it follows that any theory that purports to explain the determinants of any one form of international economic involvement is unlikely to explain the whole; nor, where that form is one of a number of possible alternatives, will it be adequately explained unless the forces explaining these alternatives are also taken into account. One should not be surprised, then, if trade theories of the neofactor brand, based on location-specific endowments, will not normally be able to explain trade in goods based on ownership-specific endowments. But neither should one be disquieted if the neotechnology and monopolistic competitive theories of trade, based on ownership specific endowments, are also inadequate where the use of such advantages is better exploited in conjunction with location specific endowments of foreign countries.

It may be reasonably argued, however, that this latter criticism would be better directed against the way in which data on international transactions are collected and presented, and the way in which the exported ownership advantages are priced. First, trade statistics usually give details of the gross output of goods exported. But where exports contain a high import content, their total value may tell us little about the use made of indigenous endowments. This deficiency can only be overcome by recording exports on a domestic value-added basis. Second, trade statistics either ignore, or classify completely separately, intermediary goods, such as technology, management and organization, which are exported in their own right. If these could be given a commodity classification, and their value added to the export of final products, then the ownership advantages of exporting enterprises would be better captured. Third, where trade takes place within the same enterprises the recorded prices may bear little resemblance to arm's length prices, and so to the value of factor inputs used. If these problems could be overcome, a combination of the neofactor, neotechnology and monopolistic competitive theories of trade would probably explain trade patterns very well.

MULTINATIONAL ENTERPRISES

So far the multinational enterprise has not been explicitly introduced into the discussion. MNEs are companies which undertake productive activities outside the country in which they are incorporated. They are, by definition, also companies which are internationally involved. The extent to which they engage in foreign production will depend on their comparative ownership advantages *vis-à-vis* host country firms, and the comparative location endowments of home and foreign countries.

Unlike location-specific endowments, which are external to the enterprises that use them, ownership-specific endowments are internal to particular enterprises. They consist of tangible and intangible resources, including technology, which itself dictates the efficiency of resource usage. Unlike location endowments many ownership endowments take on the quality of public goods, that is, their marginal usage cost is zero or minimal (hence, wherever a marginal revenue can be earned, but is not earned, they are underutilized); and although their origin may be partly determined by the industry or country characteristics of enterprises, they can be used anywhere.

What, then determines the ownership advantages which one country's enterprises possess over those of another? For our purposes, we distinguish between three kinds of advantage. The first comprises those which any firms may have over another producing in the same location. Here, Bain's (1956) classic work on the barriers to new competition provides the basic answer. Such benefits may lie in the access to markets or raw materials not available to competitors; or in size (which may both generate scale economies and inhibit effective competition); or in an exclusive possession of intangible assets, for example, patents, trademarks, and management skills, which enable it to reach a higher level of technical or price efficiency and/or achieve more market power. These advantages, then, stem from size, monopoly power, and better resource capability and usage.

The second type of advantage is that which a branch plant of a national enterprise may have over a *de novo* enterprise (or over an existing enterprise breaking into a new product area), again producing in the same location. This arises because, while the branch plant may benefit from many of the endowments of the parent company, for example, access to cheaper inputs, knowledge of markets, centralized accounting procedures, administrative experience, R&D, at zero or low marginal cost, the *de novo* firm will normally have to bear their full cost. The greater the non production overheads of the enterprise, the more pronounced this advantage is likely to be.

The third type of advantage is that which arises specifically from the multinationality of a company, and is an extension of the other two. The larger the number and the greater the difference between economic environments in which an enterprise operates, the better placed it is to take advantage of different factor endowments and market situations. I shall return to this point later in the article.

Most of these benefits, both individually and collectively, have been used by economists to explain the participation of affiliates of MNEs in the output of industries in host countries. However, while recognizing that they are interrelated, there have been few explicit attempts to explain either the basis of interrelationship or why the more marketable of the advantages are not sold directly to other firms. In consequence, not only has one of the fundamental attributes of MNEs been largely overlooked, but so also has the basis for much of the concern about the present international economic order. The substance of our thesis is not, in itself, new; it is more a reinterpretation and extension of an idea first formulated by Coase in 1937, and more recently resurrected in the literature by Arrow (1969, 1975), Williamson (1971, 1975, 1979), Alchian and Demsetz (1972), Furobotn and Pejovich (1972), McManus (1972), Baumann (1975), Brown (1976), Magee (1977a, 1977b) and, perhaps most systematically of all, by Buckley and Casson (1976).[8]

The thesis is that the international competitiveness of a country's products is attributable not only to the possession of superior resources and, in some cases, the necessity of its enterprises but also to the desire and ability of those enterprises to internalize the advantages resulting from this possession; and that servicing a foreign market through foreign production confers unique benefits of this kind. Where, for example, enterprises choose to replace, or not to use, the mechanism of the market, but instead allocate resources by their own control procedures, not only do they gain but, depending on the reason for internalization, others (notably their customers and suppliers prior to vertical integration, and their competitors prior to horizontal integration) may lose. Internalization is thus a powerful motive for takeovers or mergers, and a valuable tool in the strategy of oligopolists.

It has long been recognized that such gains may follow from vertical integration and, to a lesser extent, from horizontal integration of a firm's activities; and much of current antitrust legislation is designed to prevent or minimize abuses arising as a result. But much less attention has been paid to the type of internalizing practised by conglomerates, or that which reflects in the internal extension of a company's activities, or that associated with the internalization of resources, products or markets over geographical space.

Consider, for example, the areas in which the participation of MNEs, irrespective of their country of origin, is most pronounced in host countries. These include export-oriented primary goods sectors requiring large amounts of capital, for example, aluminium, oil, copper and/or those faced with substantial barriers to foreign marketing and distribution, for example, bananas, pineapples, coffee; technologically advanced manufacturing industries or those supplying branded consumer products with a high income elasticity of demand and subject to the economies of large-scale production; capital or skill intensive service industries, such as insurance, banking and large-scale construction; and activities in which the spatial integration of inputs, products or markets is essential to efficiency, for example, airlines, hotels. All of these not only require endowments in which MNEs have a comparative advantage, and which are difficult to acquire by *de novo* entrants, but, more pertinent to our argument, they are all sectors in which there is a pronounced propensity of firms to internalize activities, particularly across national boundaries.

What, then, are these incentives of firms to internalize activities? Basically they are to avoid the disadvantages or capitalize on the advantages of imperfections or disequilibria in external mechanisms of resource allocation.[9] These mechanisms are mostly of two kinds – the price system and public authority fiat. Where markets are perfectly competitive, the coordinating of interdependent activities cannot be improved upon; once imperfections arise or can be exploited through internalization, this becomes a possibility.

Market imperfections may be both structural and cognitive. Uncertainty over future market conditions in the absence of competitive future markets, or about government policies, is another kind of imperfection.

Structural imperfections arise where there are barriers to competition and economic rents are earned; where transaction costs are high; or where the economies of interdependent activities cannot be fully captured.

Cognitive imperfections arise wherever information about the product or service being marketed is not really available, or is costly to acquire. The cost of uncertainty may be gauged by the risk premium required to discount it, which may differ quite significantly between firms. From the buyer's viewpoint, market imperfections to avoid include uncertainty over the availability and price of essential supplies, and lack of control over their delivery timing and quality. From the seller's viewpoint, the propensity to internalize will be greatest where the market does not permit price discrimination; where the costs of enforcing property rights and controlling information flows are high; where the output produced is of more value to the seller than the buyer is willing to pay (again, possibly because of ignorance on the part of the buyer),[10] or, in the case of selling outlets, where the seller, to protect his reputation, wishes to ensure a certain quality of service, including after-sales maintenance. For both groups of firms, and for those considering horizontal integration, the possession of underutilized resources, particularly entrepreneurial and organizational capacity, which may be used at low marginal cost to produce products complementary to those currently being supplied, also fosters internalization.

At the same time, to benefit from some of these advantages an enterprise must be of sufficient size. This prompts firms to engage in product diversification or integration, which, in turn, increases their opportunities to profit from other internalizing practices such as cross-subsidization of costs and predatory pricing. One suspects that many of the advantages of conglomerate mergers are of this kind; and it cannot be a coincidence that, in recent years, takeovers and mergers have been concentrated in areas in which advantages of internalization are most pronounced.[11]

Public intervention in the allocation of resources may also encourage enterprises to internalize activities. Many policy instruments of governments, however justified in the pursuance of macroeconomic (and other) goals, may create distortions in the allocation of resources which enterprises may seek to exploit or protect themselves against. Some of these provoke reactions from all enterprises; others from only those which operate across national boundaries.

Here the analysis will be confined to two kinds of government intervention especially relevant to the behaviour of MNEs. The first concerns the production and marketing of public goods, which are not only characterized by their zero marginal cost, but by the fact that their value to the owner may hinge on the extent to which others also possess them. Under these circumstances, an orthodox perfect market is impossible, unless the purchaser relies on the seller to withhold the sale of a good to other buyers, or not to price it lower.

Some commodities and services produced by private enterprises also have the characteristics of public goods. The major example is technology – an intermediary good which embraces all kinds of knowledge embodied in both human and non-human capital (Johnson 1970). The significance of technology in the modern world economy needs no elaboration: it is the main engine of development, a leading determinant of both absolute and relative living standards, and a controlling factor in the spatial allocation of resources. Its phenomenal growth since the Second World War, especially in the field of information and communications technology, has undoubtedly facilitated the internationalization of firms, just as the railroad, telegraph and telephone helped the creation of national enterprises a century ago.[12]

It is my contention that the need both to generate innovations and ideas and to retain exclusive right to their use has been one of the main inducements for enterprises to internalize their activities in the last two decades. Governments have encouraged this by extensively subsidizing R&D, continuing to endorse the patent system and by recognizing that, in some industries, if the benefits of technological advances are to be fully exploited, not only may it be necessary to restrict the number of producers but that enterprises should be free to internalize their knowledge producing with their knowledge-consuming activities. Even without the intervention of governments, technology possesses many of the attributes for internalizing (or not externalizing) markets. At the time of its production, it is the sole possession of the innovator, who naturally wishes to exploit it most profitably; it is costly and takes time to produce but there is no future market in it; it is often difficult for a potential buyer to value as its usefulness can only be determined after it has been purchased. Yet often, for its efficient exploitation, it needs complementary or back-up resources. These qualities apply particularly to the kind of knowledge which cannot be patented, for example, financial systems, organizational skills, marketing expertise, management experience and so on.

The second example of government intervention is particularly relevant to the operations of MNEs. It both encourages such enterprises to internalize existing activities and to engage in new activities which offer the possibility of internalizing gains. It arises because of different economic policies of national governments which often lead to distortions in the international allocation of resources. Assume, for example, that an MNE wishes to maximize its post-tax profits and that corporate tax rates differ between countries. One way it can reduce its total tax burden is to capitalize on its intra-group transactions by manipulating its transfer prices so as to record the highest profits in the lowest tax areas. Other things being equal, the more internal transactions the company engages in the greater its opportunities for doing this – hence, in the case of MNEs, the added impetus to engage in a global strategy and to practise product or process specialization within its organization.

The MNE has other reasons for internalizing its operations across boundaries (Rugman 1980). These include the desire to minimize the risk and/or costs of fluctuating exchange rates; to cushion the adverse effects of government legislation or policy, for example, in respect to dividend remittances; to be able to take advantage of differential interest rates and 'leads' and 'lags' in intra-group payments; and to adjust the distribution of its short-term assets between different currency areas. Some of these benefits of internalization are now being eroded by government surveillance over transfer pricing and by the tendency for contractual arrangements between foreign and indigenous firms to replace equity investments of the former.

How far MNEs actually do manipulate intra-group prices to transfer income across national boundaries is still a matter for empirical research; so far the evidence collected is partial and impressionistic. Suffice to say there are many reasons why an MNE may wish to take advantage of such opportunities (Lall 1973), and that however vigilant the tax authorities may be in some areas, for example, the pricing of intangible assets, the difficulty of (1) estimating the extent to which a transfer of goods or services has taken place, and (2) assigning a value to them, is a very real one.

It has been illustrated, at some length, why firms, and MNEs in particular, gain from internalizing their activities, especially in respect of the production and marketing of technology. Another sector in which MNEs are particularly active is the capital intensive, resource based industries. Here, all the traditional reasons for vertical integration hold good, in addition to those which result from multinationality *per se*; the classic example is the oil industry. They imply, for the most part, a vertical division of activity of firms, though the operations may be horizontal as well, where similar products are produced. Here, too, the impetus to internalize transactions (as opposed to engaging in contractual arrangements) in the case of international vertical integration is likely to be greater than in the case of domestic vertical integration.

It must not be forgotten, however, that there are costs as well as benefits to internalizing economic activities; for an examination of these see Coase (1937) and Buckley and Casson (1976). As markets become less imperfect the net gains of internalization are reduced. The move towards externalizing the marketing of many raw materials, partly stimulated by the actions of governments, testifies to this. In his study of UK direct investment overseas, Reddaway *et al.* (1968) found that only 4 per cent of the output of UK plantation and mining affiliates, originally set up to supply the investing firms, was now directly imported by them.

It can be concluded, therefore, that the ownership advantages of firms stem from their exclusive possession and use of certain kinds of assets. Very often enterprises acquire these rights by internalizing those previously distributed by the market or public fiat, or by not externalizing those which they originate themselves. This will only be profitable in imperfect market conditions, and where it is thought the coordinating and synergizing properties of the firm to allocate resources are superior to those of markets or public fiat. It is possible to identify the source of such imperfections, both within countries and internationally, and to point to the types of activities which offer the greatest gains from internalization. Of these, the production and marketing of intangible assets and of essential location-specific resouces are the two most important. Both happen to be areas in which MNEs are particularly involved; the fact that the ownership advantages are exploited by foreign production is partly explained by location-specific endowments of the foreign country, and partly by certain ownership advantages which accrue only when a firm produces outside its national boundaries.[13]

AN ECLECTIC THEORY OF PRODUCTION

What is the link between the above discussion and other explanations of international involvement? Simply this. The neotechnology theories of trade and the knowledge theories of direct investment both emphasize the possession of superior technology as an explanation of both trade and production. The monopolistic competitive theories concentrate on some aspect of arm's length imperfect competition as the explanation for trade and investment.

It is my contention that the two approaches should be treated as complementary aspects of an eclectic theory of international involvement, which should embrace not only the product but also the factor and intermediary goods markets, and should acknowledge that the ownership advantages arise not only from the exclusive possession of certain assets, but from the ability of firms to internalize these assets to protect themselves against the failure of markets (including the consequences of this failure for competitors' behaviour) and government fiat over the rest of their activities. Because it relates to the way in which the enterprise coordinates its activities, this approach may be called a systemic theory of ownership advantages, applied to both trade and international production.[14] In favouring such an approach admittedly I may be in danger of being accused of eclectic taxonomy. I also acknowledge the interdependence between technology, imperfect competition and the internalization process, and that it is not always easy to separate cause and effect.

But in the search for a composite measure of ownership advantage a systemic approach has something to commend it. Empirically, there can be little doubt of the increase in the vertical and horizontal integration of firms and of market and product diversification, which has enabled firms to benefit from the internalization of their activities. This is demonstrated both by the increase in the concentration of enterprises in industrial economies in the postwar period and by the growing importance of the pre- and post-production activities of firms. Other data suggest that about one half of all exports of MNEs are intra-group in character.

More generally, the eclectic model can be perceived as a general theory of international production in so far as it provides an analytical framework for explaining all forms of such production. This, however, is not to assert that particular forms of international production are to be explained by the same ownership, location of internalization characteristics. This is clearly not the case, and it is readily accepted that different types of international production may call for quite different explanations. But our contention is that these should be regarded as complementary, rather than alternative, interpretations of MNE activity and of the eclectic paradigm. For this reason, I have no difficulty in reconciling seemingly competing theories within this paradigm, as, more often than not, they are seeking to explain different things.

What, then, is the positive value of the eclectic theory of international production? The theory suggests that, given the distribution of location-specific endowments, enterprises which have the greatest opportunities for and derive the most from, internalizing activities will be the most competitive in foreign markets.[15] *Inter alia* these advantages will differ according to industry, country and enterprise characteristics. Hence, the ownership advantages of Japanese iron and steel firms over South Korean iron and steel firms will be very different from those of UK tobacco firms over Brazilian tobacco firms or US computer firms over French computer firms. Enterprises will engage in the type of internalization most suited to the factor combinations, market situations and government policies with which they are faced. For example, the systemic theory would suggest not only that research-intensive industries would tend to be more multi-national than other industries, but that internalization to secure foreign-based raw materials would be greater for enterprises from economies which have few indigenous materials than those which are self-sufficient; that the most efficient MNEs will exploit the most profitable foreign markets – compare, for example, the US and UK choice of investment outlets (Stopford 1976); that the participation of foreign affiliates is likely to be greatest in those sectors of host countries where there are substantial economies of enterprise size. This theory is consistent with Horst's conclusion (1972) that most of the explanatory variables of foreign direct investment can be captured in the size of enterprise; indeed, one would normally expect size and the propensity to internalize to be very closely correlated, and MNEs to be better equipped to spread risks than national multiproduct firms.

What does the eclectic theory predict that the other theories of international production do not? Taking the theories as a group, probably very little, except so far as the independent variables fail to capture the advantages of internalization. Indeed, it could be argued that this theory is less an alternative theory of ownership advantages of enterprises than one which pinpoints the essential and common characteristics of each of the traditional explanations. There is, however, one difference of substance. The eclectic approach would argue that it is not the possession of technology *per se* which gives an enterprise selling goods embodying that technology to foreign markets (irrespective of where they are produced) an edge over its competitors, but the advantage of internalizing that technology rather than selling it to a foreign producer for the production of those goods. It is not the orthodox type of monopoly advantages which give the enterprise an edge over its rivals – actual or potential – but the advantages which accrue through internalization, for example, transfer price manipulation, security of supplies and markets, and control over use of intermediate goods. It is not surplus entrepreneurial resources *per se* which lead to foreign direct investment, but the ability of enterprises to combine these resources with others to take advantage of the economies of production of joint products.

In other words, without the incentive to internalize the production and/or sale of technology, foreign investment in technology-based industries would give way to licensing agreements and/or to the outright sale of knowledge on a contractual basis. Without the incentive to internalize market imperfections there would be much less reason to engage in vertical or horizontal integration, and again transactions would take place between independent firms. This, it could be argued, is the distinctiveness of this approach.

LOCATION

So far the discussion has concentrated on the ownership endowments of its enterprises as an explanation of a country's international competitiveness, whatever the form of the involvement. It has been argued that, although the advantages are enterprise specific, the fact that these may differ according to nationality of enterprise suggests that such advantages, though endogenous to the individual firms at that time, are not independent of their industrial structure, or of the general economic and institutional environment of which they are part. For example, US government science and education policy may be a key variable in explaining the technological lead of US firms in many industries, while, as Vernon (1974) has pointed out, innovations respond to factor endowment and market needs, which also influence the likely advantages of internalizing those innovations. The institutional arrangements by which innovations are rewarded are no less relevant.

But these country or industry variables affecting ownership advantages are not the same as the location specific endowments referred to earlier. With this interpretation, these comprise three components: the resources which can only be used by enterprises in the locations in which they are sited, unavoidable or non-transferable costs such as taxes, government constraints on dividend remission, and the costs of shipping products from the country of production to the country of marketing.

Each of these elements has received extensive attention in the literature of location theory, which usually assumes ownership endowments as the same between firms, and seeks to explain where they are exploited. Our concern here is a different one. Put in question form it is: given the ownership endowments, is the location of production by MNEs likely to be different from that of non-MNEs? The systemic theory suggests that it is, and for three reasons. First, there may be particular internalizing economies resulting from the friction of geographical space. Second, the location-specific endowments, which offer the greatest potential for internalization, are not distributed evenly between countries.[16] Third, where there are differences in the market imperfections or government policies of countries, then MNEs might be influenced by the extent to which they take advantage of these imperfections by internalizing their operations.

In elaboration of these points, four observations can be made. First, various studies have underlined the advantages of coordinating R&D activities of MNEs (Ronstadt 1977; Fischer and Behrman 1979; Lall 1979) and centralizing them in or near the markets which stimulate such activities (Michalet 1973; Creamer 1976). In the case of US-based MNE, this suggests, that for most kinds of R&D, both ownership and location endowments work in favour of a home R&D base.[17] In the case of MNEs from smaller home markets this tendency may not be so pronounced. By contrast, because the advantages of internalization are generally much less, it may be profitable to spatially disperse some kinds of manufacturing activities, especially where the production processes involved have become standardized (Vernon 1974).

Second, an MNE which produces in different market environments may well seek to coordinate its activities differently. The degree of uncertainty over local consumer tastes, future market conditions and government policy certainly varies between countries. For example, the less imperfect is the market for technology, the less likely is an enterprise to market technology-based products itself. Compare, for example, the role of foreign pharmaceutical companies in Italy, which does not recognize patent protection on drugs, with that of such companies in almost any other European country. By contrast, in some developing countries, MNEs may be reluctant to license local firms because they feel that the complementary technology is insufficient to ensure the quality control they need.[18]

Third, and perhaps most important, is the advantage that a diversified earnings base provides for an MNE to exploit differential imperfections in national or international markets and/or currency areas (Aliber 1970), *inter alia*, through transfer-price manipulation; the use of leads and lags in intra group transactions; the acquisition and monitoring of information; and the extension of benefits enjoyed by multi-plant national firms at an international level. These are some of the (potential) advantages of internalization afforded by international production, compared with international trade.

Fourth, there is the drive towards international production as part of oligopolistic behaviour (Knickerbocker 1973; Flowers 1976; Graham 1978). This is really a territorial extension of domestic strategy, and does not pose any new conceptual problems (but see Vernon 1974). Again, however, in so far as a company perceives its foreign interests to be part of a global strategy, rather than as an independent entity, the internalizing advantages may be crucial to the locational decision of both leaders and followers.

EFFECT OF MNEs ON INTERNATIONAL DISTRIBUTION

In the light of the above analysis, what might one expect the impact of the MNE to be on location of production, the international diffusion or transfer of technology and trade patterns?

There are many different views about the effect of MNEs on the international distribution of resources. Partly, these reflect differences in the perspective one takes, for example, that of a particular country or region, or that of all countries; or of the goals one is seeking to promote. We shall confine ourselves to economic issues viewed in a global context from two main viewpoints. The first is that MNEs promote a more efficient distribution of resources since, by internalizing imperfect markets, they are able to overcome distortions in the economic system such as barriers to the transfer of technology, import controls and inappropriately valued exchange rates. Moreover, in a world of uncertainty and information imperfections, their more efficient scanning and monitoring processes, and their flexibility to respond better to market signals, is a useful competitive stimulus. In short, this view extols the MNE as an integrating force in the world economy, surmounting national barriers, circumventing high transaction costs and improving the allocating of resources.

The second view asserts that, far from overcoming market imperfections, the MNEs are themselves a major distorting force in resource allocation; this is partly because they operate mostly in oligopolistic markets and partly because of their ability to bypass market mechanisms and/or government regulations (Hymer 1970). As a result, it is argued, they engage in restrictive practices, raise barriers to entry and, by their internalization and centralization of decision-taking, adversely affect the efficiency of resource allocation between countries. Far from promoting competition, the coordination of activities by entrepreneurs freezes existing production patterns, encourages agglomeration and makes it more difficult for countries to exploit their dynamic comparative advantages. Since MNEs do exert monopoly power, it is legitimate (on the lines of the optimum tariff argument) for home or host countries to impose restrictions on their activities.

The truth, in so far as it is possible to generalize, is obviously somewhere between these two extremes, with the balance steering one way or another according to:

1 the efficiency of the resource allocative mechanism prior to the entrance of the MNEs;
2 the market conditions under which MNEs compete – which will vary *inter alia* according to industry and country.

But there are certain effects of MNEs, however they may be interpreted, which do seem to have been reasonably well established in the literature, and we will now touch on three of these.

1 In some instances, MNEs have been an integrating force and have taken advantage of existing factor endowments, thus promoting the more efficient use of resources. The best example is where mobile resources of capital and technology are transferred from a capital- and technology-rich country and combined with immobile resources of labour and/materials in labour- and materials-rich countries, thereby helping these countries to exploit their dynamic comparative advantage. Other examples include what is currently happening in Europe as a result of the EC, namely, that the MNEs are rationalizing their activities to take

advantage of the economies of specialization. This is a slow process but no different, in principle, to the behaviour of multiregional (national) enterprises in the USA, which may well be one of the explanations of the greater specialization in the USA than within the EC, as demonstrated by Hufbauer and Chilas (1974).

2 There is some evidence of a spatial specialization of the activities of MNEs and, in particular, the centralization of R&D activities in the home country. Something over 90 per cent of the R&D activities of Swedish and US MNEs is undertaken in their home countries, and the proportion is probably not very different for most of the other leading investors. Hymer suggests that MNEs are encouraging the specialization of activities, not for technological as much as organizational or strategic reasons, most of which enhance the incentive to interalize R&D in the home country. But it does not necessarily follow that, without MNEs, the distribution of innovative activities would have been any the less centralized. R&D among Japanese and European enterprises has certainly been stimulated by the competition from US MNEs. The impact on the UK pharmaceutical and semiconductor industries are classic examples (Tilton 1971; Lake 1976). In the LDCs, because of the lack of indigenous competitors, the Hymer hypothesis probably holds more weight, though even here there are examples of MNEs setting up specialized R&D facilities (Behrman and Fischer 1980).[19]

3 In any analysis of the impact of MNEs on trade and location it is useful to distinguish between the different motives for foreign direct investment. Kojima (1978), for example, has distinguished between trade-oriented and anti-trade-oriented activities of MNEs. He suggests that current Swedish and Japanese investments are mainly made in areas in which the home countries are losing a comparative advantage and host countries are gaining it. These have been of two kinds; one to exploit natural resources not available indigenously, and the other to switch labour intensive activities from high labour cost to low labour cost locations. On the other hand, Kojima asserts that many foreign investments by US firms have been made to protect an oligopolistic position in world markets and in response to trade barriers, and have transferred activities from which they have a comparative advantage to where they have a disadvantage. Such investments, he claims, are anti-trade oriented and run against the principles of comparative advantage. Kojima cites here the extensive US foreign investments in the capital and technologically intensive industries.

The border between transferring a comparative advantage and creating a new one, and the Kojima distinction between trade-generating and trade-destroying investments is not altogether convincing. Moreover, his approach tends to be a static one and is couched in terms of first-best solutions. It also fails to consider vertical specialization within industrial sectors. Assuming technology (as an intermediate good) can be sold for a competitive price between independent parties, one might reasonably expect non-skilled labour intensive operations of high technology industries to be transplanted to those areas which possess such labour in abundance, and countries with an abundance of materials to utilize such materials with technology developed by nations which have a limited amount of materials. The Japanese and US patterns may be complementary to each other; their ownership and locational advantages may reflect country specific characteristics.[20] Evidence collected about the trading patterns of US MNEs (Lipsey and Weiss 1973) supports this view. The imports of US MNEs tend to be more capital intensive than those of other US firms, mainly because of the ability of MNEs to export capital and technology to undertake the labour intensive production processes of a capital intensive product in low labour cost areas.

From a normative viewpoint, the point of greater interest is the extent to which technology transfer through the coordination of the firm is preferable to that of the market, but, on this subject, there has been only limited research (Arrow 1969; Williamson 1979; Teece 1979). Yet this, as has been suggested, is a crucial issue, which both helps to explain the growth of MNEs (relative to non-MNEs) and their effect on the spatial distribution of economic activity. Assuming perfectly competitive markets are not generally feasible (nor, from viewpoints other than economic efficiency, necessarily desirable), under what circumstances is it preferable for the resource allocative process to be decided upon by markets or governments, however imperfect they may be, and under what circumstances by the internal governance of MNEs? For there is no *a priori* reason to suppose one form of resource allocation is preferable to the other. In remedying the imperfections and alleged distorting behaviour of MNEs, should not as much attention be give to removing some of the distortions of the environment in which they operate, so that they have less incentive to internalize their activities? To give a recent example, the replacement of fixed by flexible rates has decisively reduced the impetus for MNEs to engage in speculative or protective currency movements across boundaries. The candidate most in need of attention at the moment is technology. It is here that the present system of rewards and penalties leaves so much to be desired (Johnson 1970) and it is here that both the incentive to internalize by MNEs and the potential for distorting behaviour on their part in exploiting the benefits of that internalization arise.

In the last resort, however, we must acknowledge that it is not efficiency, and certainly not efficiency viewed from a global standpoint, that is the standard by which the relative merits of internalization of MNEs and imperfect markets of allocating resources is likely to be assessed. It is the effects of such patterns of resource allocation on the distribution of income between or within nations; on the relative economic powers of countries or of different groups of asset owners; on the sovereignty of one country to manage its own affairs. It is these matters which are at the centre of the arena of public debate at the moment; and it is on such criteria as these that the actions of MNEs are judged.

Some countries facing the choice offered above have clearly preferred to buy their resources in imperfect markets than through MNEs (Japan is the obvious example), while many LDCs are increasingly seeking to depackage the package of resources provided by MNEs in the belief that they can externalize the internal economies. Within the advanced countries the non-market route is generally accepted. But here, too, there are murmurings of concern, articulated not only in such polemics as *The Global Reach* (Barnet and Muller 1974) but in research studies done at the Brookings Institution (Bergsten *et al.* 1978) and by Peggy Musgrave (1975) on the effect of the (internalizing) advantages of international production on the domestic economic power of US corporations.

This particular area of the debate on the role of MNEs in trade and the transfer of technology and the location of production is still in its infancy. It is an area hazardous and not altogether attractive for the academic economist; the issues are controversial; the concepts are elusive; the data are not easily subject to quantitative manipulation and appraisal; and the standard of debate is often low. But, intellectually, it presents a great challenge, offering much scope for the collaboration not only of economists of different specialities and persuasions, but between economists and researchers from other disciplines. For these reasons alone, it deserves to attract our ablest minds.

NOTES

1 The following observation by Williams (1929) about industries which had expanded beyond their political frontiers is of interest to our discussion.

> They represent in some cases the projection by one country into others of its capital, technique, special knowledge along the lines of an industry and its market, as against the obvious alternative of home employment in other lines. They represent, in other cases, an international assembling of capital and management for world enterprises ramifying into many countries. They suggest very strikingly an organic inter-connection of international trade, movement of productive factors, transport and market organisation.

2 For further details see Dunning (1981) Chapter 3, p. 48.
3 Mainly enterprises: by a country's enterprises is meant those whose head offices are legally incorporated in that country.
4 Gross domestic product = incomes earned from domestic resources; gross national product = gross national product + income earned from assets abroad less income paid to foreigners on domestic assets.
5 Proximity to the point of sale may be treated as a location specific endowment

for these purposes; distance (implying transport and other transfer costs) is thus considered as a negative endowment.

6 See Lall (1980) for a discussion on the extent to which ownership advantages are mobile, that is, transferable across national boundaries.

7 For an elaboration of the complementarity between the neofactor and neotechnology theories of trade, see Hirsch (1974).

8 One of the most recent and stimulating contributions on these lines is contained in Swedenborg (1979). For a general reappraisal on the literature on internalization see Rugman (1980) and Teece (1981).

9 To avoid being subject to imperfections of markets when they are the weaker party to an exchange but to capitalize on imperfections when they are the stronger party.

10 Such as particularly applies in the case of transactions involving non-standard technology or information, and which are infrequent and conducted under uncertainty.

11 For a recent study of the applicability of the eclectic theory and the markets and hierarchies paradigm to the acquisition of foreign firms in Canada and that of domestic firms in the USA see Calvet (1980).

12 The transition from regional to national railroads in the nineteenth and early twentieth century was paralleled by the transition from national to multinational airlines after the Second World War.

13 We have not the space to deal with the role of internalization in prompting other forms of foreign direct investment; in some cases, the coordinating advantages of the firm clearly transcends that of the market for technological reasons, such as airlines; in others it is much more to do with controlling information among interdependent activities, such as advertising, and tourism; or as a form of oligopolistic strategy. In many cases, an investment based on technological innovation has managed to create its own barriers to entry through economies of size.

14 Licensing and other forms of contractual arrangements of intermediate products.

15 The points made in this paragraph are extended and set out in a rather different way in Tables 3.1 and 4.2 of Dunning (1981).

16 This point is elaborated in Chapter 4.

17 Lall (1979) suggests that in cases where major technological efforts on products and processes are not crucially linked to each other, international experience and cost advantages tend to promote greater reliance on foreign R&D. By contrast, in those sectors where innovation centres around product development and testing it is much more difficult to separate any major part of R&D activity from the main markets and centre of decision-taking. Michalet (1973), on the other hand, distinguishes between a specialised and imitative R&D strategy of MNEs, while Ronstadt (1977) adopts a more functional approach arguing that different types of R&D have different location needs. In a study of the overseas R&D activities of fifty-five US-based MNEs, Mansfield et al. (1979) found that such activities were increasing relative to those in the USA and were concentrated on product and process improvements and modifications rather than the discovery of new products and processes. The authors argued that one important reason – at least in the 1960s – for foreign R&D activities was that the cost of R&D inputs was considerably lower in Japan, Europe and Canada than in the USA.

18 See Chapter 5 of Dunning (1981).

19 Mainly in material processing or product adaptation to meet specialized local needs. Behrman and Fischer (1980) note that US enterprises have some R&D

facilities in Hong Kong, Argentina, Colombia, Egypt, Philippines and Taiwan, whereas Argentina, Hong Kong and Singapore are among developing countries attracting such activities by European MNEs.

20 This point is further explored in Dunning (1981) Chapter 4. Here it is worth pointing out that vertical foreign direct investment often precedes horizontal foreign direct investment (as it did in the UK and USA) and that the pattern of new Japanese investment in the late 1970s resembles much more that traditional US kind than it did in the 1960s.

REFERENCES

Alchian, A., and Demsetz, H. (1972), 'Production, information costs and economic organisation', *American Economic Review*, Vol. 62 (December).

Aliber, R. (1970), 'A theory of foreign direct investment', in C.P. Kindleberger (ed.), *The International Corporation* (Cambridge, Mass.: MIT Press).

Arrow, K. J. (1969), 'The organisation of economic activity: issues pertinent to the choice of market and non market considerations', in Joint Economic Committee, *The Analysis of Public Expenditures: the PPB System* (Washington, DC: US Government Printing Office).

Arrow, K. J. (1975), 'Vertical integration and communication', *Bell Journal of Economics*, Vol. 5 no. 1 (Spring).

Bain, J. S. (1956), *Barriers to New Competition* (Cambridge, Mass.: Harvard University Press).

Baldwin, R. E. (1970), 'International trade in inputs and outputs', *American Economic Review*, Vol. 60 (May).

Barnet, R. J., and Muller, R. E. (1974), *The Global Reach* (New York: Simon and Schuster).

Baumann, H. (1975), 'Merger theory, property rights and the pattern of US direct investment in Canada', *Weltwirtschaftliches Archiv*, Vol. 111, no. 4.

Behrman, J. N., and Fischer, W. A. (1980), *Overseas R and D Activities of Transnational Corporations* (Cambridge, Mass.: Oelgeschlager, Gunn and Hain).

Bergsten, E. F., Horst, T., and Moran, T. E. (1978), *American Multinationals and American Interests* (Washington DC: Brookings Institution).

Brown, W. B. (1976), 'Islands of conscious power: MNCs in the theory of the firm', *MSU Business Topics* (Summer).

Buckley, P. J., and Casson, M. (1976), *The Future of the Multinational Enterprise* (London: Macmillan).

Buckley, P. J., and Dunning, J. H. (1976), 'The industrial structure of US direct investment in the UK', *Journal of International Business Studies*, Vol. 7 (Summer).

Calvet, A. L. (1980), 'Markets and hierarchies: towards a theory of international business', PhD thesis, Sloane School of Management, Cambridge, Mass.

Caves, R. E. (1971), 'Industrial corporations: the industrial economics of foreign investment', *Economica*, Vol. 38 (February).

Caves, R. E. (1974a), 'Causes of direct investment: foreign firms' shares in Canadian and United Kingdom manufacturing industries', *Review of Economics and Statistics*, Vol. 56 (August).

Caves, R. E. (1974b), 'Industrial organisation', in J. H. Dunning (ed.), *Economic Analysis and the Multinational Enterprise* (London: Allen & Unwin).

Coase, R. H. (1937), 'The nature of the firm', *Economica*, Vol. 4 (November).

Creamer, D. (1976), *Overseas Research and Development by US Multinationals 1966–75* (New York: The Conference Board).

Davidson, W. H., and McFeetridge, D. G. (1980), *International Technology Trans-actions and the Theory of the Firm* (mimeo).

Dunning, J. H. (1958), *American Investment in British Manufacturing Industry* (London: Allen & Unwin).

Dunning, J. H. (1973a), 'The determinants of international production', *Oxford Economic Papers*, Vol. 25 (November).

Dunning, J. H. (1973b), 'The location of international firms in an enlarged EEC: an exploratory paper', Manchester Statistical Society.

Dunning, John H. (1981), *International Production and the Multinational Enterprise* (London: Allen & Unwin).

Fischer, W. A., and Behrman, J. N. (1979), 'The co-ordination of foreign R and D activities by transnational corporations', *Journal of International Business Studies*, Vol. 10 (Winter).

Flowers, E. B. (1976), 'Oligopolistic reaction in European and Canadian direct investment in the US', *Journal of International Business Studies*, Vol. 7 (Fall/Winter).

Furubotn, E. G., and Pejovich, S. (1972), 'Property rights and economic theory: a survey of recent literature', *Journal of Economic Issues*, Vol. 6 (December).

Graham, E. M. (1978), 'Transatlantic investment by multinational firms: a rivalistic phenomenon', *Journal of Post Keynesian Economics*, Vol. 1 (Fall).

Hirsch, S. (1974), 'Capital and technology confronting the neo factor proportions and neo-technology accounts of international trade', *Weltwirtschaftliches Archiv*, Vol. 110, No. 4.

Hirsch, S. (1976), 'An international trade and investment theory of the firm', *Oxford Economic Papers*, Vol. 28 (July).

Horst, T. (1972), 'Firm and industry determinants of the decision to invest abroad: an empirical study', *Review of Economics and Statistics*, Vol. 54 (August).

Hufbauer, G. C. (1970), 'The impact of national characteristics and technology on the commodity composition of trade in manufactured goods', in R. Vernon (ed.), *The Technology Factor in International Trade* (New York: Columbia University Press).

Hufbauer, G. C., and Chilas, J. G. (1974), 'Specialisation by industrial countries: extent and consequences', in H. Giersch (ed.), *The International Division of Labour*: Problems and Perspectives (Tubingen: Mohr).

Hymer, S. (1960), 'The international operations of national firms: a study of direct investment', unpublished doctoral thesis, MIT.

Hymer, S. (1970), 'The multinational corporation and the law of uneven develop-ment', in J. Bhagwati (ed.), *Economics and World Order* (New York: World Law Fund).

Iversen, C. (1935), *Aspects of International Capital Movements* (London and Copen-hagen: Levin and Munksgaard).

Johnson, H. (1968), *Comparative Cost and Commercial Policy Theory for a Developing World Economy* (Stockholm: Almquist and Wiksell).

Johnson, H. (1970), 'The efficiency and welfare implications of the international corporation', in C. P. Kindleberger (ed.) *The International Corporation* (Cam-bridge, Mass.: MIT Press).

Knickerbocker, P. T. (1973), *Oligopolistic Reaction and the Multinational Enterprise* (Cambridge, Mass.: Harvard University Press).

Kojima, K. (1978), *Direct Foreign Investment* (London: Croom Helm).

Lake, A. (1976), *Transnational Activity and Market Entry in the Semiconductor Industry* and *Foreign Competition and the UK Pharmaceutical Industry* (National Bureau of Economic Research: New York, Working Papers Nos 126 and 155).

Lall, S. (1973), 'Transfer pricing by multinational manufacturing firms', *Oxford Bulletin of Economics and Statistics*, Vol. 35 (August).

Lall, S. (1979), 'The international allocation of research activity by US multi-nationals', *Oxford Bulletin of Economics and Statistics*, Vol. 41 (November).

Lall, S. (1980), 'Monopolistic advantages and foreign involvement by US manu-facturing industry', *Oxford Economic Papers*, Vol. 32 (March).

Leontief, W. (1953), 'Domestic production and foreign trade; the American captial position re-examined', *Proceedings of the American Philosophical Society*, Vol. 97.

Leontief, W. (1956), 'Factor proportions and the structure of American trade: further theoretical and empirical analysis', *Review of Economics and Statistics*, Vol. 38.

Lipsey, R. E., and Weiss, M. Y. (1973), 'Multinational firms and the factor intensity of trade', National Bureau of Economic Research: New York, Working Paper 8.

MacDougall, G. D. A. (1951), 'British and American exports. A study suggested by the theory of comparative costs, Part I', *Economic Journal*, Vol. 61.

MacDougall, G. D. A. (1952), 'British and American exports. A study suggested by the theory of comparative costs, Part II', *Economic Journal*, Vol. 62.

McManus, J. C. (1972), 'The theory of the multinational firm', in G. Pacquet (ed.), *The Multinational Firm and the Nation State* (Toronto: Collier-Macmillan).

Magee, S. P. (1977a), 'Multinational corporations, the industry technology cycle and development', *Journal of World Trade Law*, Vol. XI (July/August).

Magee, S. P. (1977b), 'Technology and the appropriability theory of the multi-national corporation', in J. Bhagwati (ed.), *The New International Economic Order* (Cambridge, Mass.: MIT Press).

Mansfield, E., Teece, D., and Romeo, A. (1979), 'Overseas research and develop-ment by US based firms, *Economica*, Vol. 46 (May).

Michalet, C. (1973), 'Multinational enterprises and the transfer of technology', unpublished paper for OECD, DAS/SPR/73.64.

Muller, R. (1975), 'Global corporations and national stabilisation policy: the need for social planning', *Journal of Economic Issues*, Vol. 9 (June).

Mundell, R. A. (1957), 'International trade and factor mobility', *American Economic Review*, Vol. 47 (June).

Musgrave, P. B. (1975), *Direct Investment Abroad and the Multinationals: Effects on the US Economy*. Prepared for the use of the Sub-Committee on Multinational Corporations of the Committee on Foreign Relations, US Senate, August (Washington DC: US Government Printing Office).

Nurkse, R. (1933), 'Causes and effects of capital movements', reprinted in J. H. Dunning, *International Investment* (Harmondsworth: Penguin Readings, 1972).

Ohlin, B. (1933), *Interregional and International Trade* (Cambridge, Mass.: Harvard University Press, rev. edn. 1967).

Orr, D. (1973), 'Foreign control and foreign penetration in Canadian manufacturing industries', unpublished manuscript.

Owen, R. F. (1979), *Inter-Industry Determinants of Foreign Direct Investment. A Perspective Emphasising the Canadian Experience*, Working Papers in International Economics, Princeton University (May).

Parry, T. G. (1975), 'The international location of production: studies in the trade and non-trade servicing of international markets by multinational manu-facturing enterprise', PhD Thesis, University of London.

Parry, T. G. (1980), *The Multinational Enterprise: International Investment and Host Country Impacts* (Greenwich, Conn.: JAI Press).

Reddaway, N.B., Potter, S. T., and Taylor, C. T. (1968), *The Effects of UK Direct Investment Overseas* (Cambridge: Cambridge University Press).

Ronstadt, R. (1977), *Research and Development Abroad by US Multinationals* (New York: Praeger).

Rugman, A. M. (1980), 'Internalisation as a general theory of foreign direct investment. A reappraisal of the literature', *Weltwirtschaftliches Archiv,* Vol. 116, no. 2.

Samuelson, P. (1948), 'International trade and equalisation of factor prices', *Economic Journal*, Vol. 58 (June).

Southard, F. A. (1931), *American Industry in Europe* (Boston: Houghton Mifflin).

Stopford, J. (1976), 'Changing perspectives on investment of British manufacturing multinationals', *Journal of International Business Studies*, Vol. 7 (Fall/Winter).

Swedenborg, B. (1979), *The Multinational Operations of Swedish Firms; An Analysis of Determinants of Effects* (Stockholm: Almquist and Wiksell).

Teece, D. J. (1979), *Technology transfer and R & D Activities of Multinational Firms: Some Theory and Evidence* (mimeo), Stanford University (November).

Teece, D. J. (1981), 'The multinational enterprise: market failure and market power considerations', *Share Management Review*, Vol. 22, no. 3.

Tilton, J. E. (1971), *International Diffusion of Technology: The Case of Semi-conductors* (Washington DC: The Brookings Institution).

Vernon, R. (1966), 'International investment and international trade in the product cycle', *Quarterly Journal of Economics*, Vol. 80 (May).

Vernon, R. (1974), 'The location of economic activity', in J. H. Dunning, (ed.), *Economic Analysis and the Multinational Enterprise* (London: Allen & Unwin).

Williams, J. H. (1929), 'The theory of international trade reconsidered', *Economic Journal*, Vol. 39 (June).

Williamson, O. E. (1971), 'The vertical integration of production market failure considerations', *American Economic Review*, Vol. 61 (May).

Williamson, O. E. (1975), *Markets and Hierarchies: Analysis and Antitrust Implications* (New York: The Free Press).

Williamson, O. E. (1979), 'Transaction-cost economics: the governance of contractual relations', *Journal of Law and Economics*, Vol. 22 (October).

Wolf, B. M. (1977), 'Industrial diversification and internationalisation: some empirical evidence', *Journal of Industrial Economics*, Vol. 26 (December).

Chapter 15

Is manufacturing still special in the new world order?

Richard Brown and DeAnne Julius

The momentum is building for a global economic transformation. But the symptoms that are starting to appear are being misdiagnosed as an old disease: deindustrialization. This partly because attention is focused more on the immediate losers than the winners, especially during a global slowdown. It is partly because, at a time of economic hiatus, historical averages are poor indicators of future possibilities. However, if the old policy remedies are applies the pain of transition will be greater and last longer. This transformation is a condition – like adolescence – that will be uncomfortable while it lasts but must be allowed to run its course. Fighting the symptoms will fail and will result in worse problems to come.

THE STRUCTURAL SHIFTS

There are two interrelated shifts taking place: geographic and sectoral. Over the postwar period the geographic centre of gravity diffused outward from the USA to encompass Western Europe and then Japan. In 1950 the USA alone produced more than half of world output. By 1990 its share was less than a quarter but the above triad accounted for almost three-quarters of world GNP, measured in the conventional way. A reversal of this pattern of OECD dominance is imminent. Using non-conventional measures of world GNP (as explained below) it becomes clear that it is already happening. By the turn of the century many of today's big firms – if they are to remain big – will have more customers and more employees in poor countries than in rich ones.

The second, closely related, shift is in the sectoral pattern of employment. In nearly all rich countries the share of the labour force employed in manufacturing has passed its peak and in countries such as Germany, where it is still high, it is likely to go into steep decline. The pace and degree of change will vary across countries depending on their past structure of employment, on the flexibility of their labour markets and on the level of competition in their service industries. But the trend is universal; it is a consequence partly of the increasing demand for services but mainly of the transformation in the developing countries which is shifting both their demand patterns and their comparative advantage in international trade.

A dual shift of this magnitude raises stark concerns, especially in the rich (OECD) countries. Where will all those displaced factory workers find jobs? With productivity growth so low (historically) in the service sectors, will incomes stagnate with a shift into services? Without manufactured exports how will countries pay for increased imports? Without a manufacturing base of big, capital-intensive firms to develop new technology and generate spinoffs in skills and jobs for smaller firms, how can an economy prosper?

Some of these concerns are retreads of the deindustrialization debate that flared in Britain in the 1970s, and in the USA and Japan in the 1980s. They have recently resurfaced in all three countries and we believe – because of the structural shifts to come – they will soon spread to other countries and intensify. They will provoke misguided industrial policies and protectionism unless the concerns are addressed and the changes underway are better understood.

In the next section of this article we examine the historical analogy of the shift of modern economics out of agriculture. We then assess the three main concerns of the Manufacturing Is Special School (MISS). We follow this with a review of the key forces driving the structural change and the early evidence of its strength. The final section summarizes the implications for businesses and governments.

AN HISTORICAL ANALOGY

The European emigration to the Americas, the Industrial Revolution, the rise of mass production, the abolition of slavery, and the decline of domestic service, are examples of geographic and sectoral economic shifts over the past 300 years. Indeed, over the broad sweep of economic history, such transitions are more the norm than the exception. It would be surprising if the current period of unprecedented technological and political change did not produce something similar.

Only for the past century, however, are recorded data sufficient to permit quantitative comparison of historic and current trends. Data on six large economies show that the employment shift away from agriculture has been the most dramatic structural change this century (Figure 15.1). Although starting points were very different, the cross-country pattern and degree of convergence are striking. At the beginning of the century, 68 per cent of the labour force in Japan were employed in agriculture, compared to 44 per cent in the USA, and just 19 per cent in Britain. Those shares were halved by 1940 in the USA and UK; it took until 1960 in Japan. Despite heavy postwar protection of the sector in all three countries, the pattern of convergence continued and by 1990 the shares were 7 per cent

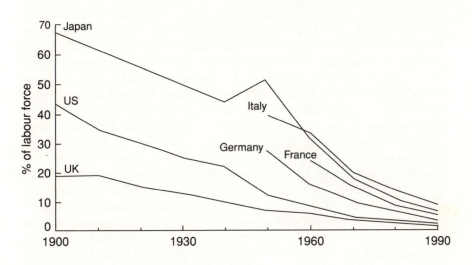

Figure 15.1 Share of agricultural employment
Source: Liesner (1985)

in Japan, 3 per cent in the USA and 2 per cent in Britain. In Germany, France and Italy (where comparable data are available only since 1950), the share of agricultural employment fell from an average of 32 per cent just after the war to 6 per cent by 1990.

This much of the story is fairly familiar. What is more surprising is that over this period the shares of employment in manufacturing did not show a corresponding rise. The structural shift in employment was not from agriculture into manufacturing. In the USA the share of manufacturing employment peaked at 27 per cent of the labour force in 1920 (when 30 per cent still worked in agriculture) and then fluctuated between 21 per cent and 26 per cent for the next 60 years. The more industrialized UK had 33 per cent of its workforce in manufacturing in 1900 and, after various ups and downs, the same percentage in 1960. In neither country was there a systematic tendency for the rate of unemployment to rise during 1900–60 despite the growth of the labour force and the shrinkage of farm jobs.

Where did the displaced agricultural workers and the new entrants to the workforce find jobs – predominantly in the service sector. Its share of employment has been growing without interruption in each of the six countries with available data: in the USA and UK since 1900 and in the other four countries since 1950 when their data begin. Again, the starting points and rates of change differ, but the trend of rising service employment is common to all.

Thus the expansion of the service base of modern market economies has been under way for most of this century. It has been absorbing agricultural labour and, in recent decades, manufacturing labour (Figure 15.2). Left to

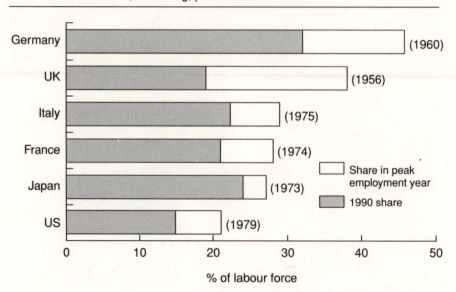

Figure 15.2 Share of manufacturing employment
Source: Liesner (1985)

market forces and assuming continued technological progress, there is little reason to suppose that manufacturing employment should follow a very different path over the next fifty years than agricultural employment has over the past fifty. Both exhibit rising productivity through labour-saving technological change. Both produce easily tradable output so that incremental productive capacity can migrate to low-cost locations. In their basic forms, both account for a shrinking share of consumer expenditure as incomes rise from subsistence to saturation levels. Although spending on food or goods may not fall, an increasing share of it will be on the service component of its value added (e.g. restaurant and ready-to-serve meals, customised consumer products and computer software).

If the agricultural analogy is correct, we may expect to see:

1 Manufacturing employment continuing to fall across the OECD, reaching levels of 10 per cent or below in most countries within thirty years. This is the average period over which agricultural employment fell from the current manufacturing share to below 10 per cent across the sample countries.

2 Faster employment falls in those countries where manufacturing employment is currently highest: Germany (a real outlier at 32 per cent), Japan (24 per cent) and Italy (22 per cent). The biggest falls so far have followed this pattern – they have been greatest in Germany and the UK, at their peak the two most industrialized countries of our sample.

In fact, projections from the agricultural anology are probably too timid. The emerging manufacturing prowess of the developing countries, discussed below, will accelerate these trends.

IS MANUFACTURING SPECIAL?

For supporters of what we call the Manufacturing Is Special School (MISS) the trends identified above are of critical concern. Their case draws on an apparently simple fact – the high growth developed economies (e.g. Germany and Japan) have been those with large and buoyant manufacturing sectors. Three main arguments have been put forward to explain this:

1 Manufacturing jobs have higher productivity and higher wages; hence a shift to the service sector reduces the growth of GDP and incomes.
2 Manufactured goods have a higher export content; a shift to services creates a balance of payments constraint on faster growth.
3 The manufacturing sector possesses externalities that create spinoff growth and jobs in other sectors – for example, through economies of scale and a greater rate of technical progress.

These propositions boil down to the claim that manufacturing has special growth-inducing characteristics not to be found in services (see, for example, Thirlwall 1982). Our claim is that even if this were true in the past it will become progressively less true in the future. We take each point in turn.

Jobs

Service sector jobs conjure up an image of a 16-year-old flipping hamburgers at MacDonalds. However brain surgeons and bankers are also service providers. So are most managers and sales people in large manufacturing companies. The statistical confusion between types of job and types of company has meant that the growing trend for big firms to contract out services that were once supplied inhouse masquerades as job losses in manufacturing. Actually this is correcting a statistical error. Meanwhile the US Bureau of Labor Statistics predicts that executives, managers, professionals and technicians will account for 41 per cent of all US job growth to 2005.

On the issue of productivity the statistical dice are again loaded in favour of manufacturing (not surprisingly, given that this is the old-established sector which historically has paid the wages of the statisticians). For example, a lot of service sector data ignore differences in hours worked, thereby underestimating the productivity of the services sector which makes more use of part-time workers. The data also fail to capture quality improvements – a dental filling today is very different from ten years ago. In most national accounts the output of the non-market services sector (e.g. public education) is calculated as the cost of inputs, thereby excluding by definition any improvements in quality or productivity. All this means that the inflation component of the growth in spending on services tends to be overestimated and hence productivity growth is understated.

However, even if service jobs were on average less productive and lower paid than manufacturing this would not be the end of the story. As countries get richer an increasing portion of income is spent on services such as travel, health and education. This increased demand bids up their value. On the supply side, some prefer jobs which are less stressful or more social and these tend to be the lower paid service jobs. A recent survey of employment in Britain found that assembly-line workers had the lowest level of job satisfaction, followed by those working with machines and monitoring equipment. Workers dealing primarily with people scored the highest job satisfaction (see Gallie *et al*. 1993). Many of the growing number of women entering the labour market prefer part-time jobs and are willing to trade off income for flexibility. Thus some of the claimed falling-off in growth following the shift to services is more apparent than real (the under-recording of quality and productivity improvements in services) and some the natural accompaniment of increased demand for leisure and flexibility.

Finally, what counts is what is happening at the margin. Here there are two changes to note. First, many of the new service sector jobs are both high value added and high paid. A recent survey of the largest 100 firms in Manchester, a city in the manufacturing heartland of the UK, found that employees in the leisure and media sectors were the highest paid and those in manufacturing the lowest (see KPMG Peat Marwick study 1993). Second, for reasons discussed below, prices and wages in manufacturing are likely to be in relative decline.

Exports

Here the MISS argues that services have a low export content and/or a low income elasticity of demand. Thus if a country experiences deindustrialization (i) its share of world export markets will fall; and (ii) its demand for imports will rise as its residents turn increasingly to foreign markets to satisfy their demand for manufactured goods. As a result growing trade and current account deficits will emerge. To avoid sustained depreciation the country will have to deflate domestic demand to bring imports back into line with exports – this in turn will hurt domestic output, including in the service sector.

What is at issue is whether services are the 'wrong' goods in this context. This is far from clear – services already account for a substantial share of world trade (albeit not as high as manufactures) and trade in services is growing faster than trade in manufactures. Invisible earnings accounted for one-third of total current account receipts of industrial countries in 1983. The IMF estimates that this share has increased by 4 percentage points since then (see World Economic Forum 1992). Furthermore, this is taking place against a background of much greater impediments to trade in services than in manufactures. Partly reflecting this, countries with a comparative advantage in the service sectors (e.g. the world's largest service exporters, the USA and the UK) are increasingly supplying these to other countries via the medium of international direct investment (IDI), with the eventual benefits of repatriated profits and dividends (some 40 per cent of the stock of outward IDI from the five major economies has been in the service sector). Again we conclude that the future will be different from the past. With service-oriented shifts in demand, widespread deregulation of service industries, and growing IDI in services, manufacturing will lose its past pre-eminence as the fountain of all foreign exchange.

Externalities

Finally we come to the third of the MISS concerns, namely that large, capital-intensive, manufacturing firms are the key to the generation of new technology and jobs throughout the entire economy. The chemicals, automobile and computer industries are classic examples where rapid change in product or process technology brought high returns to a small number of large firms. However, that phase has probably peaked for those industries. Economies of scale have been reaped, new competitors are driving down prices, and the market for some of these products is reaching maturity in the OECD countries.

Many of today's high-technology industries are in the service sector and they are driving research in new products. The communications industry creates the market for the fax machine and the cellular phone. The health industry shapes the research of pharmaceutical companies. The transport industry drives aerospace development. These examples further illustrate the growing interdependence between manufacturing and services – large corporations are contracting out important activities such as marketing and computing to the service sector, and we are buying high-technology intermediate inputs such as just-in-time distribution systems and computer-aided design (hence the rapid growth of business services). The growth of services is a natural and necessary concomitant to increased economic specialization and sophistication.

Thus during the coming decades breakthroughs in productivity and wealth creation are equally likely to spring from the service sectors. Economies of scale were at the root of the step-change advances of the 1950s and 1960s in chemicals, automobiles and consumer goods. There are already signs that economies of scope may bring similar cost savings, quality enhancement and new service products in telecommunications, finance, air transport and entertainment in the 1990s.

THE NEW WORLD ECONOMIC ORDER

Meanwhile in the developing world, change is also afoot. For many such countries the 1980s were a lost decade in terms of economic growth. There are two important reasons for believing that the future may be rather different. First, the spectacular collapse of communism shook the last vestiges of belief in centrally planned, highly redistributive, models of economic growth. Now there is no alternative to the market economy. Second, the seeds of reform are falling on well prepared soil. As the 1991 *World Development Report* noted, investing in people is a key complement to good economic policies. Between 1965 and 1988, secondary school enrolment increased from 26 per cent to 55 per cent of the school-age population in the fifty-eight middle-income developing countries, and tertiary enrolment jumped from 7 per cent to 17 per cent (see World Bank 1991). By 1988 a larger percentage of Korea's 20–24 year-olds were in higher education than were their French or German counterparts (see World Economic Forum 1992).

Sustained annual growth in the region of 5–6 per cent for developing countries as a group, as suggested in two recent studies (see World Bank 1993 and Shell 1993), is thus an entirely plausible outcome. This will have remarkable consequences for the world economic order: the centre of gravity of global consumption and production will shift from rich to developing countries. This shift will reflect in part the rapid growth in productivity (and in population) in the latter. It will also reflect changes in relative prices, wages and exchange rates.

The last point is a complex but central element in the structural shift to come. At present the use of market exchange rates can grossly understate the economic size of poor countries because the former can diverge significantly from purchasing power parity (PPP) rates. In 1990, using conventional (market) exchange rates, the combined GDP of the rich countries was 2.7 times larger than that of the non-OECD world. Using PPP estimates, it was only 1.1 times larger. Over time, however, more rapid growth in the developing world will increase wages and prices in the tradeable sectors, dragging in their wake costs and prices in the less traded sectors. Such forces will gradually move the exchange rates of developing countries towards their PPP levels, further increasing their consumer power. The consequences are far-reaching. For example, it has been estimated that by 2020 there will be more cars in today's poor countries than in today's rich ones (Figure 15.3).

The mirror image will be seen in the OECD countries. Although productivity in manufacturing will continue to rise there, the relative price of manufactured goods will fall with increased competition from developing countries. The current large differences in manufacturing labour costs will be eroded (Figure 15.4). Just as in agriculture, despite high productivity growth, the typical manufacturing job will no longer be high wage in the OECD.

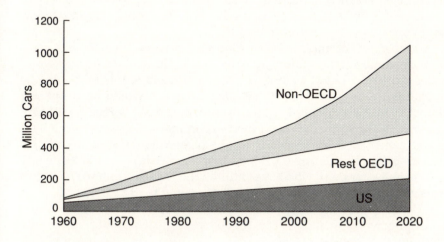

Figure 15.3 World Passenger cars
Source: Shell (1993)

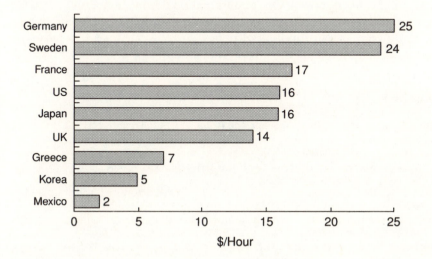

Figure 15.4 Hourly compensation in manufacturing: 1992
Source: DRI (1992)

IMPLICATIONS

Our first set of implications is for businesses (and hence for investors). More and more manufacturing companies will find themselves in highly competitive commodity-style markets. If they choose to compete on costs they will have to shift production to developing countries. If they choose to compete in high value added niches they will have to raise the service intensive customization of their products. Either route will hasten the employment shift to services in the OECD.

Our second set of implications is for policy-makers. They will face great pressure to subsidize, or failing that, to protect, the manufacturing sectors under threat. It would be a critical mistake to yield to this pressure. The agricultural experience shows that such a reaction would be costly and ultimately fruitless in stopping job erosion in the OECD. For the developing countries, being squeezed out of their export markets would stymie their growth potential. Such a setback would expose the vulnerability of new democracies in East Europe, Latin America and Asia. It would be deeply disillusioning for those who have endured the pain of economic reform in order to compete and grow through linking into world markets. Instead of providing growing markets for OECD exports and investment, the developing world would become the source of greater political instability and migratory pressures.

Rather than focusing on jobs, OECD governments should focus on people. Only by upgrading and broadening their education systems will they have workers whose productivity and flexibility will underpin their expanding service sectors. On the international front they must press for free trade in services and greater freedom in international investment. In the traditional areas of industrial policy and direct support to industry, we are asking politicians to do what they find most difficult: nothing!

REFERENCES

Gallie, Duncan and White, *Employment in Britain*, BEBC Distribution, P.O. Box 1496, Poole, June 1993.

IMS, *World Economic Outlook*, 1992.

KPMG Peat Marwick, a study of the top 100 companies in Manchester, as cited in the *Financial Times*, 4 June 1993.

Liesner, Thelma, *Economic Statistics, 1900–1983*, The Economist Publications Ltd., 1985.

Shell International Petroleum Company, Group Planning, *Global Scenarios 1992–2020*, April 1993.

Thirlwall, A. P., *Deindustrialization in the United Kingdom*, Lloyds Bank Review, April 1982.

World Bank, *World Development Report 1991: The Challenge of Development*, OUP 1991.

World Bank, *Global Economic Prospects and the Developing Countries*, 1993.

World Economic Forum, *The World Competitiveness Report 1992*, 12th edition, June 1992.
World Markets Executive Overview, DRI/McGraw-Hill, Fourth Quarter 1992.

Acknowledgements

Chapter 1 'The effects of globalization and turbulence on policy making processes', by Miriam L. Campanella from *Government and Opposition*, 1993, 28 (2), pp. 190–205. Reproduced with permission.

Chapter 2 'The determinants and dynamics of national advantage', from *The Competitive Advantage of Nations* (1990), by Michael E. Porter, The Free Press (a division of Simon & Schuster), pp. 131–75. Reproduced with permission.

Chapter 3 'Horses for courses: organizational forms for multinational corporations', by Sumantra Ghoshal and Nitin Nohria from *Sloan Management Review*, Winter 1993, pp. 23–35.

Chapter 4 'Thinking globally, acting locally', by Anthony G. Eames from *Business Quarterly*, Winter 1990, pp. 112–15.

Chapter 5 'The internationalization of the firm – four Swedish cases', by Jon Johanson and Finn Wiedersheim-Paul from *Journal of Management Studies*, October 1975, pp. 305–22. Reproduced with permission.

Chapter 6 'Business environment assessment', from *Managing International Political Risk: Strategies and Techniques* (1983), by Daniel A. Sharp, Bond Publishing, pp. 7–31.

Chapter 7 'International economic integration: progress, prospects and implications', by David Henderson, *International Affairs*, 1992, 68 (4), pp. 633–53. Reproduced with permission.

Chapter 8 'The cultural relativity of organizational practices and theories', by Geert Hofstede, *Journal of International Business Studies*, Fall 1983, pp. 75–89. Reproduced with permission.

Chapter 9 'Developing a "European" model of human resource management', by Chris Brewster, *The International Journal of Human Resource Management*, 4:4, December 1993, pp. 765–84.

Chapter 10 'Tech talk: how managers are stimulating global R&D communication', by Arnoud De Meyer, *Sloan Management Review*, 32 (3), Spring 1991, pp. 49–58.

Chapter 11 'Rattling SABRE – new ways to compete on information', by Max D. Hopper, *Harvard Business Review*, 68 (3), May-June 1990, pp. 118–25. Reproduced with permission.

Chapter 12 '*Technik*' from *Managers and Management in Western Germany* (1980), by Peter Lawrence, Croom Helm, pp. 96–9.

Chapter 13 'Finance and global competition: exploiting financial scope and coping with volatile exchange rates', by Donald R. Lessard *New Developments in International Finance* (1988), pp. 3–16.

Chapter 14 'Trade, location of economic activity and the multinational enterprise: a search for an eclectic approach', from *International Production and the Multinational Enterprise*, by John H. Dunning (1981), Allen & Unwin, pp. 21–45.

Chapter 15 'Is manufacturing still special in the new world order?', by Richard

Brown and DeAnne Julius, *The Amex Bank Review*, Oxford University Press, 1993, pp. 6–17.
Permission to reproduce Chapters 3, 6, 10, 13 and 15 has been sought but not received at the time of printing. The publisher would be glad to hear from copyright holders and will be pleased to make the necessary arrangement at the first opportunity.

Notes on sources

Chapter 1 M. L. Campanella (1993) *Government and Opposition*, 28 (2), pp. 190–205.

Chapter 2 M. E. Porter (1990) *The Competitive Advantage of Nations*, The Free Press, pp. 131–75.

Chapter 3 S. Ghoshal and N. Nohria (1993) *Sloan Management Review*, Winter, pp. 23–35.

Chapter 4 A. G. Eames (1990) *Business Quarterly*, Winter, pp. 112–15.

Chapter 5 J. Johanson and F. Wiedersheim-Paul (1975) *Journal of Management Studies*, October, pp. 305–22.

Chapter 6 D. A. Sharp (1983) *Managing International Political Risk: Strategies and Techniques*, Bond Publishing, pp. 7–31.

Chapter 7 D. Henderson (1992) *International Affairs*, 68 (4), pp. 633–53.

Chapter 8 G. Hofstede (1983) *Journal of International Business Studies*, Fall, pp. 75–89.

Chapter 9 C. Brewster (1993) *The International Journal of Human Resource Management*, 4 (4), December, pp. 765–84.

Chapter 10 A. De Meyer (1991) *Sloan Management Review*, 32 (3), Spring pp. 49–58.

Chapter 11 M. D. Hopper (1990) *Harvard Business Review*, 68 (3), May-June, pp. 118–25.

Chapter 12 P. R. Lawrence (1980) *Technik: Managers and Management in Western Germany*, Croom Helm, pp. 96–9.

Chapter 13 D. R. Lessard (1988) *New Developments in International Finance*, pp. 3–16.

Chapter 14 J. H. Dunning (1981) *International Production and the Multinational Enterprise*, Allen & Unwin, pp. 21–45.

Chapter 15 R. Brown and D. Julius (1993) *The Amex Bank Review*, pp. 6–17.

Index